P9-CJD-085

Putting Away Childish Things

Putting Away Childish Things

The Virgin Birth, the Empty Tomb, and
Other Fairy Tales You Don't Need to Believe
to Have a Living Faith

Uta Ranke-Heinemann
Translated by Peter Heinegg

HarperSanFrancisco
A Division of HarperCollins*Publishers*

This book was originally published in German under the title NEIN UND AMEN. Copyright © 1992 by Hoffman und Campe Verlag.

PUTTING AWAY CHILDISH THINGS: *The Virgin Birth, the Empty Tomb, and Other Fairy Tales You Don't Need to Believe to Have a Living Faith.* English translation copyright © 1994 by HarperCollins Publishers. All rights reserved. Printed in the United States of America. No part of this book may be used or reproduced in any manner whatsoever without written permission except in the case of brief quotations embodied in critical articles and reviews. For information address HarperCollins Publishers, 10 East 53rd Street, New York, NY 10022.

FIRST EDITION

Library of Congress Cataloging-in-Publication Data

Ranke-Heinemann, Uta, 1927–
   [Nein und Amen. English]
   Putting away childish things : the virgin birth, the empty tomb, and other fairy tales you don't need to believe to have a living faith / Uta Ranke-Heinemann ; translated by Peter Heinegg. — 1st ed.
       p.   cm.
   Includes index.
   ISBN 0-06-066860-1 (alk. paper)
   ISBN 0-06-066861-X (pbk.)
   ISBN 0-06-066847-4 (int'l. pbk.)
   1. Bible. N.T.—Criticism, interpretation, etc. 2. Bible. N.T.—Legends. 3. Jesus Christ—Rationalistic interpretations.
   I. Title.
   BS2370.R3613   1994
   225.6—dc20   93-33896
                                                        CIP

94 95 96 97 98 RRD(H) 10 9 8 7 6 5 4 3 2 1

This edition is printed on acid-free paper that meets the American National Standards Institute Z39.48 Standard.

Contents

When I was a child,
I spoke as a child,
I understood as a child,
I thought as a child;
but when I became a man,
I put away childish things.

1 CORINTHIANS 13:11

Foreword

W<small>HEN</small> I <small>WAS</small> a little girl, there was really only one question about Christianity that interested me: Is there a life after death? Sometimes I would lie awake for a long time before falling asleep and imagine myself lying in a coffin: for ever and ever and ever. . . . That childish question, that childish fear, grew as dark and difficult as the night.

In 1944, about six months before the end of the war, my family's home, my school, and the whole city of Essen had been largely destroyed by bombs. Meanwhile, even in Winterberg, where the war had driven us, there was no school that I could go to. So my mother traveled with me to Marburg, to the home of Professor Rudolf Bultmann (1884–1976). She had studied with Bultmann in the 1920s and had taken her state examination with him. She asked him whether I could stay in his house and continue my studies in Marburg. I was just seventeen, and he amiably replied that he and his wife and daughters were looking forward to having me. I stayed there until the war was over.

Bultmann would later become famous for "demythologizing the New Testament." Around that time—though the nightly air raids and other catastrophes of the war drowned them out—the first critical voices were being raised against Bultmann in the Protestant Church. One day I got a letter from Father Friedrich Graeber, in whose parish I had been confirmed and who was my father's best friend. "Dear Uta," he wrote, "Professor Bultmann doesn't believe in the resurrection. Don't let yourself be influenced by him."

Over the sparest of lunches (the usual sort back then) I asked: "Herr Professor, is it true you don't believe in the resurrection?" "Uta," he said, "you don't understand these things yet." Then he smiled, with the weary look of someone who is always being asked the same question. I concluded that he did believe in the resurrection, but evidently not in the same way other people did. I dropped the issue and put off any discussion of it till later. Besides, I already had my hands full trying to prepare for my lessons: Every Tuesday and Friday afternoon Bultmann translated Plato with me upstairs in his study—that is, I translated, and he explained to me the world of Plato's thought.

Years later, in 1954, after following in my mother's footsteps by studying Protestant theology, I emphatically left both of my parents' footsteps behind by converting to Catholicism. I wrote Rudolf Bultmann a letter, once again asking him about his belief in the resurrection of the dead. But more about that in Chapter Nine, on Easter.

The question of life after death and the memory of Rudolf Bultmann—a scholar who was unstinting in his help to others—have been with me all my life. My recollections of Bultmann came to mind when my doubts about religion began to grow and grow. But at the same time, his example has taught me that a skeptic can be a Christian, too. This book's original German title was No and Amen (Nein und Amen). In the following chapters, I say no many times to the usual concepts of faith, but that doesn't prevent me or anyone else, for all our doubts, from saying amen.

Introduction

HUMAN BEINGS WANT to believe. People are therefore the ideal soil for the seed of religion. There's nothing wrong with that, as long as they're dealing with God himself, because people can trust God not to hoodwink them. But we humans deal not so much with God as with his authorized deputies. Since they assure us that it's all for our eternal happiness and salvation, we let them tell us many tales. Believers accept without question what they're taught to believe and do, because when authority comes forward bearing a mandate from God, doubt seems to be a sin.

Christians have to deal with God's truth only indirectly, because as the catechism says: "The Catholic Church teaches us what God has revealed." Or, as a Catholic hymn puts it: "O God, I believe with all my heart / That what your Church teaches is true, / For both the written and unwritten part / Came to her directly from you." Thus Christians only get the truth secondhand, if at all. But truth that has passed through alien hands is a censored truth, and the God whom we meet at the end of a series of ecclesiastical middlemen is a censored God. The truth, or whatever remains of it, has degenerated—thanks to theologically dense Christian pastors—into a mass of misunderstood and incomprehensible teachings; in other words, into pseudofaith and superstition.

The Church calls on us to believe and not to think. Thus, throughout their lives, believers practice the mental gymnastics of saying amen to everything they're told. In a religion that blesses believers but distrusts doubters, the questioners go unblessed and arouse suspicion in more than a few believers. Yet questioning is a Christian virtue, though seldom practiced by Christians.

Still, it may be that people are no longer content with what others insist that they believe. People seem no longer to listen and to give credit to fairy tales, because their hearts and minds find it too painful.

But what are they to turn to? The Church isn't interested in understanding or enlightenment: Every variety of enlightenment strikes it as suspicious, if not worthy of damnation. The Church speaks only about the hurt done to its religious feelings. It closely monitors such hurts and is often running to the courts. Unfortunately, it pays too little attention to the hurt done to our religious intelligence, which has no legal protection. From the law's point of view, such intelligence doesn't even exist. Hence, people who long for the truth—and who mean by that more than the truths served up to them by the "servants of the servants of God"—are thrown back on their own devices.

The discussions that follow are designed to help this questing intelligence. Some people will say this harms the faith, but understanding can't harm faith; actually, it's faith that has all too often harmed the understanding. The desire to believe without damaging one's mind is, rightly viewed, an act of piety. When people who long for a more immediate, authentic, and large-scale truth simply walk away from verbose and empty sermonizing, it sometimes happens that a new truth, beautiful and gentle, dawns in their darkness. This is the truth of God's compassion, which has been obscured by the Church's many fairy tales and which is nonetheless the only truth—and the only hope.

We encounter this truth in the person of Jesus. We know neither when and where he was born, nor when he died: He is a man without a biography. We don't know how long his public activity as a preacher lasted or where exactly it took place. Strictly speaking, we don't know a whole lot more than that he was born, that there were people who followed him as his disciples, and that he was executed on the cross—the Roman version of the gallows—and thus came to a wretched end.

We don't know a lot about Jesus. But if we trace his steps, we sense that he sought—and found—God; that he wanted to reveal this God as being close to every one of us; and that he wanted to make everyone an intimate both of this God and of his or her neighbor. Anyone who cares to know also realizes that Jesus' voice is as much a living voice as ever; his truth a living truth; and his God a living God, near to us all.

This Jesus lies buried not only in Jerusalem, but also beneath a mountain of kitsch, tall tales, and church phraseology. Though he is missing and presumed dead, we must go forth and rediscover him.

CHAPTER ONE

Luke's Christmas Fairy Tale

CHRISTMAS, THE FEAST of Jesus' birth, is something like the entrance to the Christian world. It is a rich and beautiful gateway, a kind of magic door. Mysterious things lie behind this gate, things out of the tale of A Thousand and One Nights. Here, too, the setting is the Orient, and we have Oriental kings, camel caravans, a strange star, and the aroma of unknown spices.

Beyond such beautiful golden dream-images of a mysteriously transfigured day from a distant past, Christmas offers people today a completely concrete magic. It conjures up a world full of shining lights, candles, the smell of fir and spruce, and Christmas carols. For an evening or for several days, it spreads over our multifarious outer and inner human poverty the reflection of angels. And the angels proclaim a great joy.

Yet all this is just a fairy tale, because, in fact, angels never come into our everyday life to proclaim great joy. In fact, fairy tales never stand up to real life. Even that magical fairy tale of the crib and the kings and shepherds out in the fields can't withstand critical exposure to real history or a critical look at the real story of the child whose birth we recall at Christmas. That is because this story turned bitter and ended in an execution. And if we already had in the fairy tale something like the hem of an angel's garment in our hand, once we open that hand and take a look at it, we'll find it empty. That's the way fairy tales are: Their multicolored charms evaporate like a mirage.

But while this state of affairs may be troubling, we shouldn't dodge it. We can't take it for granted that it's such a bad idea to turn our backs on the fantastic images of fables and to exchange them for an unfairy-tale-like truth, which affects our life more powerfully than any fairy tale. This is the truth that Jesus preached, after he, too, had left behind the magic of childhood and entered into the pains of the world—the truth, that is, of God's love.

But as if the age of fairy tales were still with us, instead of this truth Christians are offered decorations and the colorful frippery of the fairy-tale-like entrance. We are served ersatz truth—fantasies posing as essentials, as worthy of solemn celebration. The crucial material is thus buried under Christmas kitsch and other sorts of miraculous hubbub. If the Church has dressed itself up as a sort of eternal Scheherazade, as the tireless storyteller of a thousand and one miracles, then she has exchanged the single vital miracle for trivial little miracles and has thereby committed treason.

Within the Synoptic Gospels of Mark, Matthew, and Luke (so called because their narratives offer a "synopsis" or "common perspective"), the tendency to write miraculous history is readily recognizable. Mark is the oldest of the three, followed by Matthew and Luke. The Synoptics reveal a powerful impulse to superexalt and divinize Jesus through increasingly massive incursions by heavenly powers into his life, as far back as his birth, and even his conception. It's significant that Paul, the oldest New Testament author, never mentions a virgin birth. His faith is based entirely on the crucial and comprehensive theological truth of Christ's resurrection. "If Christ has not been raised, then our preaching is in vain and your faith is in vain" (1 Cor. 15:17). If Christ had not risen, then the annunciation by the angel, the virgin birth, and any amount of miracles would have left faith null and void. But if Christ has risen, then there's no need for all these miracle stories, so Paul doesn't talk about them.

But for the later generation, which included the Evangelists, belief in the resurrection was no longer enough. They elaborated the truth of the resurrection into detailed, mutually contradictory miracle stories. In addition, in their efforts to portray Jesus as divine, they kept assigning to that divinity an earlier date.

In Mark, the earliest Gospel, which still lacks a miraculous narrative of the annunciation and birth of Jesus, the heavens open at Jesus' baptism and a voice proclaims his divine sonship. Thus, in Mark, Jesus becomes God's Son only on the occasion of his baptism. In Matthew God intervenes miraculously even before Jesus' birth. An angel appears to Joseph, although only in a dream, and brings to him the message of a divine birth. In Luke the angel appears in the flesh, if one can say that about angels. In the account of the fourth and latest Evangelist, John (which is not considered one of the Synoptics because it offers its own peculiar sequence of events), the process of the miraculous divinization of Jesus in the New Testament reaches its zenith: In John, Jesus is already preexisting God.

From the New Testament miracle stories to this day, Christianity has increasingly evolved into a miracle religion, and during this evolution, it has taken refuge in ever more bizarre curiosities and abstruse notions. These have become the standard of Christian religious understanding, so much so that nowadays a person who refuses to believe in anything but Jesus and his resurrection is a heretic in the eyes of the Church.

But now to take a concrete look at the Christmas narratives in the New Testament. The accounts in the Gospels of Matthew and Luke (the only two that report about Jesus' birth) are, with respect to time, place, and circumstances, a collection of legends. The Gospels of Mark and John have nothing to report about Jesus' birth, but begin their presentation of his life at a point when he is already a grown-up. (It should be noted that the Gospel of Luke, as well as Acts of the Apostles—both written by the same author—do not derive from Luke, the physician and companion of Paul mentioned in the Letter to the Colossians (4:14). Nor is Matthew the author of the Gospel of Matthew. The real authors of both Gospels are unknown.)

A glance at the impossibilities and contradictions that we find in the Gospel accounts of Jesus' birth will suffice to show their historical incredibility. We can begin with Luke's famous Christian story, which is read aloud in many Christian—and especially Protestant—homes on Christmas Eve: "In those days a decree went out from Caesar Augustus that all the world should be enrolled. This was the first enrollment, when Quirinius was the governor of Syria. And all went to be enrolled, each in his own city" (Luke 2:1–3).

The very assertion that there was an imperial edict calling for such a census proves the whole story a fable. No Roman emperor ever issued such a senseless command. It would have unleashed a wave of international migration, driving the inhabitants of the empire this way and that across country after country to their native cities, and then back to their current places of residence. Such a method of assessing taxes would have been absurd and unworkable.

To be sure, it was customary to take censuses and to prepare lists of citizens for tax assessments and the mustering of recruits. Such censuses were held in Rome every five years, a custom that went back to 366 B.C. Every citizen of Rome had to appear in the Campus Martius and make a declaration of his family and financial affairs to the censors. Censuses were not held at regular intervals in the provinces, but as the need arose. In such censuses, the place that people (Jewish or otherwise) came from was a matter of complete indifference to the Roman state. According to Roman law, the tax declarations had to be made in the town where the taxpayer resided or, in the case of real estate, in the town where the property was.

A census ordered by Quirinius actually did take place. After the death of King Herod in 4 B.C., Herod's eldest son, Archelaos, became "ethnarch" (prince of the people) of Judea, Samaria, and Idumea. He lived in continual conflict with his subjects. After this led to a bloodbath in the forecourt of the Temple, the people sent a delegation to Augustus to register their complaints. The emperor summoned Archelaos to Rome, deposed him, and exiled him to Galilee.

After the deposition of Archelaos, control of Judea was shifted to the Roman province of Syria in A.D. 6. That same year, the emperor appointed Quirinius governor (*legatus*) of Syria, with the special assignment of organizing the administration of Judea.

At the same time, Judea was given a regional governor, called a procurator. These administrators, by the way, had their official residence not in Jerusalem but in Caesarea by the sea. Only on high feast days, when great masses of Jews streamed into Jerusalem, did the procurators come to the city to counter any possible unrest. The best known procurator was Pontius Pilate (A.D. 26–36).

Josephus (A.D. 37/38–100/110) was a Jewish general and in A.D. 66/67 supreme commander in Galilee. In the year 67 he surrendered the fortress of Jotapata to the Romans; and after the destruction of the Temple and the end of the Jewish War (A.D. 66–70), he wrote a number of important historical works. His writings are our main source for the history of New Testament times. Josephus reports as follows on Quirinius and his census:

> Quirinius, a Roman senator who had proceeded through all the magistracies to the consulship and a man who was extremely distinguished in other respects, arrived in Syria, dispatched by Caesar [Augustus] to be governor of the nation and to make an assessment of their property. Coponius, a man of equestrian rank, was sent along with him to rule over the Jews with full authority. Quirinius also visited Judaea, which had been annexed to Syria, in order to make an assessment of the property of the Jews and to liquidate the estate of Archelaus. (Josephus, Jewish Antiquities, trans. Louis Feldman [Cambridge, MA: Harvard Univ. Press (Loeb Classical Library), 1965], XVIII, i, 1, pp. 3, 5. Hereinafter cited as JA and LCL.)

With respect to this census or tax assessment, apart from the reference to the procurator Coponius (A.D. 6–9), Josephus also makes a further mention of the year A.D. 6: "Quirinius had now liquidated the estate of Archelaus; and by this time the registrations of property that took place in the thirty-seventh year after Caesar's defeat of Antony at Actium were complete. Since the high priest Joazar had now been overpowered by a popular faction, Quirinius stripped him of the dignity of his office" (Josephus, JA, XVIII, ii, 1, p. 23). The battle of Actium (in which the future emperor Augustus triumphed over Antony and Cleopatra) took place in 31 B.C. So we are back in the year A.D. 6.

The first procurator was, as mentioned, Lucius Coponius (A.D. 6–9). Under his rule there was a violent clash with the Jewish population, caused by the very census that Quirinius had ordered in A.D. 6. The resistance to Quirinius's census was so strong that a certain Judas, nick-named "the Galilean," sparked a popular uprising in Judea and Samaria. "A Galilean, named Judas, incited his countrymen to revolt, upbraiding them as cowards for consenting to pay tribute to the Romans and tolerat-ing mortal masters, after having God for their lord" (Josephus, *The Jewish War*, trans. H. St. J. Thackeray [LCL], II, viii, 1, pp. 367, 369. Hereinafter cited as *JW*). Acts of the Apostles (5:37) reports Judas's death in the course of his uprising. Later the procurator Alexander (A.D. 46–48) had Judas's two sons, Jacob and Simon, crucified as rebels (Josephus, *JA*, XX, v, 2, p. 55).

Also in A.D. 6, and likewise in connection with this census, the ex-tremely nationalistic party of the Zealots (i.e., people deeply committed to the law of God) was founded. The party's founder and religious inspira-tion was once again Judas the Galilean, along with the Pharisee Zadok. The Zealots viewed the struggle against the rule of the Roman foreigners as a religious obligation. It is worth noting that the party was founded in Galilee, although that region of the country was not affected by the cen-sus. But well before then, Galilee had developed into a center of resistance against the Roman occupying power, and the Galileans had the reputation of being anarchists. The fact that Jesus was a Galilean probably played a decisive role in his trial and execution.

This much is certain: The census mentioned by Luke as taking place at the time of Jesus' birth actually occurred in A.D. 6. Nothing is known of any earlier census. Hence, the date provided by Luke doesn't agree with his other statement (given in Luke 1:15) that John the Baptist, Jesus' cou-sin born just six months before him, was begotten in the days of Herod (d. 4 B.C.).

Along with this discrepancy in dating, Luke also cites a false motive for the trip to Bethlehem. There would have been no such journey unless Joseph had owned property in Bethlehem. But if he had no real estate, as an inhabitant of Galilee under the tetrarch Herod Antipas, he would not have been affected by the order of the Syrian governor Quirinius. Under no circumstances could the reason for Joseph's journey be, as Luke says, that he was "of the house and lineage of David," because, as already men-tioned, that was of no interest to the Romans in this context.

Moreover, Joseph owned no property in Bethlehem. Otherwise he would have had tenant farmers or slaves. In that case he would have been a well-to-do man and could have seen to it that the child was born at the house of a tenant farmer or manager instead of in a manger. But Joseph and Mary were poor people, a couple with no possessions, as is clear from Luke's description of the purification offering for Mary: "When the time had come for their purification [here Luke falsely applies the necessity of cultic purification to both parents; only the mother was affected] according to the law of Moses, they brought him up to Jerusalem to present him to the Lord . . . and to offer a sacrifice, according to what is said in the law of the Lord, 'a pair of turtledoves, or two young pigeons'" (Luke 2:22ff.).

A sacrifice of pigeons was not the rule but the exception, and it was permitted only to poor people: "And when the days of her purification are completed, . . . she shall bring to the priest . . . a lamb a year old for a burnt offering, and a young pigeon or turtledove for a sin offering, and he shall offer it before the Lord, and make atonement for her; then shall she be clean" (Lev. 12:6ff.). If Mary's offering of pigeons isn't just another fantasy of the Gospel writer, then it's clear proof of how poor the couple was. In any case, we can't have Joseph, on the one hand, owning property in Bethlehem to justify his trip there and, on the other hand, Mary offering the sacrifice prescribed for the poor.

But if there was no census around the time of Jesus' birth—assuming he was born during the reign of Herod—then there would be no reason at all for Joseph to expose his pregnant wife to the hardships and dangers of such a trip immediately before her delivery. Consequently we can say that Joseph and Mary never took any trip at this time for this reason. That means that if Joseph and Mary were living in Nazareth, Jesus was born not in Bethlehem but in Nazareth. But Bethlehem is important for Luke (just as it is for Matthew) as the birthplace of Jesus because it is the city of David. Luke wants to make the birth of Jesus in Bethlehem plausible by fabricating the story of the census. But since he handles the facts arbitrarily, the facts themselves refute him. Hence, there was no vain search for lodging, and no child in the manger, no shepherds, and no ox and ass on the scene.

Even if we were to suppose for a moment that there was such a census at the time cited by Luke—namely, in the reign of Herod—the idea of a woman in the ninth month of pregnancy going on such a trek immediately before giving birth would be absurd. Joseph's behavior in exposing his wife and unborn child to mortal danger would have to be labeled as incomprehensibly reckless. This is especially true when we consider that Mary's presence at a tax assessment was not in the least required, since only heads of families were obliged to register. Furthermore, such assessments did not take place on a fixed date, but were stretched over a period of weeks and even months, so there was no need to hurry.

If we follow the Gospel account, it's altogether impossible to understand why Joseph didn't take better precautions for the birth. For example, he didn't arrange things so that when "the time came for her to be delivered" she could stay with her relative Elizabeth (who, according to the New Testament, lived only a few kilometers away) and give birth to her son there. But presumably this relative of Mary's was herself a creature of legend.

Moreover, the road taken by Mary and Joseph (at first only the husband is named: "And Joseph also went up from Galilee, from the city of Nazareth, to Judea," Luke 2:4) for the supposed census was a difficult and dangerous journey of about 130 kilometers. As for the hardships, we need only imagine the last part of the journey, from Jericho to Jerusalem. (We have to assume that they took the simpler route through the Jordan Valley, and not the steep up-and-down path through the mountainous—and hostile—country of Samaria.) We are told that Jesus himself went to Jerusalem via Jericho (Mark 10:46). Jericho is about 250 meters beneath sea level, Jerusalem about 750 meters above. In the rainy season—that is, the winter—making any progress over the waterlogged roads was unthinkable. Therefore, it is also absurd to imagine the Christmas story as taking place in December ("The snow lay on the ground, / The stars shone bright").

The road was dangerous, too, because brigandage was widespread at the time, and individuals and small groups were in constant danger of being assaulted. The story of the man who was traveling from Jerusalem to Jericho and fell among robbers, as told by Jesus (Luke 10:30), is very much taken from everyday life. But it's highly unlikely that anyone from Nazareth would have gone with Joseph and Mary to Bethlehem for a census: There is no reason to assume that a fairly large number of property owners from Bethlehem lived in Nazareth, of all places. Larger groups or caravans of travelers could be gotten together for protection against robbers only around the greatest feast days.

But there is no word—the very idea is out of the question—of the tax assessment's taking place precisely during one of the three greatest festivals (Passover, Shavuoth, and Succoth) when Jewish pilgrims went to Jerusalem. Because if they had had to be assessed anywhere except in Jerusalem, either their religious obligation to go on pilgrimage would have prevented them from meeting their political obligation to be assessed or, vice versa, their political obligation to be assessed would have prevented them from meeting their religious obligation to go on pilgrimage. This religious duty to travel as a pilgrim applied to everybody (with a few exceptions): "All are obliged to appear at the three main festivals in the Temple, except for the deaf, the insane, minors, neuters, hermaphrodites, women[!], slaves, the lame, the blind, the sick, the very old, and those who are incapable of walking up to Temple Mount with their own feet" (quoted in Joachim Jeremias, *Jerusalem zur Zeit Jesu* [1969], p. 87). In short, the assessment cannot have taken place during any one of the three great festivals.

At other times when pilgrims didn't come to Jerusalem in great crowds, there were thousands upon thousands of accommodations available for the night. Jerusalem was a tourist city of unique dimensions. The eighth of the ten miracles which take place at the sanctuary was believed to be that there was always enough room, and no pilgrim ever said to another, "The throng is so great that I can't find lodging for the night in Jerusalem." Actually, that wasn't completely true. It is reported that "no one was ever crushed to death in the Temple court, except on a Passover during the time of Hillel, when an old man was crushed; and so it was called the Passover of the Crushed Man" (quoted in Jeremias, *Jerusalem*, pp. 89, 95).

With so much room in Jerusalem, there was no need to go to Bethlehem, which Luke describes as full to overflowing, because Bethlehem lay close to Jerusalem (about eight kilometers). And it wasn't even necessary to go to Jerusalem itself. All the surrounding villages, including those between Jerusalem and Bethlehem, were prepared to welcome strangers.

Thus the author of Luke is guilty of discrepancies if not downright nonsense. But he tops it off with his jumbled dates. As we have already seen, he puts Jesus' birth in the time of Quirinius's census, which took place in A.D. 6, while he locates all the events of Jesus' infancy in the reign of Herod. But Herod died in 4 B.C., so Luke erred either by placing the birth of Jesus in the time of Quirinius's tax assessment (A.D. 6) or by placing it in the time of Herod (d. 4 B.C.). Evidently, one of the dates must be wrong, unless they're both wrong. If we wish to continue seeing Luke's accounts of angelic messages and so forth as historical events, we would have to take a large leap of faith: We'd have to assume that while on verifiable matters of historical fact Luke tells all sorts of fairy tales, on all supernatural matters—which by definition can never be checked—he simply reports the facts. By his arbitrary treatment of history, Luke has shown himself to be an unhistorical reporter—a teller of fairy tales.

Here is another instance of how the historical data supplied by Luke are unreliable. Luke also provides a date for the beginning of Jesus' public activity: He makes it coincide with the appearance of John the Baptist. But once again the numbers are confused. At the beginning of chapter 3 Luke says: "In the fifteenth year of the reign of Tiberius Caesar, Pontius Pilate being governor [procurator] of Judea, and Herod being tetrarch of Galilee, and his brother Philip tetrarch of the region of Iturea and Trachonitis, and Lysanias tetrarch of Abilene, in the high-priesthood of Annas and Caiaphas, the word of God came to John the son of Zechariah in the wilderness."

To the particulars: Tiberius (42 B.C.–A.D. 37) became emperor on 19 August A.D. 14. Thus the fifteenth year of his reign fell between August A.D. 28 and August A.D. 29. Pontius Pilate was procurator of Judea from A.D. 26 to 36. Herod Antipas was tetrarch (meaning a ruler over a portion—originally a fourth—of a country) of Galilee from 4 B.C. to A.D. 36. His brother Philip was tetrarch of Iturea and Trachonitis from 4 B.C. to A.D. 34. We know little more of Lysanias than that he died sometime between A.D. 28 and 37. So far, so good: The year 28/29 is possible.

But what Luke adds to this is impossible: "in the high-priesthood of Annas and Caiaphas." First, Luke strangely makes a singular "high priest" out of the two men. Second, everyone takes the date to mean the term of office, not the lifetime of the two. But Annas's term of office ended in A.D. 15. Then he was removed from office by the Roman procurator Valerius Gratus (A.D. 15–26), the predecessor of Pontius Pilate (Josephus, *JA*, XVIII, ii, 2, p. 29). Caiaphas's term in office began in A.D. 15. Between A.D. 15 and 18 came the four brief terms in office of four different high priests.

Luke obviously had no idea of the actual historical dates. Thus he practically asserts that Jesus was active, on the one hand, in the years from A.D. 15 to 18 (the minimum time frame in which both Annas and Caiaphas were high priests), and, on the other hand, in A.D. 29. Nowadays scriptural commentators avoid the problems of the false dating "in the high-priesthood of Annas and Caiaphas" by explaining that one of the high priests (Annas) was actually not in office, but still alive and, in fact, still influential, when Jesus began his public career in the year 29.

But while such commentators suppose that Luke may not have meant to be so precise as his language sounds, when he says that Jesus was active during the term of office of Annas and Caiaphas, later theologians took him quite literally. We can see this, for example, by glancing in the famous *Ecclesiastical History* of Eusebius, bishop of Caesarea in Palestine (d. 339). Eusebius takes Luke to mean what he says—namely, that Jesus' activity spanned the years from Annas to Caiaphas. But at the same time, he sticks to the year 29. Thus Eusebius provides the following nonsensical account:

> *When Tiberius Caesar was in the fifteenth year of his reign . . .
> the divine Scripture [commentary: Luke's imprecision has by
> now become "divine"] says that he [Jesus] completed the whole
> time of his teaching while Annas and Caiaphas were high priest,
> showing that the whole time of his teaching was bounded by the
> years which cover their administrations. Since, then, he began
> in the high priesthood of Annas and continued to the reign of
> Caiaphas the intervening time does not extend to a full four
> years. . . . Four high priests intervened in succession between*

Annas and Caiaphas. (Ecclesiastical History, *trans. Kirsopp Lake [Cambridge, MA: Harvard Univ. Press (LCL), 1992], I, x, 2-6, p. 77)*

For a long time, church historians followed this dating maneuver. The theologians swallowed with scarcely any difficulty whatever was written in the Gospels. Thus in his *Catena Aurea,* the "Golden Chain," an exposition of the Gospels, Thomas Aquinas, the most important theologian of the Middle Ages (d. 1274), borrowed Eusebius's preposterous dating. Thomas placed Jesus' public activity both in the fifteenth year of the reign of Tiberius (A.D. 29) and in the four years from Annas to Caiaphas, A.D. 15 through 18 (*Commentary on Luke,* 3:1-2).

In fact, we don't have one solid biographical notice of the year of Jesus' birth. There definitely were historians in his day who could have reported on this—Josephus, for example; but he doesn't mention Jesus. The writers who tell us about Jesus, the four Evangelists, are not really interested in Jesus' biography. Thus, as far as the concrete data of his birth are concerned, Jesus entered history almost like a phantom. And since we also don't know the year of his death, he stepped out of history in the same uncertain blur. We have nothing concrete in hand, only the traces that he left behind in the religious landscape of Palestine.

In conclusion, one more note on the annunciation, as described by Luke (1:26ff.). Here the angel Gabriel doesn't give his own name, as he does in the scene with the father of John the Baptist, Zachariah (Luke 1:19). Nevertheless, Mary immediately identifies him as Gabriel. He has come to Nazareth and prophesies that she will conceive a son. Mary has one objection: "How shall this be, since I know not man?" (that is, have had no sexual relations with a man) (Luke 1:34). Mary should at least have known her own husband, Joseph. But this embarrassed translation, "since I know not man," which we find in both Catholic and Protestant Bibles, is inaccurate, since the English word *know* means a purely intellectual operation, unlike the New Testament Greek word. Furthermore, whether translated clearly or vaguely, the phrasing of Mary's objection proves to be, upon closer inspection, a literary invention out of the mouth of an artificial figure.

Admittedly, Mary's words "since I have no sexual relations with a man" do correctly render her objective situation. But subjectively or psychologically, such a manner of speaking is completely inconsistent. Objectively or legally speaking, Mary was forbidden to have sexual relations with a strange man. That would have meant adultery and a capital crime. As for her own husband—although he already was legally her husband—Mary was still a kind of fiancée. Joseph had not yet taken her home to his house. Sexual intercourse between an engaged couple, while not forbidden, was still unusual. So Mary's objection correctly conveys the actual situation.

But psychologically this sentence can never have been spoken, because it states that Mary has relations neither with her husband nor with any other man. Conversely, she sees that the angel's message presupposes her having intercourse either with her own husband or with a stranger. She does *not* say the only thing that she could have said: "since I have no sexual relations with *my husband.*" Instead she says, "with *man,*" meaning with any man. This indifference, this placing of marital and extramarital relations on the same level, proves that Mary's objection to the angel is a literary invention, as we shall see once again in the chapter on the Virgin Mother.

Appendix

The house of the holy Virgin in Nazareth was transported by angels from Nazareth to Europe on the night of 9 May in the year 1291. It first arrived in Raunitza (Dalmatia), between Tersato and Fiume. In the morning, the inhabitants of Raunitza saw to their great astonishment the house (which was built in a strange architectural style) standing on a spot where no house had stood before. In the house they found a cross on an altar and a statue of the holy Virgin. The bishop of the region, who lay sick in bed, recovered his health at once and told everyone about the revelation he had received. The governor of Fiume, Nicolaus Frangipani, sent a delegation to Nazareth, which was informed by the locals that the holy house had disappeared from Nazareth. The foundation, which was still intact, matched the outline of the strange house in Raunitza.

All this was taken down in sworn testimony and may be read in the archives of Fiume. The entire proceedings were published. But after three years and seven months, on the night of 10 December 1294, the house vanished from Raunitza and suddenly appeared on the other side of the Adriatic near the city of Recanati in Italy. Shepherds had seen it glide over the sea. Later, however, the house moved on, since, along with many pilgrims, many criminals also felt attracted to the site. It first moved two kilometers and then another 150 meters, toward Loreto, where it plumped itself down on a public highway. There it stands to this day. "Over the course of the centuries the Holy House of Loreto has passed all examinations, both historical and scientific, with flying colors; and it is humanly certain that this is the same house in which Mary, the Queen of Heaven, dwelled in Nazareth" (Heinrich Joseph Wetzer and Benedikt Welte, *Kirchenlexikon* [1893], VIII, 147).

Pope Julius II (1503–12) had the famous Bramante design a marble covering for the house in 1510. Popes Leo X (1513–21), Clement VII (1523–34), and Paul III (1534–49) had the designs executed. Later popes, namely, Pius V (1566–72) and Sixtus V (1585–90), built a splendid basilica over the house. Unfortunately, the wonder-working image was stolen by the French in 1797, but Napoleon had it returned in 1801. In memory of the pious event of the "conveyance of the holy house of Mary, the Mother of God, wherein the Word was made flesh," Innocent XII—after a thorough investigation by appropriate committees—established a feast of the Holy House with its own mass in the year 1699. It was at first merely a regional affair, but it was extended to Tuscany in 1719 and by Pope Benedict XIII (1724–30) to the Papal States, Venice, and all Spanish possessions. Pilgrims to the Holy House received, and still receive, many indulgences.

In November 1887 a famous saint-to-be visited the Holy House of Loreto. It was Saint Thérèse de Lisieux, also called Thérèse of the Child Jesus or little Saint Thérèse, to distinguish her from "big Saint Teresa" of Avila. At the age of fifteen, she entered the Carmelite order, and she died in 1897, after a hard life in religion, at the age of twenty-four. Little Saint Thérèse reported on her trip to Loreto in her diary:

After leaving Venice, we arrived in Padua where we venerated St. Anthony's tongue and, at Bologna, the body of St. Catherine whose face is marked with the kiss of the Child Jesus. I was full of happiness when we set off to Loreto. The Blessed Virgin chose well when she placed her house there. . . . What shall I say about the holy house? I was deeply moved to be under the very roof which had sheltered the Holy Family, and to be looking at the walls on which Our Lord had gazed and walking on the ground once moistened by St. Joseph's sweat, and to be where Mary had carried Jesus in her arms after carrying Him in her virginal womb. I saw the little room of the Annunciation and I put my rosary in the dish used by the Child Jesus. (The Autobiography of St. Thérèse of Lisieux: The Story of a Soul, *trans.* John Beevers [New York: Doubleday, 1989], pp. 79-80)

CHAPTER TWO

Matthew's Fairy Tale of Jesus' Childhood

THE NARRATIVES OF Jesus' infancy in Matthew and Luke were put together late in the 1st century A.D. But the usual term "infancy narratives" is fundamentally incorrect, because we never learn what sort of a child Jesus was—for example, was he lively or quiet? These stories are mainly concerned with his miraculous birth.

The well-known Catholic New Testament scholar Karl Hermann Schelke finds it quite natural that these birth stories should have been composed so late:

> Of the four Gospels—at least in the form we have them today, written in Greek—the Gospel of Mark is the oldest, probably written before A.D. 70, the year Jerusalem was destroyed. The Gospel of Mark has no infancy narrative. This absence is striking, but it would be jumping to conclusions to say that the infancy narratives are a later and most likely legendary accretion. First, the resurrection of Christ had to be proclaimed and, along with that, the dreadful cross, which was staring everyone in the face, had to be explained and overcome.... Only then did the authors' interest turn to the hidden events of Jesus' early childhood. That explains why only the later Gospels of Matthew and Luke

have infancy narratives. ("Die Kindheitsgeschichten Jesu," in
Bibel und zeitgemäßer Glaube *[1967], II, 14)*

Schelke argues that the infancy narratives emerged so late not because they were legends, but because before then people were busy with other things. First the resurrection had to be proclaimed, and in this way the death of Jesus was "explained and overcome" by the end of the first century (Schelke dates the Gospels of Matthew and Luke around A.D. 80). Only then could these two Evangelists turn to new areas of interest.

But even if Christians had "explained and overcome" the death of Jesus more quickly, the infancy narratives, to which they could have turned that much sooner, would still be legends. On the other hand, there are some people who still can't "explain" the death of Jesus on the cross, much less "overcome" it, and who have a hard time with the way the theologians "explain" and "overcome" it. But more on that subject later. In any event, the infancy narratives are unaffected by all this and remain, now as ever, legends.

Matthew has "Jesus of Nazareth" (where he probably was born, in fact) born in Bethlehem, the city of David, but he tells an altogether different story from Luke's. First of all, Matthew places the events exclusively in the time of Herod. Thus for Matthew the latest possible date for Jesus' birth would be 4 B.C., since Herod died in that year.

Matthew knows nothing about a census ordered by Augustus, which Luke needed simply to get Mary and Joseph to Bethlehem, the city of David. For Matthew, Mary and Joseph do not live in Nazareth; they are in Bethlehem from the outset, so he has an altogether different problem from Luke's. Luke, in order to have "Jesus of Nazareth" born in the city of David, has Mary and Joseph travel to Bethlehem, while Matthew's "Jesus of Nazareth" somehow had to arrive in Nazareth from Bethlehem. This happened, says the Evangelist, so "that what was spoken by the prophets might be fulfilled, 'He shall be called a Nazarene'" (Matt. 2:3).

This prophecy, however, has one cosmetic defect: It doesn't exist. Since even actual Old Testament passages available to Matthew shouldn't be taken as prophesying a concrete person, a nonexistent scriptural passage can a fortiori not be taken as referring to Jesus. The prophecy, therefore, is based on Matthew's total misunderstanding of a passage from Isaiah (11:1), where the Messiah is called a *nezer* (branch); in other words, a branch from Jesse's (father of David) "stump." Matthew reads into "nezer" the city of Nazareth, and so Mary and Joseph had to move to Nazareth.

As the motive for this change of residence Matthew doesn't cite the chaos due to the census of Augustus or anything like that. Instead he chooses the motif of flight, although he adds an intermediary stop. Jesus flees from King Herod to Egypt and then, out of fear of his successor, to Nazareth. Of course, he could have fled to Nazareth immediately; but for the sake of fulfilling another prophecy (Hos. 11:1), he first had to flee to Egypt: "Out of Egypt I called my son." So at some point Jesus has to be called out of Egypt. But first, of course, he has to get there, and so we have the flight from the child-murderer Herod into Egypt. In passing, it might be noted that Hosea's "son" in Egypt has nothing to do with an individual son; it means the entire people of Israel.

But before both flights (to Egypt and to Nazareth) come Herod's persecutions, and these in turn are connected to the grand visit from the East. After Matthew mentions, only briefly, the birth of Jesus—he has no specific information—he begins his actual narrative with astrological events: "Now when Jesus was born in Bethlehem of Judea in the days of Herod the king, behold, wise men [astrologers] from the East came to Jerusalem" (Matt. 2:1). Presumably they came from Babylon and wanted to look for the newborn king of the Jews, whose star they had seen. This brings Herod on stage.

Evidently the star, in the meantime, has not been functioning properly. After the Magi see the star in the East, it lights their way up to Jerusalem, but it doesn't shine again until after their visit with Herod. It then goes before them till it reaches the home of the child they are seeking, in Bethlehem. Had the star shone continuously, or had it begun to shine again only a little sooner, or had it shone while detouring around Jerusalem, then the fatal visit to Herod would have been superfluous. Moreover, the new king of the Jews would not have been exposed to the danger of death by the star's temporary power failure. In any case, for the children of Bethlehem, who according to Matthew were murdered by Herod, the heavenly star turns into a fatal star indeed.

As for the star's illuminating the road from Jerusalem to Bethlehem, that was entirely unnecessary, since Herod had already informed the Magi about the city they were looking for. The star was needed only to find the exact house number, so to speak. On this matter Hermann Samuel Reimarus (d. 1768), the father of modern skeptical commentators on the Bible, observed long ago: "A comet with a tail is too high to point to a specific house" (*Apologie oder Schutzschrift für die vernünftigen Verehrer Gottes* [1972], II, 536).

The framework of Luke's account has no time for the whole story of the star and the Magi. Since Herod has all the male children killed "who were two years old or under, according to the time which he had ascertained from the wise men" (Matt. 2:16), at least one year must have passed between the birth of Jesus and the visit of the Magi. Jesus would have been going on two. Strangely enough, however, as we know from the Church's depictions of the adoration of the Magi, Jesus was still lying in the manger—no doubt he wasn't a very active child. In this phlegmatic feature of his character Jesus obviously took after his father, who after all this time was still sitting tight with his young family in the stable.

According to Luke, though, everything was quite different. After forty days—that is, after the legally required purification of the mother—Mary and Joseph return directly to Galilee (Luke 2:39). But this forty-day period wasn't long enough to contain either the visit of the Magi to the one- to two-year-old baby Jesus or the ensuing flight to Egypt after the slaughter of the Innocents. And to that extent fairy tales do, after all, approach the truth, at least indirectly, because here one fairy tale refutes the other.

The ancient world was full of stars announcing important events, especially the birth of great men. At first, the notion of being led by stars was an absolutely everyday matter; every nation that sailed the sea was familiar with it. But since these guiding signs were understood as divine signs, they were early on considered as pointing to divine dignity that transcended the usual measure of human greatness.

Suetonius (ca. A.D. 70–?) reports not specifically about a star but in general about a "miraculous sign" in connection with the birth of Augustus. Referring to Julius Marathus, the freeman and secretary of Augustus, Suetonius writes:

According to Julius Marathus, a public portent warned the Roman people some months before Augustus' birth that Nature was making ready to provide them with a king; and this caused the Senate such consternation that they issued a decree which forbade the rearing of a male child for a whole year. However, a group of senators whose wives were expectant prevented the decree from being filed at the Treasury and thus becoming law—for each of them hoped that the prophesied King would be his own son.

Suetonius tells us further:

Then there is a story which I found in a book called Theologumena, *by Asclepias of Mendes. Augustus' mother, Atia, with certain married women friends, once attended a solemn midnight service at the temple of Apollo, where she had her litter set down, and presently fell asleep as the others also did. Suddenly a serpent glided up, entered her, and then glided away again. On awakening, she purified herself, as if after intimacy with her husband. An irremovable coloured mark in the shape of a serpent, which then appeared on her body, made her ashamed to visit the public baths any more; and the birth of Augustus nine months later suggested a divine paternity. Atia dreamed that her intestines were carried up to Heaven and overhung all lands and sea; and Octavius [Augustus' father], that the sun rose from between her thighs.* (The Twelve Caesars, *trans. Robert Graves [Baltimore: Penguin, 1957], pp. 100–101)*

The same narrative elements that appear in connection with the birth of Jesus also turn up here with reference to Augustus: a miraculous sign, conception without a man, a dream vision of the husband, persecution by the rulers.

Schelke, too, points to parallel star-signs in the history of religion:

According to Virgil [d. 19 B.C.], in the Aeneid II, 694ff. *Aeneas was led by a star on his journey from Troy to Latium. According to the commentary of Servius [ca. A.D. 400] on the* Aeneid X, 272 *a comet appeared in the sky when Augustus took command. Then, we are told, a great joy was shared by all the people. The description of the star of the Magi, as it appears, disappears, and reappears can be labeled a legendarily stylized narrative. (Schelke, "Die Kindheitsgeschichten Jesu," p. 16)*

From this standpoint, the Gospel account of this sort of miraculous star appearing at the birth of Jesus is no longer even a miracle.

The church father Origen (d. 253) positively demands a star for Jesus' birth:

It has been observed that at great events and the most far-reaching changes of history stars of this kind appear which are signifi-cant of changes of dynasties or wars, or whatever may happen among men which has the effect of shaking earthly affairs. We read in the book on comets by Chaeremon the Stoic [1st century B.C.] how comets even appeared when good events were about to happen, and he gives an account of these. If then a comet, as it is called, or some similar star appears at new dynasties or other great events on earth, why is it amazing that a star should have appeared at the birth of a man who was to introduce new ideas among the human race and to bring a doctrine not only to Jews but also to Greeks, and to many barbarian nations as well? (Con-tra Celsum, trans. Henry Chadwick [Cambridge: Cambridge Univ. Press, 1953], I, 59, p. 54)

Ever since the time of Kepler (d. 1630), astronomers have speculated that the star of Bethlehem might be the rare triple conjunction of Jupiter and Saturn that occurred in Pisces in May, October, and December during the year A.D. 7. But this possibility is out because Matthew says there was only one star, not many. Also, a conjunction wouldn't travel from Jerusalem to Bethlehem in order, as Matthew asserts, to come to rest over a house. Only a fairy-tale star can do that, and a very low-flying fairy-tale star at that, because there's no way to determine over which house a star in the sky is "resting."

In this context it's worth noting what Pope Leo I (d. 461) has to say about the star. In a display of a Christian anti-Judaism that had been quick to develop, Leo writes that the star was invisible to the Jews because of their blindness (Sermon XXXV, 1). That must have been an enormous blindness, because in the Church's view the star was of an enormous size. The church father Ignatius of Antioch (d. ca. 110) writes: "A star shone in heaven beyond all the stars, and its light was unspeakable, and its newness caused astonishment, and all the other stars, with the sun and moon gathered in chorus round this star, and it far exceeded them all in its light" (*Letter to the Ephesians*, XIX, 2, in *The Apostolic Fathers*, trans. Kirsopp Lake [Cambridge, MA: Harvard Univ. Press (LCL), 1976–77], p. 193). In the apocryphal *Protevangelium of James* (ca. 150) the Magi describe the star to Herod as follows: "We saw how an indescribably greater star shone among those stars and dimmed them, so that they no longer shone; and so we knew that a king was born for Israel" (21; in Edgar Hennecke, *New Testament Apocrypha*, ed. Wilhelm Schneemelcher, various translators, 2 vols. [Philadelphia: Westminster Press, 1963], I, 386. Hereinafter cited as *NTA*).

For the New Testament writers and especially for Matthew, the Old Testament is a book full of prophecies of Jesus. Matthew takes every conceivable pain to show how these prophecies have now been fulfilled, even though sometimes he has to stretch the evidence to make his point.

As for Bethlehem, which as the city of David was inevitably mentioned in connection with the future Messiah, Matthew adds yet another prophecy, this one by Micah. Micah speaks of Bethlehem as the birthplace of a future "ruler of Israel" (5:1). (Incidentally, one must distinguish between the high priest, singular, and the high priests, plural: The latter are members of a consistory made up of priests and lay noblemen, which was subordinate to the ruling high priest.) The scribes knew this prophecy and so were able to tell Herod the birthplace of the newborn king: "And you, Bethlehem, in the land of Judah, are by no means least among the rulers of Judah; for from you shall come a ruler who will govern my people Israel" (Matt. 2:6). Actually, the original text of Micah says just the opposite: "But you, O Bethlehem Ephrathah, who are little to be among the clans of Judah." Furthermore, upon closer inspection, the link between Jesus and this ruler prophesied by Micah proves to be quite tenuous. Micah is talking about a bloody leader in war. His men "shall rule the land of Assyria with the sword, and the land of Nimrod with the drawn sword" (Mic. 5:6). The well-known Catholic Pattloch Bible doesn't shrink from providing this slaughter-filled section from Micah (8th century B.C.) with the heading "Birth and Activity of the Messiah." The text of Micah goes on to characterize this messianic "activity": "like a lion among the beasts of the forest, like a young lion among the flocks of sheep, which when it goes through, treads down and tears in pieces, and there is none to deliver" (Mic. 5:8). Because of this prophecy, Jesus was finally born in Bethlehem (or perhaps wasn't born there).

Whenever Matthew thinks he's found something in the Old Testament, he strives to find events in the life of Jesus that could be read as its fulfillment, and if necessary, he makes up such events. Such contrived fulfillments of old prophecies are called fulfillment legends. It's a bit like the old song where the jealous lover says that he saw Esau sitting on a see-saw—evidently just for the sake of the rhyme.

One especially curious fulfillment of an Old Testament prophecy cited by Matthew may be inserted here, although it occurs only toward the end of Jesus' life, in connection with Jesus' entrance into Jerusalem. Matthew views this entrance as a fulfillment of a prophecy in Zech. 9:9: "Rejoice greatly, O daughter of Zion! Shout aloud, O daughter of Jerusalem! Lo, your king comes to you; triumphant and victorious is he, humble and riding on an ass, on a colt the foal of an ass."

"Foal of an ass" is an explanation of "colt." The text speaks of a single ass, but because Matthew mistakenly thinks that Zechariah is talking about two asses, he also mistakenly translates: "This took place to fulfill what was spoken by the prophet, saying, 'Tell the daughter of Zion, Behold your king is coming to you, humble and mounted on an ass, and on a colt, the foal of an ass" (Matt. 21:4–5). Accordingly, Matthew also has Jesus tell the disciples earlier: "Go into the village opposite you, and immediately you will find an ass tied, and a colt with her; untie them and bring them to me. And if anyone says anything to you, you shall say, 'The Lord has need of them.'. . . The disciples went and did as Jesus had directed them. They brought the ass and the colt and put their garments on them, and he sat thereon" (Matt. 21:2ff.). On both beasts!

Theologians have struggled (in vain) to make sense of this senseless passage. As the officially approved Catholic religion textbook *Patmos-Synopsis* (1968) says: "In this way Matthew bears witness to his faith that the episode corresponds to the will of God. . . . Obviously it is very important to Matthew that the Old Testament promise is fulfilled down to the slightest detail" (p. 13).

Thus Matthew's odd misunderstanding of a passage from the Old Testament gets theologically sanitized by taking it as a sign of faith "that the event corresponds to God's will." But invoking the will of God to smooth over error is uncalled for. There's no point in looking for the will of God in nonsense; we have enough to do searching for it in what does make sense. But any Christian can bring God and what makes sense together. Often enough theologians see nonsense as the tea leaves that they are supposed to read in order to divine the will of God.

But Jesus himself had more healthy common sense than such theologians, as we can see in a saying of his contained in the apocryphal Coptic *Gospel of Thomas,* which was rediscovered in 1945 in Nag Hammadi (Upper Egypt) and which has all the marks of authenticity. The saying goes: "It is impossible for a man to mount two horses" (logion 47, *NTA,* I, 291).

The two-asses theology might put too much of a strain on, say, eight- or nine-year-old pupils in grammar school. But the theologians have thought of that too, and so instead of riding around on both beasts at once they prefer to switch from theology to zoology. Thus in his *Commentary . . . on the Catechism for the Third and Fourth Grades* (1966, p. 166), Joseph Solzbacher works up Jesus' entrance into Jerusalem with the ass and her colt as a sort of meditation on kindness to animals. Wishing to spare religion teachers a "detailed exegesis," Solzbacher writes: "Did Jesus sit on the ass? On her colt? On both? . . . Jesus rode on the colt, only on the colt. Without its mother the colt would have bucked and refused to move, and no one could have ridden it."

Another fulfillment of a prophecy is the horrible story of Herod's murder of the little boys in Bethlehem. But we need not mourn these deaths. The whole story, like that of the three wise men from the East, is just a fairy tale, and it takes place only because of a prophecy. Matthew writes: "Then was fulfilled what was spoken by the prophet Jeremiah: 'A voice was heard in Ramah, wailing and loud lamentation, Rachel weeping for her children; she refused to be consoled, because they were no more'" (Matt. 2:17–18; Jer. 31:15). Matthew ignores the fact that Jeremiah is talking about Ramah, a place eight kilometers north of Jerusalem, not at all about Bethlehem, which lies eight kilometers south of the capital. Also Jeremiah is not talking about the murder of children, because in Jeremiah Rachel's sons are captured, and the prophet promises: "Your children shall come back to their own country" (Jer. 31:17).

We run into the story of the slaughter of the Innocents at other times and in different places. It contains a widespread motif of fairy tales and legends. Matthew borrows the essential features of the story from Exod. 1:15–16. In so doing, he uses the form that this tale about Moses acquired in later Jewish culture, as told, for example, by Josephus:

> One of the sacred scribes—persons with considerable skill in accurately predicting the future—announced to the king that there would be born to the Israelites at that time one who would abase the sovereignty of the Egyptians and exalt the Israelites, were he reared to manhood. . . . Alarmed thereat, the king, on this sage's advice, ordered that every male child born to the Israelites should be destroyed by being cast into the river. (JA, trans. H. St. J. Thackeray [Cambridge, MA: Harvard Univ. Press (LCL), 1991], II, ix, 2; p. 253)

This persecution of the children of Israel by Pharaoh supplies the pattern for Herod's persecution of the children of Bethlehem.

Matthew enriches his fairy tale of the slaughtered Innocents with a few other quotations from the Old Testament that refer to a later stage in the life of the grown-up Moses. Moses has to flee from Pharaoh because he has killed an Egyptian (Exod. 2:12ff.) and stays away until God informs him that he can return without danger: "For all the men who were seeking your life are dead" (Exod. 4:19). "For those who sought the child's life are dead" (Matt. 2:20). "So Moses took his wife and his sons and set them on an ass, and went back to the land of Egypt" (Exod. 4:20). "And he [Joseph] rose and took the child and his mother, and went to the land of Israel"

(Matt. 2:21). Thus Matthew fits together the events in Exod. 1:15f., in the embellished form available in his own day, as well as the sentence from Exod. 4:19–20, and makes them over into a new event.

But such proof that a Gospel story has been borrowed from elsewhere is not enough to embarrass the theologians. Hermann Schelke, for instance, writes: "The tradition of Moses' miraculous childhood has evidently influenced the account of Jesus' childhood. But these findings from history have a theological content. This is a way of expressing the idea that Jesus is a new Moses" ("Die Kindheitsgeschichten Jesu," p. 17). Under this motto of "theological content" one may transcribe many things from many sources and turn Jesus into a copy of any number of possible predecessors. In this case, however, the comparison of Jesus to Moses already limps because, unlike Moses, Jesus has not killed anyone.

We're aware of many foul crimes committed by Herod, but the slaughter of the Innocents isn't one of them. This is merely a Christian calumny. Besides, this massacre wasn't even needed as a practical measure, because, after all, everyone in Bethlehem must have known to which house with which little boy (of the, say, twenty to thirty such infants in town) the star and the caravan had made their way.

But even if we take the slaughter of the Innocents at face value, we have to ask why, although God saved his own son by sending an angel to warn Joseph in a dream, he left the sons of other fathers and mothers to die. But perhaps that's an unchristian question. Pope Leo I, the Great (d. 461), in any case takes a positive view of the matter: God had already given the dead infants "the dignity of martyrdom" (Sermon XXXI). Why Mary and Joseph themselves, after the warning dream, didn't warn the parents of other children must likewise remain an open question. Perhaps they thought as positively as Pope Leo the Great would later do.

Although the slaughter of the Innocents ascribed to Herod is a fairy tale, in a sense we can still label him a child murderer, because he had three of his own children executed under accusation of conspiring against their father: in 7 B.C., his sons Alexander and Aristoboulos by his second wife, Mariamne (whom he had killed in 29 B.C. for adultery); and, five days before his own death in 4 B.C., his oldest son, Antipater, by his first wife, Doris. Herod had been married to a total of ten wives. His murderous behavior is said to have made Augustus remark that he would rather be Herod's pig than his son. The point of the joke is that in Greek, which cultivated Romans spoke at the time, the words for pig (*hys*) and son (*hyios*) sound alike. As a Jew, Herod didn't eat pork, but he did murder his sons.

Despite the fascination felt by all readers and hearers of the story of the wise men—those magical, fortune-telling Oriental priests—the whole scenario was still too pale and threadbare: People wanted to learn more about these mysterious visitors to Bethlehem. The Church took care to remedy this deficiency, and the believing public has had its pious hunger for knowledge appeased with an extensive, continually growing choreographic embellishment, in a sort of illustrated-magazine theology. In this way one of the central fairy-tale images of Christianity came into being; and not a few people see in this familiar picture of Christmastide—with its fantasies of the manger and the ox and the ass, "round yon Virgin mother and child, holy infant so tender and mild," etc.—the very center of Christianity.

To begin with, nobody even knew how many Magi had come from the East, but this gap was the first to be filled. From the three gifts mentioned in Matthew's Gospel—namely, gold, frankincense, and myrrh—readers inferred three givers. There were three Magi (Origen, *In Gen. hom.*, XIV, 3). For Pope Leo the Great (in his "Sermons for the Epiphany") the number three was definitively fixed.

The Magi gradually evolved into kings, a process capped by Caesarius (d. 542), bishop of Arles (the Gallic Rome), the most influential 6th-century prince of the Church. By the 8th century their names were known: Caspar, Melchior, and Balthasar. They were, respectively, a young man, a mature man, and an old man. Likewise, from the 8th century on, it was known that they came from the three parts of the known world: Europe, Asia, and Africa.

Their names served to fend off ghosts and demons. The night before the feast of the Three Kings is Befana (from Epiphania), the last of the twelve nights of Christmas, when evil spirits fly through the air. To this day, the blessing of the Three Kings wards off evil from house and home. Three Kings magical spells were useful against plagues, misfortune, and fire. The initial letters of their names on church bells beat back storms, and European inns with names like "star" and "crown" still promise travelers a safe place to stay. The star of Bethlehem has thus forfeited much of its great and holy glow and has been commercially profaned.

One of the Three Kings is still alive and full of beans in the Kasperltheater (the Punch and Judy show in northern Europe). In 1164 the archbishop of Cologne, Rainald von Dassel, who was also an imperial chancellor (d. 1167), had the relics of the Three Kings brought by brute force to Cologne from Milan. He happened to be on a campaign with Frederick I, Barbarossa, in Italy, and in this way he united the unholy deeds of war with the holy deed of robbing relics. What star, lucky or otherwise, had previously led the Three to Milan is unknown. Who found them—and where—and who ever had the fantastic idea that the relics were the actual bones of the Magi is swathed in darkness. There is a tradition that the Empress Helena, the mother of Emperor Constantine, who occasionally had visions of holy places and objects, sent them as a gift to Milan. But that's another fairy tale.

For those who believe it, the Three Old Magicians now lie quiet and dead in a golden coffin in the lofty cathedral at Cologne on the Rhine, waiting for time to pass away. Some nightly visitors to the cathedral even think they sense mysterious things happening around the casket on Twelfth Night. Some go so far as to claim that for a moment they see a strange light shining like a sort of star on the coffin, but others again maintain that it's only a stray reflection from the streetlamps of Cologne.

CHAPTER THREE

The Virgin Mother

THE VIRGIN AND the Angel: It's an image for poets and painters. A poet composed it, and time and again painters have painted it in their different ways. The messenger from God and the girl, still virginally distant from concrete human existence, on the threshold between childhood and womanhood, still framed by a space full of expectation and hope and ready dreams. . . . The image grows into a magical human and religious fantasy that has always fascinated us.

Working from a similar fantasy, the old astrological religions placed the constellation of Virgo in the heavens as a weaver of fertility. The Egyptians raised Isis to the altars; the Greeks exalted Dike as Astraia—the star virgin—or as Demeter or Tyche. This fantasy also gave birth to many other ancient goddesses: for example, Artemis, the goddess who not only protects chaste young men, but is also the mistress of youth, marriage, and birth. Athena was a virgin, a goddess without a mother, who like the virgin Nike came forth from the head of Zeus. Nemesis and Dike, as virgins, are the inaccessible and independent goddesses of justice.

Many other kindred spirits might be named. With all of them, the idea of goddess and virgin was at once the twofold resonance and expression of the one ancient longing, born of human dreams, for an unearthly and supernatural existence. Virginal, too, is the great Virgin of

Christianity, Mary. For many Catholics, much as the Church might protest, she is, even if unofficially, the great Christian goddess.

The Virgin Mary, however, was not originally a Christian idea. She made her way into the religious edifice of Christianity, so to speak, on a roundabout route through territory inhabited by pagans and Gentile Christians. The images mentioned above are without exception non-Jewish. Such ideas remained alien to Judaism and the original form of Jewish Christianity. Jewish Christians did not believe in the virgin birth of Jesus (see Chapter Twelve on Acts of the Apostles).

In all myths of redemption, virgins have constantly played a special role as the expressive symbol of the new, pure beginning of a new and better world. One such extremely ancient notion is that of virgins who bear divine child redeemers. "The redeemer king appears everywhere as the son of a virgin" (Gerhard Kittel, *Theologisches Wörterbuch zum Neuen Testament* [1954], V, 828, n. 21). Cardinal Joseph Ratzinger writes: "The myth of the marvelous birth of the redeeming child is in fact spread all over the world." He speculates that "the confused hopes of humanity for the Virgin-mother" have been taken up by the New Testament (*Einführung in das Christentum* [1968], p. 224). Thus even Cardinal Ratzinger recognizes that the myth of the virgin birth has nothing specifically Christian about it.

For the "overshadowing" of Mary by the Holy Spirit there were in fact many prior and competing images. According to the standard Protestant reference work *Religion in Geschichte und Gegenwart,*

> *The most varying cycles of myths and legends tell of sons of the gods who are born of the union with an earthly woman. According to ancient Egyptian tradition Amon-Ra begets with the king's consort the divine child who will exercise a splendid royal power throughout the land. Babylonian kings, Greek heroes (Heracles, Asclepius, among others), and Roman emperors were all begotten by gods. Greek religion laid special stress on the virginity of the mother impregnated by the god. . . . And the birth legend of Jesus must likewise be put into this historical religious context. ([1929] III, 569-70. Hereinafter cited as RGG.)*

Karlheinz Deschner offers a beautiful example from Persian mythology of the begetting of the son of a god: "Lady, spoke a voice, the great Helios has sent me to you as the announcer of the generation that he will carry out in you. . . . You will be the mother of a . . . little child, whose name is 'Beginning and End'" (*Abermals krähte der Hahn* [1987], p. 79).

Thus in the New Testament we find the same pattern that occurs more frequently in the ancient myths: The redeemer is the son of a virgin. It had all begun, if we follow Luke, in Nazareth, a little town in Lower Galilee. This was a place about which nobody had ever heard anything. The story involved a girl, twelve years old or so, actually just a child. The proper Jewish name of this girl was Miriam, later Latinized into Maria (Mary). The girl was engaged to a man named Joseph, who was supposed to have come from the line of David.

Jewish girls usually got engaged when they were twelve or twelve and a half years old. If the girl was any older and still hadn't found a husband, her mother might well panic and her father get gray hairs. An engagement was the first phase of getting married, which was followed after somewhat more than a year by the bride's being taken to her fiancé's home. Engagement counted as marriage, not de facto but de jure: The fiancée was already the man's wife. If the man died before bringing her home, she was already his widow.

Infidelity by the fiancée was considered adultery. If the husband demanded that she be taken before the court and punished, a harsh sentence loomed ahead: A girl between twelve years and a day up to twelve years and six months would be stoned along with her lover. An older girl would be strangled; a younger one was considered a minor and went unpunished. Fortunately, the scribes had added on so many conditions to the penal provisions for adultery by the fiancée (Deut. 22:23–24) that the punishment was scarcely possible anymore: At least two witnesses had to prove that they had warned the adulterous pair about the consequences facing them, and that the couple had nevertheless continued in their sin.

Yet executions did take place. An engaged daughter of a priest—according to Lev. 21:9 harsher penalties were in order for priests' daughters—was burned to death for adultery. Rabbi Eleazar ben Zadok (born shortly after A.D. 35) witnessed this scene as a young boy (Joachim

Jeremias, *Jerusalem zur Zeit Jesu* [1969], p. 201). This execution occurred in the reign of King Herod Agrippa I (A.D. 41–44).

Herod Agrippa I, by the way, was a grandson of Herod the Great (d. A.D. 4) and Mariamne, a son of Aristoboulos (murdered A.D. 7) and a brother of Herodias, who prompted the beheading of John the Baptist. (The scene of Salome's dance, followed by her request for the head of the Baptist [Mark 6:17–29] is characterized by Bultmann as "a completely legendary account . . . , while Josephus reports that Herod, in the face of the crowds that streamed to the Baptist, was afraid that John would stir up the people to rebellion, and he forestalled this by executing him" [*Jesus* (1926), p. 27].) Herod Agrippa I is mentioned in Acts of the Apostles (12:2): "He killed James the brother of John with the sword."

As for Joseph, naturally he could never have provided the legally requisite evidence of Mary's infidelity. The only possibility left to him was to separate from his fiancée by drawing up a bill of divorce, because it turned out that this girl, Mary, who was engaged to him but had not been brought home as his bride, had become pregnant. But this wasn't infidelity, it was a virginal conception.

We meet this virginal pregnancy in the New Testament in two different versions: a longer, more colorful one in chapter 1 of the Gospel of Luke, and a shorter, plainer one in chapter 1 of Matthew. In the latter, however, the scene is laid not in Nazareth but in Bethlehem. As we saw, Matthew does have the couple head to Nazareth, but only after several years. Except for the passages in Matthew and Luke, the virginal conception and birth are mentioned nowhere else in the New Testament. On the contrary, in Paul, the oldest Christian author, we find a hint of the opposite of the virgin birth: "Born of a woman," says Paul of Jesus in Gal. 4:4, *not* "born of a virgin."

Now to Matthew, which says simply: "She was found to be with child of the Holy Spirit" (Matt. 1:18). It's clear that the situation described here is different from the one in the Gospel of Luke, where an angel appears and announces the conception. Matthew's Gospel must be talking about a point several months after the conception. Otherwise, the conception could not have been "found"; only the pregnancy itself could be found. That the pregnancy had come about through the "Holy Spirit" could not be "found"—it first had to be revealed. But there is no mention of any announcement taking place, or of Mary's being informed in any way about an impending pregnancy, or of her being enlightened during the pregnancy itself about its nature and importance. It seems that she wasn't asked, that nothing was said to her, and so she had no way of knowing anything. Thus she looks like a minor standing on the fringe of the event. Throughout the entire story she says not a single word. She was "found" to be pregnant. Evidently she also hadn't told her husband, Joseph, about the pregnancy until her condition became obvious.

Not until later is the fact that this pregnancy is from the "Holy Spirit" revealed to Joseph by an angel in a dream. Even then nobody speaks with Mary herself, and once again she says nothing. But in view of the situation, of course, there had to be some talk. And while Mary has no decision to make, the decision is made for her. When the angel appears to Joseph, he informs him as if he were Mary's master, who now has to determine what is to be done. The fate of a woman lies entirely in the hands of a man. But at least the dream angel can move Joseph to change his original plan, so he doesn't repudiate his bride but keeps her instead.

Furthermore, in Matthew's version the order to name the child Jesus is given to Joseph, whereas in Luke it is for the mother to name the child. The whole scene, therefore, is tailored to fit Joseph. He is the main—and only—protagonist in the narrative. Through the mute mother, the story of Jesus' birth becomes a story for men and a rather bald one at that. Perhaps that is why Matthew's version gave pious imaginations so little to feed on.

People who consider Matthew a historical author might wonder why God got this girl, unasked and uninformed, into a situation of public shame, with every appearance of being an adulteress. That is a question that the theologians who take this fairy tale for a historical document have never dealt with and hence have no answer for. Which tells us something about their male theology.

In Luke the first one to be informed is not Joseph but, as befits such cases, Mary. Luke's version contradicts Matthew's in other ways, too. Matthew speaks only about an angel in Joseph's dream, while in Luke a real angel appears. A dream angel differs from a real angel about as much as a dreamt-of lottery jackpot differs from a real one. In Luke, Mary doesn't stand silently on the fringe; she's alive and at the center of the picture.

In the following centuries this impressive story by Luke left a unique mark on both folk piety and theology through the rich imaginative unfolding of the image of the "Virgin Mary" and of the message of the angel. By comparison with the Lucan narrative, the rest of the New Testament—apart from the story of the Passion—left a much feebler trace in the popular piety and teaching of the Catholic Church.

This exaggerated stress on Mariology has often turned the meaning and content of Christian doctrine absolutely upside down. The Catholic *Kirchenlexikon* by Heinrich Wetzer and Benedikt Welte, for example, presents a summa of this theological perversion: "The whole center of gravity of Christian faith rests on the fact that Mary conceived and gave birth as a virgin, made fruitful through the operation of the Holy Spirit. Everything that has been subsequently taught and believed about the deliverance from sin and liberation of the human race through the blood of Jesus Christ 'as the unblemished Lamb of God' is based on this fact" (VIII, 719–20).

Thus the angel came to her and said: " 'Hail, O favored one, the Lord is with thee.' But she was greatly troubled by the saying, and considered in her mind what sort of greeting this might be" (Luke 1:28–29). The angel's name was Gabriel, says Luke. He was a man, because Gabriel means "man of God" or "hero of God," and a hero is always a man. There are no female angels, just as there are no female devils; only the devil's grandmother brings a little femininity into the masculine Inferno.

In real life, angels never come to visit virgins, not today and not back then. But let's listen to the biblical angel anyway: "And behold, you will conceive in your womb and bear a son, and you shall call his name Jesus. He will be great, and will be called the Son of the Most High. And the Lord God will give to him the throne of his father David" (Luke 1:31–32).

In these verses we have a partially verbatim borrowing from passages in the Old Testament, for instance, from Gen. 16:17ff., where the "angel of the Lord" comes to Hagar, Abraham's concubine, and says, "Behold, you are with child, and shall bear a son; you shall call his name Ishmael." The angel of the Lord also appears to the (unnamed) wife of Manoah, Samson's mother, who had previously been barren, and speaks to her: "You shall conceive and bear a son . . . for the boy shall be a Nazirite to God from birth" (Judg. 13:3ff.). And in Gen. 17:19 God himself comes to Abraham and announces, "Sarah your wife shall bear you a son, and you shall call his name Isaac."

But Mary raises an objection and says to the angel: "How shall this be, since I know not man?" (Luke 1:34). Of course, this dialogue between Mary and the angel never really happened. It has been constructed by Luke on an Old Testament model. The Catholic New Testament scholar Gerhard Lohfink called attention to this as far back as 1973 in his *Sachbuch zur Formkritik: Jetzt verstehe ich die Bibel besser*. He points out that it's important to observe the literary genre used in the annunciation scene, so as not to get the wrong idea that this is a real conversation between Mary and the angel Gabriel. Rather, Luke employs a familiar Old Testament schema for narratives about a divine calling that consists of four elements.

Among other examples, Lohfink cites the story of the calling of Moses (Exod. 3:10–12), in which these four stylistic elements can be found. First, God *speaks* to Moses: "Come, I will send you to Pharaoh that you may bring forth my people, the sons of Israel, out of Egypt." Second, Moses answers him with an *objection*: "Who am I that I should go to Pharaoh, and bring the sons of Israel out of Egypt?" Third, God *sets aside the misgivings*, saying: "But I will be with you." Fourth, God *gives a sign of authentication*: "This shall be the sign for you, that I have sent you: when you have brought forth the people out of Egypt, you shall serve God upon this mountain."

These same four structural elements can be found in Mary's annunciation scene. Especially important in this context is point two—the objection by the person receiving the revelation: "How shall this be, since I know not man?" Then follow point three—the removal of misgivings by an explanation, "The Holy Spirit will come upon you"—and point four, the sign of authentication, the final feature of the Old Testament stories of calling. Mary will recognize from the pregnancy of Elizabeth, now well on in years, that God will fulfill his promise.

But although the dialogue of Mary and the angel was not a real one, the words Luke puts in Mary's mouth have a genuine theological content. Actually, readers should be struck by how uncatholic, as it were, Mary's argument is. To Mary, the message announced by the angel about the conception of the Son of God is unimaginable because she has not had intercourse with a man. To her mind, therefore, intercourse with a man is a necessary prerequisite for the promised birth of the son of David—the two things are unalterably connected—whereas for Catholic theology, it's precisely the other way around: Intercourse with a man and the birth of a divine son are mutually exclusive.

If we could take the report of the annunciation as historical, we would then have to acknowledge that Mary had more theological understanding than two thousand years of Catholic virgin birth theology—that is, stork theology. With her question, Mary clearly raises an issue that, admittedly, most contemporary theologians have gotten around to discussing, but one that the Catholic bishops, and least of all John Paul II, still don't understand: From Mary's standpoint, Jesus' divine sonship doesn't exclude his natural sonship. For Mary, one is impossible without the other.

In asking her question, she might have had in mind (legendary) events from the Hebrew Bible, in which conception takes place through God's creative intervention—without excluding the participation of a male begetter. Through such divine intervention a son is born to the ninety-year-old Sarah and the one-hundred-year-old Abraham (Gen. 17:17); and the sterile Rebekah bears her sons Esau and Jacob through God's intervention (Gen. 25:21).

The notion of a virgin birth was wholly alien to Judaism, and Jews expected no such thing from their hoped-for messiah. On the contrary, they hoped for a messiah who would be born a human being. "In the Messiah," says the Jew Trypho in Justin Martyr (d. ca. A.D. 165), "we Jews all expect that Christ will be a man of merely human origin. . . . If this man appears to be the Christ, He must be considered to be a man of solely human birth" (*Dialogue with the Jew Trypho*, 49). Thus if Mary had in any way wished to connect the message of the angel with Jewish messianic expectations, she would have been thinking of anything *but* a virgin birth, since that would have been in direct conflict with what the Jews were hoping for.

In any event, Luke's Mary is in no danger of falling prey to the misunderstanding that the Catholic Church began disseminating early on—namely, that the divine sonship was based on the virgin birth or in some way related to it. Catholics have often made this connection, but, theologically speaking, it is false.

> *According to the faith of the Church, the divine sonship of Jesus is not based on the circumstance that Jesus had no human father. The doctrine of Jesus' divinity would not be violated if Jesus had been the product of a normal human marriage. For the divine sonship that faith speaks of is not a biological, but an ontological, fact; it is not an event in time, but in God's eternity.* (Ratzinger, Einführung, p. 225)

This acknowledgment may be self-evident to most theologians and even to Cardinal Ratzinger, but it remains widely unknown to the hierarchy and an all but total secret among so-called simple believers. The notion that the divine sonship depends upon the virgin birth can be found, for example, in the writings of Cardinal Höffner, who maintains that if Jesus had had a human father, then he would not be at once "true God and true man" (*Ruhrwort*, 4 July 1987, p. 11). A glance at any halfway modern book on dogmatic theology would have shown the cardinal that his fears are unfounded: "So it would be no infringement on God if his Son, insofar as he exists in the divine nature, has God as his father, but insofar as he exists in human nature, had a human father" (Michael Schmaus, *Katholische Dogmatik* [1955], V, 138). That was exactly how Mary saw things when she assumed that intercourse with a man was a necessary prerequisite for the birth of God's Son.

But apart from the question of whether God's Son need be born of a virgin, Luke's story, written by a Greek and subject to Hellenistic influences, does in any case tell of a virgin birth. And though that might be pointless to Judaism, which finds the idea of a virgin birth alien, it could prove very useful to Christianity with regard to its Hellenistic environment. Such a miraculous birth could serve as proof that their redeemer was divine, and so the Christians could match parallel notions of a re-deemer from ancient myths. On this point the Catholic theologian Karl Adam, who could never be suspected of heresy, writes:

> The myth of the supernatural begetting of pre-eminent, mythi-cally transfigured personalities is no doubt ... so deeply rooted that at least within the Hellenistic world pious believers would not have been able to bear a purely natural origin of a cultic being. It would seem that within the morally purified Christian imaginative world this long-established belief in a supernatural birth would automatically translate into belief in a virgin birth. (Quoted in Bernard Bartmann, Dogmatik [1920], I, 445.)

In the annunciation of the birth of Jesus, the Evangelist Luke ex-presses himself in a thoroughly Hellenistic fashion, that is, the child is to be begotten through God's Holy Spirit, namely, God himself. The text lit-erally says, "Therefore the holy begotten one will be called the Son of God." But since many translators are put off by the concept of "begetting," with reference to God, as too pagan, sexual, and inappropriate, they skip over this heathenish-sounding embarrassment and turn instead to the final product of the divine begetting: the child who is born. Most transla-tions speak of Mary who gives birth rather than of God who begets. The widely used Revised Standard Version of the Bible has: "Therefore the child to be born will be called holy, the Son of God." And the German Catholic-Protestant "Unity Translation" translates: "And so the child will be holy and called Son of God."

But that's not in the original Greek text. The Catholic dogmatic the-ologian Michael Schmaus tries to put down what Luke means and writes uninhibitedly: "What is otherwise achieved through the action of a male was effected in Mary by God's almighty power" (Katholische Dogmatik [1955], V, 107). But what is "achieved through the action of a male"? Every-body knows that: The man contributes the semen, which is indispensable for generation. But this picture of God as a semen donor is not only repel-lent, it doesn't properly reflect what Luke meant. His imagination was not quite so simple.

Despite the pagan, Hellenistic language of "begetting," Luke's and Matthew's idea of a virgin birth is much more profound. The birth of Jesus was not supposed to imply any notion whatsoever of human generation. There was no male contribution here, there was no human contribution at all. The making of Jesus was to be exclusively God's creative work, comparable to the creation of Adam from a lump of clay. A woman, however, is not a lump of clay. The whole miraculous narrative of the virgin birth was composed at a time when nothing was known of the female ovum. The ovum was first discovered in 1827 by a physician named K. E. von Baer, who was a professor of medicine in Königsberg and St. Petersburg. The story of the virgin birth could be composed only at a time when the woman was thought to play a wholly passive role. Until the discovery of the ovum, theologians, including Luke and Matthew, thought that women were nothing more than something like the soil, the flower pot, the petri dish into which the man placed the seed, out of which the child then grew. Such thinking was rooted in Aristotelian biology, which viewed the woman as an empty vessel for the masculine principle. Males did all the work of generation (see Uta Ranke-Heinemann, *Eunuchs for the Kingdom of Heaven* [New York: Doubleday, 1990], pp. 186ff.).

Even today we don't speak of a woman's "begetting" (i.e., actively creating), we say that women "get" or "are made" pregnant. We still treat women as passive partners in reproduction: They can only conceive (or receive) or prevent conception.

Thus, following this ancient model, Matthew and Luke could think that if an earthly father was excluded from the begetting of Jesus, then God alone would be the active force. They had no idea that to generate a person, two equally active partners were needed, so that even if the man was replaced by God, God would still not be the only active principle.

Ever since the discovery of the ovum—and with it of the woman's share in reproduction—the traditional idea of the virgin birth as an image of God's lonely creative action has become indefensible. It's different with the image of the creation of Adam from the earth, which still makes perfect sense. Nobody finds it inappropriate when, gathered at a graveside, we hear the words "Ashes to ashes, dust to dust . . ."

The idea of a concerted action between God and a woman was obviously not what Matthew and Luke had in mind when they told their stories of the virgin birth. That would have meant a sexual relationship of God with a woman. And even if this wasn't exactly the same thing as sexual relations between a man and a woman, it would have been uncomfortably similar. Thus if people had known about a woman's ovum back then, they would have had to reject it as part of the Incarnation just as much as they did a man's semen. Both ovum and semen destroy the basic idea behind the biological virgin birth, with God in charge of everything.

Thus ignorance served as the foundation for the idea of a virgin birth from the Holy Spirit in a sex-free domain. After the discovery of the ovum, any further claim that Mary gave birth virginally reduces God's role to that of a mere male substitute.

The doctrine of the virgin birth in a biological sense locks the Church into insoluble theological problems—assuming it wishes to take the facts of gynecology into consideration. But on this subject the Church still follows Aristotle. Because if it acknowledged the existence of the ovum, then it would have only two choices: either change the Creed to read, "50 percent conceived by the Holy Spirit," or, should the Church continue to deny Mary an ovum, then she becomes not Jesus' mother but his foster mother or, to put it crudely, a rented womb.

In addition, we have to consider the following: In the case of a virginal conception the first cell in Jesus' organism would have to be a female cell. And if this female cell miraculously were to begin to divide without the intervention of a man, so that a human being came into existence through further cellular division, then such a virginal pregnancy must inevitably issue in the birth of a female person. So at some point before Jesus was born, an originally female fetus would have to be transformed into a masculine fetus. But then, always assuming Mary's conceiving and giving birth as a virgin, we'd have to think about—or believe in—a transsexual mutation of Jesus, in other words, a metamorphosis of Jesus from a female into a male. Not even Pope John Paul II has gone as far as this dogmatic extrapolation. Yet in strict logic it's unavoidable.

Back to the birth stories of the New Testament. As a foundation for the legend of the virgin birth, Matthew, in line with his habit of finding everything connected to Jesus already predicted in the Old Testament, uses a passage from Isaiah (8th century B.C.). Although he interprets it as a prophecy of Mary's virgin birth, Isaiah in fact says nothing whatsoever about this. The supposed promise of a virgin birth doesn't match the Hebrew text. Isaiah 7:14 says, "Behold, a young woman shall conceive and bear a son, and shall call his name Immanuel."

That the word "virgin" appears in Matthew (1:23) derives from the Greek translation of the Bible, which was made in the 3rd century B.C. The so-called Septuagint translates the Hebrew word *alma* (young woman) with the Greek word *parthenos* (virgin). Like the English "Miss," *alma* can, but need not, mean virgin, just as any young woman might, but need not, be a virgin. But even if Isaiah had been speaking of a virgin, that would never have meant a virginal conception—he says nothing about any such thing. The passage merely says that the mother of the expected child was a virgin before he was conceived, not that the conception took place in some supernatural manner or that the mother would continue to be a virgin.

It's not clear which young woman or virgin Isaiah was thinking about when he spoke with King Ahaz in Jerusalem during the Syro-Ephraimite War of 734 B.C. He told the king about the "sign" of a young woman who would become pregnant, but in any case he was speaking of his own time, of an event in the very near future, not seven centuries away. A sign so belated obviously couldn't have been any kind of signal to the king. Isaiah says of the child Immanuel: "He shall eat curds and honey when he knows how to refuse the evil and choose the good. For before the child knows how to refuse the evil and choose the good, the land before whose two kings you are in dread will be deserted" (7:15–16).

None of this applies to Jesus, but to the years 733–32 B.C., when Assyria had conquered the two kingdoms of Damascus and Northern Israel. With that, the danger threatening King Ahaz was over. And the young woman's child Immanuel was in fact still little and unable to discern good from evil, living, as Isaiah says, on curds and honey. Isaiah was not talking about Mary, nor did Mary name her child Immanuel.

After the annunciation, Mary has, so to speak, one more great scene to play, at the visit to her legendary cousin Elizabeth. (The existence of her cousin—and hence the whole account—is legendary. This is proved by the historically more credible report in the Gospel of John that Jesus and John the Baptist did not know each other [John 1:33].) Six months before the visit, the angel Gabriel had likewise appeared to Elizabeth's husband, Zechariah, and had announced the birth (though a natural one) of a son, John the Baptist. Actually, this conception was not so natural after all, because the unfavorable conditions already met with in Sarah and Rebekah—on the one hand, advanced age, and on the other, infertility—had created a double problem for Elizabeth. The miracle was thus all the greater.

Zechariah is initially not quite able to believe the angel's message, and so he allows himself to ask the stupid (vis-à-vis an angel) question, "How shall I know this? For I am an old man, and my wife is advanced in years?" At that moment it escapes God's attention that Zechariah's question was being posed simply because of the above-mentioned Old Testament "calling" schema. This dictated that the announcement by God or an angel had to meet with an objection. But God evidently saw in this a serious sin and instantly punished him for his effrontery, striking him dumb. Thus we read in most translations: "And he made signs to them and remained dumb" (Luke 1:22). This is correct, but the Greek word for "dumb" can also mean "deaf" as well as "deaf and dumb." God obviously had made Zechariah not just dumb, but deaf and dumb. Luke 1:22 tells us that he couldn't speak; and Luke 1:62 shows that he couldn't hear, because there Zechariah's relatives make signs to him, "inquiring what he would have him [the child] called." Thus he was deaf as well. God even lengthens his sentence, because Zechariah remains deaf and dumb not just until John's birth but until his circumcision (Luke 1:64).

The story is not an especially compassionate one, because it has God whacking humans on their mouth and ears when they don't immediately understand things and ask questions in order to understand. Fortunately, God didn't make Mary deaf and dumb for her similarly skeptical question, "How shall this be, since I know not man?" (Luke 1:34). Otherwise she could never have recited her "Magnificat" (My soul magnifies the Lord) at Elizabeth's house.

But she couldn't have spoken it as she does unless she had previously done extensive editorial spade work. The Magnificat could never have been formulated spontaneously. It is a tissue of quotations from the Old Testament. "My heart exults in the Lord," says Hannah, the mother of Samuel, who has long waited in vain for a child. She has promised God that if she has a child, she will dedicate this son completely to God. Her prayer is answered, and when she later brings him to the Lord, she recites her Old Testament Magnificat (1 Sam. 2:1–10).

The next verse comes from Hab. 3:18: "I will rejoice in the Lord" (from the so-called Psalm of Habakkuk). The verse after that is again taken from the mouth of Hannah, though this time it is a request she made of God before he gave her her son (1 Sam. 1:11): "If thou wilt indeed look down on the affliction of thy maidservant . . ." "For behold all generations will call me blessed" is a variation on the words of Leah, which she cries out after her maid Zilpah, acting as her representative, has borne Jacob a son (Asher): "For the women will call me happy" (Gen. 30:13). "Holy is his name" is found in Ps. 111:9. "And his mercy is on those who fear him from generation to generation" comes from Psalm 103:17. In Psalm 89:13 we find the arm of God. From 2 Sam. 22:28 we know that "God scatters the proud in the imagination of their hearts." The fact that he puts down the mighty from their thrones can be found in Eccles. 10:14, as well as in Ps. 147:6, Job 5:11, and Ezek. 21:31. We are told by Ps. 107:9 and 1 Sam. 2:5 that "He has filled the hungry with good things." We read in Ps. 134:11 that "He has sent the rich away empty." We find the conclusion distributed among Isa. 41:8, Ps. 98:3, Mic. 7:20, and Gen. 17:7.

At first the Magnificat was probably put not into Mary's mouth but Elizabeth's. By changing verse 46 from "Elizabeth said" to "Mary said," the whole song of praise was reshaped. In a few old Latin manuscripts it is still attributed to Elizabeth. This is only logical, because the whole context doesn't fit Mary at all. The Magnificat is essentially modeled on the prayer of Hannah, who, just like Elizabeth, has long waited for a child. This situation doesn't apply to Mary, and it makes no sense when she repeats the thanksgiving of an older woman who has long been childless. And verse 56, which immediately follows the Magnificat, "And Mary remained with her," means by "her" the woman who has just spoken, namely, Elizabeth. Furthermore, in verse 58 the neighbors and relatives of Elizabeth expressly take up and repeat the notion of God's "great mercy" for Elizabeth from the Magnificat.

Then there is the fact that Zechariah, after recovering his speech, intones a song of praise and thanks, "Blessed be the Lord God of Israel" (Luke 1:68–79). This, too, consists purely of quotations from the Old Testament, which may suggest that in the original situation both parents gave thanks for the birth of their long-desired son in their own individual song of praise.

One final point on the greeting that Elizabeth extends to Mary: "Blessed [in Greek *eulogemenē*] are you among women" (Luke 1:42). This, too, is a quotation from the Old Testament, from the Book of Judges 5:24, where we read, "Most blessed of women be Jael." But this may evoke mixed feelings in Luke's audience. Jael, after all, was the woman who killed the Canaanite general Sisera, as he rested in her tent, by hammering a tent peg through his temple (Judg. 5:26). The phrase "blessed among women" may give the reader a brief shiver.

It might be objected that this sort of parallel is too farfetched. But strangely enough, in Catholic liturgy and teaching the Church has often presented similar heroines as models for Mary, and Mary has been covered with the same praise previously given to murderous heroines from the Old Testament. The custom has lasted to this day. For example, the Gradual of the mass for the Immaculate Conception says of Mary: "You are the exaltation of Jerusalem, you are the great glory of Israel, you are the great pride of our nation." This blessing was originally directed to Judith after she had single-handedly beheaded the drunken Holophernes in his sleep (Jth. 15:9). In the same Gradual, another blessing meant for Judith is applied to Mary: "You are blessed by the Most High God above all women on earth." These words are spoken by Uzziah right after Judith lifts high the severed head of Holophernes and shows it to the people (Jth. 13:18).

In Catholic Mariology and "the liturgy Judith and Esther are seen above all as images of Mary" (Schmaus, *Katholische Dogmatik,* p. 163).

Esther's achievement was considerably greater than Judith's, insofar as she was a crucial agent in the killing of 75,810 men (the enemies of the Jews), "with their children and women" (Esther 8:11). In a later passage Esther says: "And let the ten sons of Haman be hanged on the gallows" (Esther 9:13). As an "image of the immaculately conceived [Virgin]" (Schmaus, *Katholische Dogmatik*, p. 164), this mass murderess has her holy place in the liturgy for the feast of the Apparition at Lourdes.

There are still more models for Mary in Catholic Mariology. One is Deborah, who played a successful part in the extermination of the Canaanites (Judg. 4:4–5:31) and the above-mentioned Jael. According to Mariologist Alois Müller, all four, Judith, Esther, Deborah, and Jael, are "by doing such deeds symbolic prefigurations of Mary's redemptive motherhood" and "typological prefigurations of Mary's chosenness" (*Mysterium salutis* [1969], III, 2, 397). This homicidal Mariology may well give us pause.

The real life of Mary was lived far away from angelic visits and the pose of warrior-heroines. We are told of Jesus' circumcision after eight days (Luke 2:21). The events of the circumcision, the sacrifice of purification, and the redemption of a firstborn son were perfectly normal happenings for a Jewish family at the time. This normalcy is interrupted by an event in the Temple, namely, the appearance of pious old Simeon, who recognizes in the child the hoped-for Messiah.

In the legend of the twelve-year-old Jesus in the Temple, his parents fail to show any understanding. When Jesus speaks of his heavenly Father, they don't know what he is talking about (Luke 2:50). This contradicts the story of the annunciation, which in turn shows that Luke has woven together different strands of tradition. Among these the one on which this passage was based knows nothing about the virgin birth.

We hear nothing more about Joseph in the rest of the New Testament, but Mary does appear in various passages. The two most striking encounters are reported in the Gospel of John and are likewise legendary: Mary at the marriage feast at Cana, and then Mary beneath the cross, with the beloved disciple.

The marriage feast at Cana is a Hellenistic fairy tale applied to Jesus (see Chapter Six, on Jesus' miracles). The scene beneath the cross is not a historical, but a fictitious, theological-symbolic representation. The three other Evangelists credibly report that Mary and the "beloved disciple" did *not* stand beneath the cross. According to them, none of the male disciples were there, and the women stood at some distance. But Mary wasn't with them. If anyone is looking for the reason why she wasn't there, there may have been a quite natural one: There wasn't enough time for Jesus' mother in Galilee to hear about the trial and sentencing of her son, and then to make the journey from Galilee.

Judging from the Gospels, mother and son were not at all on good terms. The same holds for Jesus' relations with the rest of his family. "A prophet is not without honor," says Jesus, "except in his own country" (Mark 6:4). There should be no doubt that this was his own personal experience, because "even his own brothers did not believe in him" (John 7:5). His family actually resorted to violence to stop his preaching; and his mother, as the context shows, was on their side: "Then he came home. . . . And when his family heard it, they went out to seize him, for people were saying, 'He is crazy' [most often translated politely as 'He is beside himself']" (Mark 3:19, 21).

Instead of the family that did not believe in him, those who did believe in him became his real family.

> *While he was still speaking to the people, behold, his mother and his brothers stood outside, asking to speak to him. But he replied to the man who told him, "Who is my mother, and who are my brothers?" And stretching out his hand toward his disciples, he said, "Here are my mother and my brothers! For whoever does the will of my Father in heaven is my brother, and sister, and mother!" (Matt. 12:46ff.)*

We find similar material in the parallel passages of Mark 3:31ff. and Luke 8:20ff.

The scene depicted in Acts, where we see Mary (in Jerusalem) for the last time in the New Testament, could be historical. If so, then the family members would have arrived there in the meantime. It seems to have been a gathering of mourners, where the apostles met "with the women and Mary the mother of Jesus, and with his brothers" (Acts 1:14). We don't know when his mother and his brothers came to believe in the son and brother, but now they sat together and prayed.

Now, in Jerusalem, all the traveling and straying were over. The things that separated them were past, and all their pain had fallen silent in the last great pain. In their mourning she was once again entirely his mother, and the dead man was once again entirely her son.

CHAPTER FOUR

The Angels

THE ANGEL ENTERED Mary's house and said, "Hail, O favored one!"

He hadn't knocked; angels never do. The door had been open anyway. The hot sun stood high in the sky, the shadows in the house barred the way to its heat. It was noon in Nazareth, and the dusty village road was silent, as still as if there were nobody else in the world, or rather as if there was no world at all. It was the time of the noonday demons as well as, evidently, the noonday angels. Angels, we know, cast no shadow, but suddenly something like a shadow fell onto the entranceway to the house. And then there he was, saying, "Hail!" He didn't give his name, nor did the girl ask him, but she knew it without having to ask. It was Gabriel, the "hero of God."

The rest of us, who have never been visited by angels, would be only too glad to know more about him. For example, we'd like to know what he looked like, whether he was tall or short, fat or thin, whether he looked like a normal young man or more like an astronaut. Or perhaps he wasn't young at all, but as old as the world. It would have been an ideal opportunity for the Evangelist to tell us a bit more about him and about angels in general. For instance, we might have learned how they manage to make themselves visible, since they're pure spirits; perhaps, too, how come there are only men angels. Angels are called Michael or Gabriel or Raphael, no one has ever heard of an angel named Priscilla or Annemarie.

Let's turn from the gentle image of the girl and the angel and try to find out more about Gabriel. There are a few things about him in the Book of Daniel (composed around 164/165 B.C). There he is the angel who interprets Daniel's vision for him, one who "gives wisdom and understanding" (Dan. 9:22). Supplying such information and the annunciation in Nazareth go very well together.

In chapters 10 to 12 of Daniel, however, Gabriel puts in an altogether different sort of appearance, a much less gentle one this time. In Dan. 10:5–6 we read, first, about how he looked and spoke. Daniel describes him: "Behold, a man clothed in linen, whose loins were girded with gold of Ophaz. His body was like beryl [or olivine, in which case Gabriel was definitely green], his face like the appearance of lightning, his eyes like flaming torches, his arms and legs like the gleam of burnished bronze, and the sounds of his words like the voice of a multitude."

Unfortunately, Gabriel couldn't stay very long with Daniel, since he had to go off to do battle with both the patron angel of Greece and the patron angel of Persia (Dan. 10:20). Well, at least we know that angels wage war against one another, which makes them somewhat human.

For further details we can consult the Book of Enoch (a Jewish compendium of various texts from 170 B.C. to the beginning of the Christian era), a book much loved by the early Christians. Although it didn't become part of the Bible and is now considered one of the so-called apocryphal Scriptures, it had every right "to claim to be chosen among the holy books" (Lexikon für Theologie und Kirche [1957], I, 712. Hereinafter cited as LThK). In Enoch 10:9 we read: "To Gabriel also the Lord said, Go to the bastards [descendants of fallen angels], to the reprobates, to the children of fornication, the offspring of the Watchers [or angels], from among men: bring them forth and send them against one another. Let them perish by mutual slaughter; for length of days shall not be theirs" (trans. Richard Lawrence [Oxford: Oxford Univ. Press, 1838], p. 10).

We later learn (40:9) that Gabriel is, after Michael and Raphael, the third of the four "angels of the countenance," who stand immediately before God. According to Enoch, the name of the fourth is Phanuel. In this passage Gabriel is characterized as the one "who is in charge of all forces" (*Book of Enoch*, p. 41.)

Gabriel was in charge of the element of fire, and many believed that he was made of fire. At the same time he was considered "the harshest angel," and he was also labeled simply "terror," because he carried out God's judgments on humans (Hermann Strack and Paul Billerbeck, *Kommentar zum Neuen Testament aus Talmud und Midrash* [1965], II, 92). "Every angel is terrible," says Rilke in his second *Duino Elegy*. This is especially true of Gabriel as terror personified.

In the *Scroll of the War Rule*, one of the Dead Sea Scrolls (2nd or 1st century B.C.), the name of the angel Gabriel serves as the inscription on the shields as the great war of revenge is about to break out (1QM IX, 15–16; A. Dupont-Sommer, *The Essene Writings from Qumran*, trans. G. Vermes [Oxford, UK: Basil Blackwell, 1961], p. 183. Hereinafter cited as *TEWFQ*; see Chapter Seventeen on Jesus and the Dead Sea Scrolls).

But in Luke's annunciation scene, Gabriel shows none of his harshness or his propensity to annihilate humans and other angels. The blood on his hands, if angels have hands, can't been seen here. His harshness softens, his terror turns amiable. Still, he has to say, "Do not be afraid." Quite obviously the girl was frightened by such a frightful apparition.

According to Jewish scholars of the first centuries of the Christian era, Gabriel was, along with Michael, one of the angels who were not affected by the passing of time. About the other angels Rabbi Chelbo (ca. A.D. 300) said: "Never has a choir of angels up there intoned a song of praise for the second time. Every day God creates a new division of angels, they sing a new song before him, and then they fade away." Other rabbis also taught this doctrine of the daily disappearance of the angels (Strack and Billerbeck, *Kommentar*, II, 91). It's too bad if angels have to die and thus become a sort of throwaway sacred species.

Gabriel, as it happens, is of interest not just to Jews and Christians. He also plays an important role in Islam, because it was Gabriel who dictated the Qur'an to Muhammad. Later, when Muhammad ascended into heaven, "Gabriel held back the Temple Rock, which wanted to follow

Muhammad into heaven, and impressed the mark of his hand on it" (*LThK*, IV, 484).

Among Christians Gabriel later enjoyed a career as the patron saint of all messengers, post office employees, and newspaper boys. In 1951 Pope Pius XII declared him the guardian angel of radio and telecommunications, including TV.

As for the names of angels, only Michael, Gabriel, and Raphael have prevailed. The Roman Synod under Pope Zacharias in 745 forbade any other names. It banned the use of Uriel, Ragull, Tubuel, Inias, Tubuas, Sabaoc, and Simiel, all contributed by a certain Adalbert, who had been branded a heretic. Adalbert had claimed that one day in Jerusalem a letter from Christ inscribed with these names had fallen out of heaven and into his hands. But it was no use. The Synod declared that these were the names not of angels but of demons (Joseph von Hefele, *Konziliengeschichte* [1858], III, 506–7).

In addition, the Synod of Laodicea in Phrygia (in the second half of the 4th century) had spoken out against the cult of angels. The Synod proclaimed that "Christians should not leave the Church of God and neither venerate angels nor introduce the worship of angels" (chap. 35; Hefele, *Konziliengeschichte* [1855], I, 743). On this point it was following the Letter to the Colossians, which also attacks the cult of angels: "Let no one disqualify you, insisting on self-abasement and worship of angels" (Col. 2:18).

The realm of the angels, with its various classes and categories, is rather complicated. Apart from the messengers—the word *angel* means "messenger"—hosts of military angels populate heaven. In the Old Testament the following groups of angels can be distinguished: Cherubim, Seraphim, Erelim, Hayot, and Ofannim (*Jüdisches Lexikon* [1982], II, 399). There were guardian angels for each individual person (Gen. 21:17), as there were for entire nations; thus Michael serves as the guardian angel of Israel (Dan. 12:1). According to the Talmud, there were many billions of angels, and every Jew "is accompanied by two thousand, and others think as many as eleven thousand" (*Jüdisches Lexikon*, II, 401).

Owing to the complexity of the subject, complete clarity and general agreement are lacking in Catholic angelology. In the meantime, some types of angels from the Old Testament have been lost. In their place new choirs have been added on. As for the different kinds or classes of angels, they are listed, in descending order: Seraphim, Cherubim, Thrones, Dominations, Virtues, Powers, Principalities, Archangels, and, lowest of all, simple "angels."

There have been disputes about the exact number of "choirs." Some Church Fathers speak of from five to eight, others again of nine or more. Cyril of Jerusalem (d. 386) speaks of nine, as do Athanasius (d. 373), Ambrose (d. 397), Basilius (d. 379), John Chrysostom (d. 407), and Jerome (d. 419/420). Pope Gregory I, the Great (d. 604), fixed the number at nine (*Hom. 34 in Ev.*), and he was backed up by the medieval Scholastics, of whom the greatest, Thomas Aquinas (d. 1274), sets the standard to this day in matters of theology. Pope Gregory I, however, affirmed that the Virtues and Principalities had switched places.

Angels are originally pagan creatures, because belief in them is older than belief in the God of the Bible. When no one as yet knew anything about this God, much was already known about the existence of angels. In texts from ancient Ugarit, a city-state in northern Syria inhabited as far back as the New Stone Age (in the 4th and 3rd millennia B.C.), we meet creatures with the function of divine messengers. Among the Assyro-Babylonians, too, there were angels and messengers and servants of the gods. This traditional idea of a kind of heavenly royal household was taken over in the Hebrew Bible, where it underwent a colorful development.

Some details that apply to all angels may be of general interest. "As spiritual entities that do not consist of bodily parts, angels cannot, like the body, fill up a space so that their parts correspond to the parts of space. Instead they are located completely in their specific space and with equal completeness in all parts of this space." Thus says the *Kirchenlexikon* of Heinrich Joseph Wetzer and Benedikt Welte (IV, 521), invoking Saint Thomas Aquinas (*S.Th.* I q. 52 a. 2), who as an expert on angels bears the honorary title "Doctor angelicus."

According to Thomas, the angels have no need of language, since "the volition by which one angel presents his inner acts to another is already sufficient in itself" (*S.Th.* I q. 107 a. 1). Thus the language of the angels is a purely spiritual one. For humans, angels are silent creatures.

Furthermore, when an angel appears to a human being, he carries out none of his own vital acts with the body he has taken on. Instead, because he uses the body in which he appears only as an instrument, he carries out only mechanical imitative acts without an inner principle of life (*S.Th.* I q. 51 a. 2 ad 2).

Angels are like human beings in that their knowledge varies: Some know more, others less. But angels can learn, too, and so the lower angels are taught by the higher angels.

We have further information about two choirs of angels, namely, the Seraphim and, in particular, the Cherubim. The Seraphim appeared to the prophet Isaiah when he was called by God (Isa. 6:2). "Above him [God] stood the seraphim; each had six wings: with two he covered his face, and with two he covered his feet, and with two he flew. And one called to the other: 'Holy, holy, holy is the Lord of hosts. . . .' And the foundations of the thresholds shook at the voice of him who called, and the house was filled with smoke" (Isa. 6:2–6). But we learn little else of consequence about the Seraphim.

We meet the Cherubim right at the beginning of the Bible, right after the expulsion of Adam and Eve from Paradise. God posts Cherubim on the east side of Paradise to keep humans from the path to the Tree of Life. In Ezekiel we find an extensive description of these angels. According to the prophet, the Cherubim are humanlike creatures, each of which has a head with four faces: "The first face was the face of the cherub, and the second face was the face of a man, and the third the face of a lion, and the fourth the face of an eagle" (Ezek. 10:14). The creatures had four wings and round feet. Alongside each Cherub was a wheel. Without turning, they could go in all directions. When they went, the wheels went with them. When they flew, the wheels flew along, and as they flew, a mighty roar arose. When the creatures stood still, however, the wings didn't move. Between the wheels was fire. No doubt the angels Ezekiel describes had some technical apparatus at their disposition. No wonder Erich von Däniken surmises that what we have here is an encounter with alien astronauts. On the choirs of angels the Bible has no further details to give us.

But the devil is an angel, too; and nobody has been so unfairly treated and demonized as the devil. No wonder popular parlance feels sorry for "the poor devil." In the Old Testament, where he barely appears and plays only a marginal role, he is one of the "sons of God" (Job 1:6), which is another name for an angel. He has not been cast out by God or fallen away from him. He may not be among the number of those angels who "stand before God," as the Bible says of Gabriel, for instance; but he does belong to the group that has immediate contact with God and that has been integrated into heaven's royal household.

The devil fulfills on God's behalf the function of an accuser of humans. He does this in the case of Job, whose piety he mistrusts. In the Old Testament *Satan* is a Hebrew legal term and means "accuser before the court" or "adversary." Thus Satan is something like a heavenly public prosecutor. The Greek translation renders Satan as the *diabolos,* meaning "accuser, calumniator," because people readily feel calumniated whenever they're charged with anything. *Diabolos* is the source of the English "devil," the German "Teufel," the Italian "diavolo," and so on. The serpent in Paradise, by the way, was not the devil. It was merely a harmful demon or simply a symbol of temptation. Only later was the serpent reinterpreted by the popular mind to mean the devil.

In connection with Catholic canonization trials, the term *devil's advocate* is still in use today. This is a jocular label for the Church's attorney general, but it hits the nail on the head and restores the old notion of Satan. Naturally the *advocatus diaboli* doesn't want to do evil; rather, he is a canon lawyer who has the job of being an adversary in the interest of discovering the truth. Hence, he collects whatever can be used to object to the canonization: He is Satan in the original sense.

Only in one tiny passage of the Old Testament, in the First Book of Chronicles (21:1), is Satan blamed for instigating anyone to sin: Here he seduces David into taking a census of the population. God was against censuses. But in a parallel passage to this episode in 2 Sam. 24:1, it is God himself who seduces David into committing the sin of census taking. Thus Satan is still not really a power separate and distinct from God.

Not until the post–Old Testament, late Jewish Scriptures, that is, in the last two hundred years before Christ, are God and Satan directly pitted against each other. The accuser is turned into an adversary of God and the head of a God-hating kingdom, hence an evil principle pure and simple.

In other words, human fantasy is putting more and more distance between God and Satan, in order to free God from the burden of evil. In the Book of Enoch, borrowing from an old legend about the union of heavenly men (meaning angels) with human women (cf. the *Nephelim* in Gen. 6:14—yet another case for Mr. von Däniken), there is a dark, fantastic passage about the fall of the angels. According to Enoch, the ringleader of the fallen angels is Satan. The whorish offspring of angelic lust are the demons, spirits who cause nothing but sickness and harm.

In the New Testament, Satan bears all the negative, God-hating features that he didn't acquire in Judaism until just before the Christian era. Satan is now a superhuman power of evil. The original distinction between Satan and demons is still largely maintained in the New Testament. But starting with the church fathers it becomes increasingly blurred. Possession by demons and the Devil becomes one and the same. This whole late Jewish, New Testament, and Christian specter is alive and well today in the minds of bishops and other simple folk.

The belief in the Devil as the cause of evil is a superstition. Man has invented the Devil to get himself off the hook. Man doesn't want to be responsible for his actions, but he remains the only responsible party. He and nobody else is the Prince of Hell on earth—which is not to diminish the power of evil and even the devilishness of evil in the world.

By contrast, Christians have always seen evil in the world as a proof for the existence of the Devil. In his book *Vor dem Bösen ratlos?* (Helpless in the Face of Evil?), Herbert Haag quotes Bishop Graber of Regensburg. Apropos of the famous case of possession that occurred in the little Bavarian town of Klingenberg in the 1970s, when a supposedly possessed girl student was exorcised, upon recommendation of the bishop of Würzburg, and died in the process, Bishop Graber said: "If the Evil one does not exist, then man alone is responsible." Humans don't want to bear the sole responsibility; they'd prefer to bear none at all. "Can God have created man such a monster?" the bishop goes on to ask, and immediately he answers his own question: "No, he can't, because he is love and goodness. If there is no Devil, then there is no God."

But this theological flight of fancy, which makes the existence of the Devil absolutely necessary for the existence of God, only shifts the problem. As Haag rightly stresses, "The bishop seems to have forgotten for the moment that according to the Church's teaching the Devil too is a creature of God . . . and therefore God has made a monster after all" (Haag, *Vor dem Bösen ratlos?* [1978], p. 246).

These days, by the way, Italy is weathering an invasion of demons. One of the best-known exorcists in Italy is Father Gabriel Amorth, a Paulist priest and member of the Papal International Marian Academy in Rome. By his own account, since 1986 twelve thousand possessed persons or their family members have turned to him for help. For this reason he applied to the Italian Bishops Conference for the establishment of a central office for training and coordination of exorcists. In an interview with the Italian magazine *Oggi* on 1 June 1992, Father Amorth points out that John Paul II is also an active exorcist. He reports that the pope "certainly" undertook two exorcisms in 1984 and has likewise driven out devils more recently, as he had done before in Poland.

Speaking of recent exorcism trials in Germany: On 24 April 1978 *Der Spiegel* quoted the following words from the Hamburg *Bildzeitung:* "The public prosecutor awarded the four accused [of participating in the lethal exorcism] a lesser degree of accountability—because of their deep religious faith."

The question of the origin of evil, of what causes the tears and deviltries of the world, the question that no theologian has so far managed to answer, is one that humans have always posed. The Christian apologist Lactantius, who in the year 317 was called to Trier by Constantine to be the tutor of Prince Crispus, cites an argument by the Greek philosopher Epicurus (d. 271/270 B.C.):

> *Either God wants to get rid of evil, but he can't; or God can, but he doesn't want to; or God neither wants to nor can, or he both wants to and can. If God wants to, but can't, then he's not all-powerful. If he can, but doesn't want to, he's not all-loving. If he neither can nor wants to, he's neither all-powerful nor all-loving. And if he wants to and can—then why doesn't he remove the evils?* (De ira Dei, *chap. 13)*

On the question of the origin of evil, the theologians have always opted for the second possibility, that God can get rid of evil, but for whatever reason he doesn't want to. The theologians prefer to deduct points from God's compassion rather than from his omnipotence. A powerful God finds more supporters than a compassionate God. This is because people model their image of God on their own image. And potency and power mean a great deal to them—sometimes they mean everything—while compassion means less, and sometimes nothing at all. But we should rethink all this. God can't banish evil unless he drowns the human race. And so all he can do is mourn.

CHAPTER FIVE

Jesus' Genealogies

CHRISTIANS ARE OCCASIONALLY offered proof of things that either nobody wants proved or that can't be proved to begin with. In the case of the genealogies in the Gospels of Matthew and Luke, we find both. To prove that Jesus was descended from Adam, as Luke does, is totally superfluous, since everybody is descended from Adam. But it can't be proved why Jesus, having been descended from Adam by way of this rather than that ancestor, is the redeemer of the world. One can no more read the meaning of Jesus as the redeemer of the world from the list of his ancestors than one can read it from tea leaves.

Josef Kürzinger provides an example of such tea-leaves theology in the widely read Catholic Pattloch Bible, where he annotates Luke's genealogy of Jesus: "Tracing back the genealogy through Abraham back to the first man . . . in Luke is supposed to show Jesus as the universal Redeemer, sent to save pagans too." This sort of tracing can't demonstrate a universal Redeemer because of the simple fact that all Jews are descended from Adam through Abraham.

If the man whom Christians call the Son of God absolutely has to show that he is the son of Adam, Abraham, David, or anybody else, that reduces his importance to a rather paltry human yardstick. In that case,

Jesus' relationship to God is no longer the sole decisive factor; instead his descent from some ancestor or other becomes the whole point. But the meaning of Jesus can't be measured by criteria reminiscent of those used for race horses, where having an Arabian stallion in the pedigree may carry some weight. Jesus is not a thoroughbred.

In fact, with his genealogical certificate Jesus is robbed of all uniqueness, for all Jews were sons of Abraham, and many Jews were sons of David. In his *Apologie oder Schutzschrift für die vernünftigen Verehrer Gottes*, Samuel Reimarus (d. 1768) rightly observes that he would like to see anyone prove the following point: He says that even if Jesus' descent from David were to be accepted, the question would still remain "whether . . . he would therefore have to be the sole Savior of Israel ahead of the many others who were and still are David's descendants. Whether the promises of a Savior from David's line contain such personal features all of which apply to this Jesus and to nobody else" ([1972] II, 255).

Not only can this never be proved, but, on the contrary, there definitely were more authentic sons of David in Israel. That is because the whole claim to Jesus' being a son of David, which in both genealogies is traced through Joseph and not Mary, gets snagged on the Catholic doctrine of the virgin birth. It's a kind of theological schizophrenia when the good Catholic may, indeed should, say, "Jesus is the son of David," but may never say, "Jesus is the son of Joseph"—when Jesus is the son of David only through Joseph. But if Jesus is not a real, authentic son of Joseph, then neither is he a real, authentic son of David. And vice versa: If Jesus is only a putative son of Joseph, then he's only a putative son of David. If Joseph is only Jesus' foster father, as the Catholics call him, then David is only Jesus' foster ancestor.

The genealogies of Jesus come from a time when Joseph was still considered Jesus' physical father. Matthew places this sort of genealogy at the beginning of his Gospel (1:1–17), immediately before his story of the virgin birth (1:18–25). But the early Church increasingly tended to treat the ancient image of the virgin birth in crude biological terms. But this renders the whole Joseph genealogy problematic. It's not just Jesus' brothers and sisters from the same Gospel (Matthew 13) who become a permanent burden, but this genealogy with Joseph as the real father of Jesus.

The problem of Jesus' brothers and sisters was provisionally solved around A.D. 150 by the *Protevangelium of James* (which made them step-brothers and stepsisters). And around 400 Jerome provided the definitive solution by making them all Jesus' cousins, as we shall see in the chapter on the Apocrypha.

The problem with the genealogy of Joseph as the real father of Jesus was already noted, if not solved, by whoever did the final editing of the Gospel. Matthew suddenly segues to Mary: "and Jacob the father of Joseph the husband of Mary, of whom Jesus was born, who is called Christ" (Matt. 1:16). (Christ [*Christos*] is the Greek word for Messiah [the anointed one].) But to prevent a break in the chain of ancestors Jesus is now descended from Mary, though no longer expressly from Joseph. Luke adopts a similar tactic: "being the son (as was supposed) of Joseph, the son of Heli" (Luke 3:23).

This brushing aside of the Joseph problem creates a new problem: the fact that between Joseph and Jesus the chain is broken, never to be restored, even though, according to Luke, it's supposed to lead all the way back to Adam; and, according to Matthew, to Abraham. But for Catholic theologians there's no problem at all. The difficulty is solved by Christian fairy tales. They either say that these are Mary's genealogies (or at least one of them is Mary's genealogy), though the text contradicts this, or, in more recent times, they prefer an explanation that could only make readers familiar with Jewish law shake their heads: "Joseph was admittedly not Jesus' father by blood—as Matthew 1:18–23 makes clear—but in a legally valid sense and hence the acknowledged (by Matthew) bearer of the line of descent." Thus Josef Kürzinger in the Pattloch Bible.

On the second genealogy (Luke 3:23–38) Kürzinger writes: "According to the Jewish notion of law, someone could count as a 'son' not only by blood but also by other relationships, as well as by legal adoption." The quotation marks around the word *son* are from Kürzinger, since he himself has no doubt noticed that in Jewish law Jesus could have been at most a "son" in quotation marks.

Under the heading "Adoption" the *Jüdische Lexikon* explains in the very first sentence: "Adoption is alien to Jewish law. Both the legal concept and the technical term for it are lacking." The *Jüdische Lexikon* then proceeds to speak of levirate marriage (*levir* meaning "brother-in-law"). By this arrangement "the child of a (previously) childless widow, born from marriage with a brother of the deceased husband" counts legally as the son of the dead man. This Old Testament institution clearly shows that there must be a blood relationship between the two men in order for the child to be considered as belonging to the ancestral line of the deceased. The blood relationship is respected even after death.

The *Jüdische Lexikon* correctly notes that the "absence of adoption in Jewish law . . . is probably traceable to the fact that the Law is not in principle oriented to monogamy, and only reckons with the child's natural ties, based on birth. The actual blood relationship is the basic criterion, regardless of any legal recognition on the side of the father." Putting it plainly, adoption wasn't necessary in Judaism, since the husband could always entrust several wives with maintaining his ancestral line.

Catholic theologians, by contrast, assert that adoption by Joseph could make Jesus a descendant of David. This seems immediately reasonable to the modern reader, who lives in a first-name-basis society, where descent scarcely plays a role anymore. But it's wrong to infer back from our individualized, self-made–man or –woman society to the conditions of the ancient Jewish world. Anyone who takes this logical leap overlooks the great importance genealogies based on biological ties had for a full-blooded Israelite in the time of Jesus.

A good many civil rights were bound up with a flawless genealogy, as Joachim Jeremias points out, for example, in the chapter "The Civil Rights of the Full-Blooded Israelite" in *Jerusalem zur Zeit Jesu* (1969, pp. 332ff.). The most important privilege was this: Such a person's daughters were allowed to marry priests. Furthermore, all important public offices of honor and trust were reserved to the full-blooded Israelite. That included membership in the higher courts of justice, that is, the Sanhedrin, as well as any one of the twenty-three-member criminal courts and the seven-member local executive boards of the Jewish communes, and so forth. In all these cases the genealogies were scrutinized before conferring an office on anyone.

As part of this system, which placed such value on the noble chain of blood relationships, the choice of a wife played a major role. One of the main reasons for this was precisely the fact that any dubious birth could not, as it is in modern Western countries, be integrated into the ancestral succession by means of adoption. Twice every year, on the 15th of Ab (around August) and on the Day of Atonement, there was a dance of the virgins of Jerusalem in the vineyards surrounding the city, a sort of bridal show. Only women took part in it (mixed dancing was unknown), including the daughters of the leading families, even the daughters of the high priest. The young girls wore borrowed white garments so that those who didn't have suitable dresses wouldn't be put to shame.

Obviously wealth was not supposed to be the principle of selection—nor beauty either. Significantly, the song that the girls sang as they danced ran: "Young man, lift up your eyes and look carefully to what you are choosing, turn your eyes to the family tree! Charm is mutable, beauty is a fleeting breath, a woman who fears the Lord will be praised" (Hermann Strack and Paul Billerbeck, *Kommentar zum Neuen Testament aus Talmud und Midrash* [1965], II, 381).

Even a wife whose birth was as good as her husband's and who had a good pedigree could prove to be a blot on the escutcheon through external circumstances. If, for example, she became a prisoner of war (where rape was always a possibility), she could no longer guarantee a pure descent. The son of a woman prisoner of war was considered illegitimate and unsuitable for the office of priest.

The high priest John Hyrcanus (134–104 B.C.) and his son, the high priest Jannaeus (103–76 B.C.), were accused by their opponents of being descended from a bloodline that disqualified them for the office of high priest. Josephus describes the situation in the case of Hyrcanus: "Hyrcanus was a disciple of theirs (the Pharisees), and was greatly loved by them. Once he invited them to a feast and entertained them hospitably." When the crowd became suitably mellow, he asked them if they had any criticism to offer of his conduct. "But they testified to his being altogether virtuous. . . . However, one of the guests, named Eleasar, who had an evil nature and took pleasure in dissension, said, 'Since you have asked to be told the truth, if you wish to be righteous, give up the high-priesthood and be content with governing the people.' When Hyrcanus asked why, he was told: "Because we have heard that your mother was a captive in the reign of Antiochus Epiphanes.' But the story was false" (*JA*, trans. Ralph Marcus [Cambridge, MA: Harvard Univ. Press (LCL), 1987, XIII, x, 5, pp. 373, 375). Perhaps Hyrcanus's mother hadn't been captured by the enemy in war. But if she had, then according to Jewish law Hyrcanus could not be a lawful high priest.

Since the Jews paid so much attention to the mother, especially to her lineage, it's striking to see how in Matthew and Luke Mary's genealogy goes completely by the board. Thus from the standpoint of Jewish law, Jesus' family was unacceptable. On the paternal side—assuming the virgin birth—his father wasn't his father, and on the maternal side the pedigree was unknown.

All that could be said about his mother sounds—again if we take the reports of the virgin birth as factual assertions—rather like what Plutarch (d. ca. A.D. 120) wrote in his Life of Lysander: "There was a woman in Pontus who professed to be pregnant by Apollo, which many, as was natural, disbelieved, and many also gave credit to" (*The Lives of the Noble Grecians and Romans*, trans. John Dryden, rev. Arthur Hugh Clough [New York: Modern Library, 1932], p. 542. Hereinafter cited as *Lives*).

The paternal lineage of Jesus as the son of David has a dubious final link if Joseph wasn't Jesus' father. But it also has a dubious origin, that is, as far as the messianic promises go, which is the whole point here. For his own greater glory David had ascribed (or had others ascribe) to himself the promise that a messiah would be born from his descendants. It's safe to assume that a court poet or prophet (the percentage of flatterers always being higher in kingly palaces than in the abodes of ordinary citizens) was behind such a promise. In an inspired moment, which proved useful for all concerned, some royal retainer would have hit upon this crowning glory for the king; and this "prophecy" later found its way into the Books of Samuel.

In 2 Sam. 7:11ff. the prophet Nathan promises an everlasting reign to David's posterity: "The Lord will make you a house. . . . And your house and your kingdom shall be made sure forever before me; your throne shall be established for ever." David immediately accepts this idea and for his part shows his gratitude to God by making a promise: "And now, O Lord God, confirm for ever the word which thou hast spoken concerning thy servant and concerning his house, and do as thou hast spoken; and thy name will be magnified for ever" (2 Sam. 7:25–26). Religion promises eternal duration to the ruling house, and the ruler promises the same to religion.

Thus the messiah is defined as the redeemer-king for Israel, the ideal king who will achieve God's dominion over all nations and will establish a kingdom of peace. He will also be the descendant of a particular ruler (in this case David), who is made the standard against which the future messiah must be measured. This was the extreme limit that the glorification of a human being could reach. Up till this point, no one in Israel had ever thought of such a thing, because Israel was the last nation in the Middle East to get a monarchy. Never before had the messiah been so firmly attached to a specific family in Israel, and never before had he been yoked to a royal propaganda carriage, as he was now under David.

At least a handful of court poets were active in David's reign. We learn this from another story, the famous tale of David and Goliath, the giant from Gath, the shaft of whose spear was as thick as a weaver's beam (1 Sam. 17:4ff.). David the shepherd boy killed the ten-foot-tall (six cubits and a span) Philistine with a sling, a deed that from time immemorial, like many other killings, has been considered heroic. It wasn't: That sort of sling wasn't a toy but a deadly weapon of war. Even today a child with a weapon, a pistol, for example, can kill a giant.

But this much can be said positively for David: He did no such thing. One of the court poets merely imputed it to him. Goliath was killed by someone else, and his name, too, made its way into the Books of Samuel. This person was no shepherd boy, but a soldier, now forgotten and inglorious. "And there was again war with the Philistines at Gob; and Elhanan, the son of Jaareoregim, the Bethlehemite, slew Goliath the Gittite, the shaft of whose spear was like a weaver's beam" (2 Sam. 21:19). Nobody mentions Elhanan anymore, but David the soldier, the "shepherd boy," became king and the ancestor of the messiah.

The hope for the messiah is an old one. The tears and torment of humanity have always led it to hope for a savior to liberate and redeem men and women from all their misery. There is even a famous moment of messianic expectation in the Roman poet Virgil (d. 19 B.C.), in whose fourth

Eclogue we read: "We have reached the last Era in Sibylline song. Time has conceived and the great Sequence of the Ages starts afresh. Justice, the Virgin, comes back to dwell with us, and the rule of Saturn is restored. The Firstborn of the New Age is already on his way from high heaven down to earth" (*Latin Literature: An Anthology,* ed. Michael Grant and trans. E. V. Rieu [Harmondsworth, UK: Penguin, 1986], p. 135).

In the Old Testament the word *messiah* ("anointed") did not at first have the weight that it later acquired, especially with Christians. Kings and high priests were called anointed (i.e., by God). Even the Persian king Cyrus received this title. God, in fact, speaks a heavenly blessing over Cyrus: "Thus says the Lord to his anointed, to Cyrus, whose right hand I have grasped, to subdue nations before him, that gates may not be closed: 'I will go before you and level the mountains . . . that you may know that it is I, the Lord, the God of Israel, who call you by your name" (Isa. 45:1ff.).

The mention of Cyrus, founder of the Persian empire (539 B.C.) may remind us of the brilliant festivities commemorating the twenty-five hundredth anniversary of the Persian Empire, celebrated in Persepolis by the late Shah Reza Pahlavi. Sic transit gloria mundi. In any case, Cyrus is made so much of in the Old Testament because he let the Jews return to their homeland from their Babylonian captivity. He was also a popular figure because he and his successors provided the Jews with financial support for rebuilding their Temple (destroyed during the siege of Jerusalem by the Babylonians under Nebuchadnezzar in 586 B.C.) and resuming their Temple cult.

According to Christian interpreters, God did exactly what he had promised in the messianic prophecy of 2 Sam. 7:11ff. Hence, Jesus wouldn't be what he is if he weren't the great-great-great-etc.-grandson of David. This descent from David is therefore much more important than the person of Jesus himself, whose image in the Gospels is thoroughly neglected. Paul, for instance, has practically nothing to report about Jesus' life, but he does mention that Jesus was a son of David (Rom. 1:3).

We don't have a CV of Jesus, but we have two genealogies, one in Matthew and the other in Luke. Still, one has to choose between them because over long stretches they are contradictory and mutually exclusive.

It doesn't take a detailed argument to show that a genealogy going back to the first human being must be pure fantasy. This is what Luke does. He traces Jesus' lineage backward into the past and goes all the way to Adam. Matthew traces that lineage forward, from Abraham to Joseph.

From Abraham to David the genealogies are in agreement and match the family trees cited in the Old Testament (1 Chron. 2:1–14). But at that point Matthew and Luke go their separate ways. Matthew follows the line of ruling kings through Solomon and his son and successor Rehoboam, as found in 1 Chron. 3:5–19. Luke, by contrast, traces the line through Nathan, a son of David who never reigned as king. At the time of the Babylonian exile (586–536 B.C.) the two lists again coincide, this time in the figure of Shealtiel, though they give him different fathers. Starting with Shealtiel's son Zerubbabel, the lists again deviate and follow their course through two different sons of Zerubbabel, not meeting again till they get to Joseph, the father of Jesus (see Jeremias, *Jerusalem*, pp. 325–26).

People have made the weirdest attempts to reconcile the two irreconcilable lists of Jesus' ancestors. Catholic theologians, among others, have sweated mightily over this task. Many pious minds have been especially troubled by the fact that it isn't even clear who Jesus' grandfather was, since Matthew says he was Jacob and Luke says he was Heli (Eli).

As far back as Christian antiquity there was a great deal of fiddling and fixing with this. In his *Ecclesiastical History*, Eusebius (d. 339), who was a Father of the Church, writes that "each of the faithful has been zealous in making guesses on these passages" (*EH*, I, vii, p. 55). Nowadays believers are still fiddling with the problem. Unbelievers are luckier, since they can spend their time on more useful things. Now here they are, the two contradictory lists, from David to Jesus (the dates given for the reigns of kings are only approximate):

1 Chronicles	Matthew	Luke
(3:5–19)	(1:1–17)	(3:23–38)
David 1004–965	David	David
Solomon 965–928	Solomon	Nathan
Rehoboam 928–911	Rehoboam	Mattatha
Abijah 911–908	Abijah	Menna

1 Chronicles	Matthew	Luke
Asa 908–867	Asa	Melea
Jehoshaphat 867–846	Jehoshaphat	Eliakim
Joram 846–843	Joram	Jonam
Ahaziah 843–842		Joseph
Joash 837–798		Judah
Amaziah 798–769		Simeon
Azariah	Uzziah (=Azariah)	Levi
Jotham 741–733	Jotham	Matthat
Ahaz 733–727	Ahaz	Jorim
Hezekiah 727–698	Hezekiah	
Manasseh 698–642	Manasseh	
Amon 641–640	Amos (=Amon)	
Josiah 639–609	Josiah	Eliezer
Jehoiakim 608–598		Jesus
Jeconiah	Jeconiah	Er
	Elmadam	
	Cosam	
	Addi	
	Melchi	
	Neri	
Shealtiel	Salathiel	Salathiel
Zerubbabel	Zerubbabel	Zerubbabel
	Abiud	Rhesa
	Eliakim	Joanan
	Azor	Joda
	Zadok	Josech
	Achim	Semein
	Eliud	Mattathias
	Eleazar	Maath
	Matthan	Naggai
		Esli (Hesli)
		Nahum
		Amos

1 Chronicles	Matthew	Luke
		Mattathias
		Joseph
		Jannai
		Melchi
		Levi
		Matthat
	Jacob	Heli (Eli)
	Joseph	Joseph

In Matthew's list of ancestors the last king before the exile is Jeconiah (Jehoiachin). But Jeconiah had been cursed by God: "Write this man down as childless, a man who shall not succeed in his days; for none of his offspring shall succeed in sitting on the throne of David" (Jer. 22:30). Thus God forbade the posterity of Jeconiah to be the source of the messiah. So as a descendant of David, Jesus could be the messiah, but not as a descendant of Jeconiah. Yet the angel Gabriel seems not in the least disturbed about the old curse hanging over Jeconiah when he says to Mary, "The Lord God will give him the throne of his father David" (Luke 1:32). One text in the Bible occasionally flies in the face of another.

Matthew points out that Jesus' lineage consists of three times fourteen generations. He evidently sees some higher meaning in this, although no one knows exactly what. To arrive at his magic number of fourteen, however, he has to engage in a little manipulation by erasing certain kings before David and Jesus, such as Ahaziah, Joash, and Amaziah, who reigned between Joram and Azariah (1 Chron. 3:11–12). Dropping these kings might also have seemed appropriate to Matthew because they had all been cursed by God (1 Kings 21:21; 2 Kings 9:8). King Jehoiakim has been inadvertently omitted because his name sounds like that of his son Jehoiachin.

In view of his Potemkin-village list of ancestors from Abraham to Adam, Luke, as mentioned, has no credibility at all. But in other places, too, his list proves to be largely a fantasy: For the time of the kings he cites the names of Joseph, Judah, Simeon, and Levi, four of the sons of Jacob and eponymous ancestors of the tribes of Israel. Joachim Jeremias rightly observes that

> the custom of using the names of the twelve progenitors of the na-
> tion as personal names did not appear until after the Exile (ca.
> 536 B.C.).... When Luke cites the names of Joseph, Judah,
> Simeon, and Levi one after the other in the early period of the
> monarchy as descendants six through nine, this is an anachro-
> nism that proves the pre-exilic portion of Luke's genealogy to be
> historically worthless. (Jeremias, Jerusalem, pp. 330-31)

While both Matthew and Luke supply different lists of ancestors, they are in perfect harmony on one point: Their genealogies bear witness to a male religion. Jesus' lineage is made up almost exclusively of men. Both Evangelists present the birth of Jesus as a virgin birth, and yet at the end of their lists stands not the mother but a man who isn't even supposed to be the real father. And this is the person who guarantees the noble pedigree. A false father, a foster father, a putative father, a supposed father, an adoptive father, anything is better and more important than a real mother. Her descent plays not the slightest part in the story.

Women practically never appear in the two genealogies of Jesus: In Luke, except for Mary, there are none at all. In Matthew only four are mentioned: "Perez and Zerah by Tamar" (Matt. 1:3), "Salmon the father of Boaz by Rahab" (Matt. 1:5), "Boaz the father of Obed by Ruth" (Matt. 1:5), and one woman who is cited without a name, "the father of Solomon by the wife of Uriah" (Matt. 1:6), meaning Bathsheba. The four women, then, were first of all, Tamar, who committed incest when she seduced her father-in-law, Judah, and bore him two sons (Genesis 38); second, the pagan prostitute Rahab (Josh. 2:1); third, Ruth, who of course was not a prostitute but a foreigner from Moab; and fourth, the wife of Uriah, with whom David committed adultery.

Thus the four women listed in the genealogy all have a flaw, as theologians seldom fail to point out. They also regularly stress the presence of such women in the Gospels as clear proof of God's mercy. Catholic and Protestant writers are in fraternal accord when it comes to evaluating the significance of the feminine side of Jesus' family tree. Thus the Protestant theologian Gerhard Kittel writes: "The naming and choice is by no means accidental, but deliberate. By citing these names the Evangelist wishes to point to something . . . [to the fact] that the genealogy of Christ, by embracing the history of Israel, bears witness not just to its highlights, but at the same time to the sin and unworthiness that . . . run through those highlights" (*Theologische Wörterbuch* [1950], III, 1).

The well-known Catholic New Testament scholar Karl Hermann Schelke makes an almost verbatim discovery: "The naming and choice of the four women cannot be an accident; it is in fact deliberate. The Evangelist is thereby pointing out that the genealogy of Christ, by embracing the history of Israel, is bearing witness not only to its brilliant moments, but also to the sin and unworthiness in this history" ("Die Kindheitsgeschichten Jesu," in *Bibel und zeitgemäßer Glaube* [1967], II, 22).

In other words, "its brilliant moments" are based on the men who remain once the four women are subtracted. And the "sin and unworthiness" of Israel likewise boil down to a handful of women. Actually, there are enough male examples of "sin and unworthiness" in Jesus' lineage, quite apart from the fact that being a foreigner (Ruth) is no sin and that it takes two to commit adultery. The twain in this case are David and Bathsheba, though he is a bright spot in the genealogy and she is a stain upon it.

But upon closer inspection, the idea of descending from David may not seem so brilliant. Apart from the adultery he committed with Bathsheba's help, David did quite a few dubious things on his own. Before he became king, David was given to plundering and pillaging: "And David left neither man nor woman alive" (1 Sam. 27:9, 11). Once he was king, he maintained his penchant for murder. For example, he averted a famine by having the two sons whom Rispah had borne to Saul—Armoni and Mephibosheth—and five grandsons of his predecessor, Saul, executed by the Gibeonites. Evidently God demands human sacrifices to prevent evil, which gives the pious an opportunity to get rid of rivals.

And he gave them into the hands of the Gibeonites, and they hanged them on the mountain before the Lord, and the seven of

them perished together. [This story is one of the saddest in the
Old Testament.] . . . Then Rispah the daughter of Aiah took
sackcloth, and spread it for herself on the rock, from the begin-
ning of harvest until rain fell upon them from the heavens; and
she did not allow the birds of the air to come upon them by day,
or the beasts of the field by night. (2 Sam. 21)

"From the roof of the royal palace" David watched Bathsheba, Uriah's wife, taking a bath. "And the woman was very beautiful. And David sent and inquired about the woman. And one said, 'Is this not Bathsheba, the wife of Uriah the Hittite?' So David sent messengers and took her; and she came to him, and he lay with her." Later David wrote to his commander, Joab: "Set Uriah in the forefront of the hardest fighting, that he may be struck down and die." And so Uriah was killed. "When the wife of Uriah heard that Uriah her husband was dead, she made lamentation for her husband. And when the mourning was over, David sent and brought her to his house, and she became his wife, and bore him a son. But the thing that David had done displeased the Lord." The son died, but their second son was the future King Solomon (2 Samuel 11–12).

Because of the crime against Uriah, a curse from God was pronounced on David and his descendants. "Why have you despised the word of the Lord, to do what is evil in his sight? You have smitten Uriah the Hittite with the sword. . . . Now therefore the sword shall never depart from your house, because you have despised me" (2 Sam. 19:9–10). This passage, if read carefully, can be understood as the opposite of a messianic promise from God, who evidently judged the murder of Uriah more harshly than the theologians did Bathsheba's adultery: "Now therefore the sword shall never depart from your house." Unending war and a prince of peace are mutually exclusive.

Appendix

The New Testament genealogies of Jesus make it clear that Christians place a great deal of value on the fact that Jesus the Jew is descended from David

the Jew. Only with this family tree does Jesus seem right to them—in other
words, their whole Christian faith rests upon a Jewish lineage. For themselves, however, Christians have often tried to do exactly the opposite sort
of research, hoping to prove that they are *not* descended from David or
any Jew whatsoever. For some Christians, having a family tree completely
different from Jesus' has at times been of vital importance. People in the
Hitler era were not the first to learn how accursed a Jewish bloodline
could be. Long before that (and all the way into the 19th century, indeed
for some as late as 1946), many Spaniards had had that bitter experience.
For them, as we shall see, the family tree of Mary, measured forward in
time, played a crucial role similar to the one played by the family tree of
Joseph, measured backward.

In 1492, the year America was discovered, "los reyes católicos" of
Spain, Ferdinand and Isabel, drove the Jews from the country. The alternative was baptism or banishment. But for the Jews who converted under
pressure, preferring baptism to exile, their problems didn't end there. For
one of the first actions taken by the "Catholic sovereigns" back in 1478 had
been the setting up, with the help of a papal bull, of the Castilian Inquisition. The goal of the Inquisition, whose tribunal first met in Seville in
1480, was to ferret out the forcibly converted Jews who were suspected of
secretly practicing Jewish customs in their homes. For example, the use of
olive oil rather than lard in the kitchen aroused suspicion and was taken to
be a sign of backsliding to Judaism. In fact, this was the evidence most
widely reported to the Inquisition by informers (Léon Poliakov, *L'Histoire
de l'Antisémitisme* [1961], II, 187). The investigation in Seville lasted seven
years, and seven hundred *marranos* (pigs—that is, converted Jews) were
burned at the stake.

But baptized Jews who managed to escape the envious claws of Old
Christians and the Inquisition still faced difficulties, starting with their
family tree. In 1547 the archbishop of Toledo, Juan Martínez Siliceo, former tutor to the crown prince (later Philip II), wrote a treatise on "purity
of blood" (*limpieza de sangre*). In it he demanded that all persons seeking
to be clerics prove that they were not descended from Jews.

Henceforth even those entering a religious order had to furnish expensive proofs of racial purity. The founder of the Jesuits, Ignatius Loyola

(d. 1556), was able to block this requirement during his lifetime, but from 1592 onward the proof of racial purity was required for entrance into the Jesuit order all over the world. And this requirement was finally abolished in 1946 (cf. Friedrich Heer, *Gottes Erste Liebe. Die Juden im Spannungsfeld der Geschichte* [1981], p. 511).

The Spanish Moor (meaning a descendant of Spanish Muslims) Don Cosme and his two brothers Don Fernando and Don Juan, head of the rich and influential house of Abenamir in Valencia, lost their large fortune. In 1578 Don Cosme complained, "I have paid 7,000 ducats; and today I have nothing left with which to finance the lies of witnesses" (Poliakov, *L'Histoire*, II, 331).

This situation led to the creation of a major cottage industry: that of the *linajudos*, or ancestor researchers. In 1655 there was a suit against the ancestral research operation of Don Fernando de Leiba, because "those who do not apply to this concern are made out by it to be nephews of Luther or Mohammed." One contemporary complained about how expensive it was to pay witnesses—both for those whose blood was "pure" and those whose blood wasn't. The former had to pay to keep their blood pure, the latter to make it pure (Poliakov, *L'Histoire*, II, 283).

In 17th-century Spain there were people buzzing around in all directions throughout the country, searching the archives of different places for proof of the purity of their own blood and the impurity of their opponents'. In a letter to Philip IV (1621–65), an anonymous Inquisitor called the king's attention to the fact that by that time the question of racial purity was at the bottom of nine out of every ten civil and criminal trials (Poliakov, *L'Histoire*, II, 284).

In 1681 the Grand Inquisitor Valladares forbade noble families to hire New Christian wet nurses, who would ruin the children with their milk. In 1772 a law was passed that anyone who intended to be a lawyer, teacher, or even a simple scribe had to show a certificate of racial purity. Only after 1835 did this slowly cease to be enforced.

A few Jewish families, to be sure, succeeded in proving that they had resided in Spain even before the crucifixion of Jesus. Some indeed established that they had fled to Spain immediately after the Flood, and hence could not be "murderers of God" (Poliakov, *L'Histoire*, II, 284). The members of the Virgin Mary's family were likewise considered racially pure. That was the case of the descendants of the famous Solomon Halevi. This highly cultivated and influential rabbi of Burgos, who had converted to Christianity in 1391, became the Christian bishop of Burgos. He took the name of the apostle Paul and called himself Pablo de Santa María, since he was convinced that he was descended from the line of Mary the Mother of God. This conviction turned out to be extremely useful later on for his own descendants. He died in 1435 in the odor of sanctity, and his tomb became a shrine visited by pilgrims.

In 1604 Philip III published a dispensation in favor of Don Pedro Osorio de Velasco and other descendants of Don Pablo de Santa María. The dispensation was based on the "miraculous conversion of Pablo de Santa María, on the venerable age of this conversion, and on the nobility of his blood, which according to tradition went back to the ancestral line of Our Lady" (Poliakov, *L'Histoire*, II, 227).

CHAPTER SIX

Miraculous
Fairy Tales

IN THE CASE of a messiah or a man people made out to be the Messiah, there were, as Jews in Jesus' day saw it, and there are, as many Christians see it today, certain criteria and hallmarks to look for. People thought then, and still do today, that such criteria could be found in Old Testament prophecies, such as, "Then the eyes of the blind shall be opened, and the ears of the deaf man unstopped" (Isa. 35:5). Thus the first criterion is the power to work miracles, which people expect from a messiah, and the ability to do them is the gauge with which a messiah must be measured. Nobody believes a messiah unconditionally. Faith, too, calls for guarantees. If a messiah works no miracles, nobody will follow him. In any case, that's the basic principle, and there is only one alternative: ascribing to the messiah figure miracles that he never performed. And it won't be a big help if he himself objects to the addiction to miracles: He will be supplied with them anyway.

Jesus never wanted to be a messiah (see Chapter Seventeen, "Jesus and the Dead Sea Scrolls"); he also rejected the notion that miracles proved the truth of his message. "Unless you see signs and wonders, you will not believe" (John 4:48). For him faith based on miracles is no faith at all, and so faith in miracles isn't faith either. When the Pharisees come and demand from him a sign from heaven, he rebuffs them: "Why does this generation seek a sign? Truly, I say to you, no sign shall be given to this generation" (Mark 8:12). And, "An evil and adulterous generation seeks for a sign" (Matt. 12:39, also 16:4; cf. Luke 11:29).

That Jesus rejected miracles as a way of legitimizing his mission is reflected in the Apostolic Letters, above all those of Paul, the earliest New Testament writer, which say nothing about any miracles by Jesus. Meanwhile, as far as the Gospels are concerned, Jesus' aloofness from miracles did him no good: According to the four Evangelists, he did more than enough miracles to be recognized as the Messiah. Thus they claim that he fully satisfied both the ancient and modern expectation of miracles.

But why not take Jesus' criticism of such expectations and hence of miracles themselves as something more than mere rhetoric or an editorial addition? If we do so, we shall have to regard the wonders attributed to him as the result of a naive addiction to miracles on the part of the authors of the Gospels and their sources. This is especially the case when the miracles border on magic or when we run into miracles that were reportedly done at other times by other miracle workers.

Let's begin with the miracle at the marriage feast of Cana. In John this miracle of changing water into wine stands at the beginning of Jesus' public career. We don't know where Cana was located, only that the miracle had to do with a rather large amount of water and a rather large amount of wine—"six stone jars, each holding twenty or thirty gallons," so all told anywhere from 120 to 180 gallons of wine. This is a miracle that the other three Evangelists know nothing about, or in any event say nothing about. And it doesn't match the other miracles of Jesus reported in John, which involve healing or helping people in distress. Unless, of course, it's genuine human distress when people who are already drunk (John 2:20) have nothing left to wet their whistle with.

David Friedrich Strauß rightly called this miracle a "luxury miracle" (*Das Leben Jesu* [1837], II, 226). John's account stresses that it was wine of the finest quality, not mere table wine. This makes the miracle all the more astonishing. It was not, however, a model miracle for all Christians. This was shown several centuries later when a certain teetotaling Bishop Macarius performed a precisely contrary miracle: Invited to dine by Abbot

Peregrinus, he was presented with a glass of wine, which he drained only after changing the wine into water.

Many people have written many pages about the miracle of Cana, about what it means and what it reveals. Theologians have, as it were, turned the water in the jars not into wine but into ink. But to date no one has quite figured it out. We may assume therefore that it simply describes a kind of conjuring trick. If instead of turning water into wine, Jesus had performed any other kind of magic at the wedding, such as turning tin into aluminum, we'd be puzzling in the very same way over what it meant. And it would mean just as much and just as little as it already does. Hence, we shouldn't lose ourselves in profound speculation, but simply recognize what has really happened: Such magical miracles were invented and imputed to Jesus. Incidentally, some people are disturbed that Jesus snapped so rudely at his mother in this episode and even refused to call her Mother: "O woman, what have you to do with me?" (John 2:4). But anyone fretting about this can rest assured that Jesus never did anything of the sort.

But how did this miracle story ever come about? The date the Church celebrates the feast of this miracle can supply us with a helpful hint. It's 6 January, the feast of the Epiphany. *Epiphania* means "appearance" in Greek and refers to the revelation of the Lord's power. In pagan antiquity 6 January was the day celebrating the revelation of a different divine power and wine miracles performed by a different god: It was the feast of Dionysus, the Greek god of wine:

> In fact the motif of the story, the transformation of water into wine, is a typical motif of the Dionysus legend, in which this miracle serves to highlight the god's epiphany. And hence it is timed to coincide with the date of the feast of Dionysus, from January 5th to 6th. In the ancient Church this affinity was still understood, when . . . the 6th of January was taken to be the day that the marriage feast was celebrated at Cana. (Rudolf Bultmann, Das Evangelium des Johannes [1962], p. 83)

Plainly put, in the legend of the marriage at Cana Jesus reveals his divine power in the same way that stories had told of the Greek god

Dionysus. The 6th of January became for Christians the feast of the power revelation (epiphany) of their God, thereby displacing the feast of Dionysus's epiphany. As Bultmann says, "No doubt the story [of the marriage feast at Cana] has been borrowed from pagan legends and transferred to Jesus" (Bultmann, *Das Evangelium*, p. 83). On his feast day, Dionysus made empty jars fill up with wine in his temple in Elis; and on the island of Andros, wine flowed instead of water from a spring or in his temple. Accordingly, the true miracle of the marriage feast at Cana would not be the transformation *by* Jesus of water into wine, but the transformation *of* Jesus into a sort of Christian wine god.

John, by the way, took the miracle of the wine from a collection of Jesus' miracle stories, working portions of this collection, in a somewhat unbalanced fashion, into his Gospel, as Bultmann shows (*Das Evangelium*, p. 78). The miracles recounted in this collection were numbered. The first one was the wine miracle and is also registered as such in John (2:11: "This, the first of his signs, Jesus did at Cana in Galilee"). The second miracle in the collection is the cure of the son of the official in Capernaum, and it is likewise labeled in John as number two (4:54: "This was now the second sign that Jesus did"). But in the meantime John had long since mentioned several other miracles of Jesus, as we see in John 2:23: "Now when he was in Jerusalem at the Passover feast, many believed in his name when they saw the signs that he did."

To our taste the most sympathetic miracles are the miraculous cures of the sick. Presumably Jesus really was a healer, a kind of physician: *Iasthai* ("to heal") is what the Evangelists call his activity. For speakers of Greek (which was the international language then and of course the language of the entire New Testament), the very name of *Iesous* reminded them of *iasthai*. In the Ionic future, *iesomai* (I will heal), or the substantive, *iasis* (healing), the similarity couldn't fail to capture the attention of anyone who knew Greek.

Despite all the legendary embellishment and exaggeration, there is an undeniable historical core to accounts of Jesus' activity as a physician. But Jesus did not accept the notion, widespread in the ancient world, that the essence of sickness lay in a scheme of guilt and punishment—sickness as God's way of punishing us.

Ancient Jewish theologians drew up catalogs in which guilt and sickness were juxtaposed as cause and effect. For example: "There are three kinds of dropsy: when it results from lewdness, the body is hard; when it results from hunger, the body is bloated; when it results from a magic spell, the body is emaciated." "Every judge who accepts a bribe and twists justice will not die at an advanced age without his eyes going blind. See Exodus 23:8: 'And you shall take no bribe, for a bribe blinds the officials.'" Rabbi Jochanan (d. A.D. 270) said: "The plagues of leprosy come about from seven things: calumny, bloodshed, perjury, fornication, pride, robbery, and envy." A rabbi said: "Whoever engages in intercourse by the light of a lamp will have epileptic children." Rabbi Acha (ca. A.D. 320) said: "When a man sleeps with his wife in the days of her menstruation, his children will be struck with epilepsy." Rabbi Jochanan ben Dahabai (ca. A.D. 180): "Why do children become lame? Because the parents turn their table upside down [that is, woman on top, man beneath]. Why do they become deaf? Because the parents talk during intercourse." The later Rabbi Jochanan (d. A.D. 279), by the way, rejected this regimentation of marital sex (Hermann Strack and Paul Billerbeck, *Kommentar zum Neuen Testament aus Talmud und Midrash* [1965], II, 196, 529).

By challenging such superstitious connections, Jesus humanized the phenomenon of sickness and disability. When he sees a man blind from birth, he is asked: "Rabbi, who sinned, this man or his parents, that he was born blind?" (John 9:2). To which Jesus answers: "It was not that this man sinned, or his parents" (John 9:3). Thus he views a sick man not as someone being punished, but, in a thoroughly enlightened sense, simply as someone who must be helped.

For the benefit of the sick Jesus turns against the religious tradition of his people and cures diseases even on the Sabbath, even when the disease is not acute or life threatening. The prevalent Pharisaic teaching maintained that healing on the Sabbath was permitted when the illness was life threatening, but when there was no danger in delaying treatment, it was unconditionally forbidden (Strack and Billerbeck, *Kommentar,* I, 623).

The Roman historian Tacitus (d. A.D. 120) provides a vivid and sympathetic account of two miraculous cures that occurred in Alexandria during a visit by Emperor Vespasian in A.D. 69.

During the months while Vespasian was waiting at Alexandria for the regular season of the summer winds and a settled sea, many marvels occurred to mark the favor of heaven and a certain partiality of the gods toward him. One of the common people of Alexandria, well known for his loss of sight, threw himself before Vespasian's knees, praying him with groans to cure his blindness, being so directed by the god Serapis, whom this most superstitious of nations worships before all others; and he besought the emperor to deign to moisten his cheeks and eyes with his spittle. [Note: Jesus, too, uses spittle to cure a blind man; see Mark 8:23, John 9:6.] Another, whose hand was useless, prompted by the same god, begged Caesar to step and trample on it. Vespasian at first ridiculed these appeals and treated them with scorn; then, when the men persisted, he began at one moment to fear the discredit of failure, at another to be inspired with hopes of success by the appeals of the suppliants and the flattery of his courtiers; finally, he directed the physicians to give their opinion as to whether such blindness and infirmity could be overcome by human aid. Their reply treated the two cases differently: they said that in the first the power of sight had not been completely eaten away and it would return if the obstacles were removed; in the other, the joints had slipped and become displaced, but they could be restored if a healing pressure were applied to them. Such perhaps was the wish of the gods, and it might be that the emperor had been chosen for this divine service; in any case, if a cure were obtained, the glory would be Caesar's, but in the event of failure, ridicule would fall only on the poor suppliants. So Vespasian, believing that his good fortune was capable of anything and that nothing was any longer incredible, with a smiling countenance, and amid intense excitement on the part of the bystanders, did as he was asked to do. The hand was instantly restored to use, and the day again shone for the blind man. Both facts are told by eyewitnesses even now when falsehood brings no reward. (Histories, trans. Clifford H. Moore [Cambridge, MA: Harvard Univ. Press (LCL), 1979], IV, lxxxi, pp. 159, 161)

In this report we can find all the essential prerequisites for a miraculous cure: (1) The healing is effected not by a supernatural power to work miracles on the part of the healer, but by the *patient's attitude of expectation*. Crowds didn't stream toward Jesus because he healed many people; rather, because crowds streamed toward him, he healed many people. Whereupon still more people came streaming and he healed still more, and so on. It was a spiraling pattern of miracles. (2) People's expectations are particularly focused on *rulers and other eminent personalities*. For example, the kings of France, the successors to the Roman emperors, were expected to heal the sick. In the great court of Versailles, for instance, Louis XIV touched about twenty-four hundred sick people on 22 May 1701. The kings of France were accustomed to touching the sick (specifically those suffering from scrofula) with the words "May God heal you! The king touches you!" (Dieu te guérisse! Le roi te touche!) The reputation for extraordinary qualities surrounding a ruler or famous person and the expectations that the sick have of him escalate and reinforce each other.

This correlation is quite infallible. For, as Tacitus observes, a failed cure is not blamed on the thaumaturge; the cause in all cases is sought in the sick person. The same is true of Jesus: When he fails to work miracles, this is explained by the people's lack of faith. Hence, working miracles was hardest for Jesus in his hometown, because there the least was expected of him. In Tacitus we also find the description of the third component of a miraculous cure, namely, *the eyewitnesses:* They stick to their story that Vespasian cured both sick people even later on when testimony so flattering to the emperor could be of no advantage to them.

Miraculous cures are a complicated business because, apart from the expectations of the sick, the environment and, above all, the witnesses play a critical role. Witnesses can attest to things because they have seen them or because they think they have seen them. Witnesses can pass over in silence things they have seen. Witnesses are capable of not seeing things that they must have seen, because there is no greater blindness than the kind that refuses to see. What prompts witnesses to swear to something that may be false, even when they can no longer immediately profit by it, is again an issue that Tacitus ignores. He likewise leaves open the question of whether or in what sense he, Tacitus himself, considers miraculous cures possible.

It is no wonder that people afflicted by sickness and pain should evidence a prerational readiness to believe in miraculous cures. This has always been true, and it was true back in Alexandria during the visit of Emperor Vespasian. It also applies to Jesus, with the further condition that, as we have seen, people especially looked forward to seeing miraculous cures from the Messiah.

Jesus was not the first healer-savior. The Greek god of medicine, Asclepius, likewise was called Savior of the world (*soter tes oikoumenēs*). Since the 6th century B.C.E., his sanctuary in Epidauros had been the Lourdes of the ancient world. Beginning in the 5th and 4th centuries B.C. the devotees of Asclepius covered the Mediterranean basin with a network of almost five hundred cultic and healing centers, among them the one at Kos. His temples were hung with votive tablets from grateful cured patients, each citing the disease and the remedy that the god had revealed to the sick person in a dream while he or she slept in his sanctuary.

The most famous physician of antiquity, Hippocrates (d. ca. 370 B.C.) came from Kos, from an Asclepiad (medical) family resident there. Asclepius was not just a miraculous healer, as in his sanctuary in Epidauros; he was also the patron and protector of an enlightened guild of physicians. Even today the staff of Asclepius, the caduceus, with its two intertwined serpents, is the symbol of medical science.

After the epochal turning point in the age of Constantine (d. 337), when Christianity became the state religion and began to destroy the other religions, the Divine Physician of Christians superseded the pagan god Asclepius. Bishop Eusebius of Caesarea (d. 339), court reporter and biographer for Constantine, the first Christian emperor, tells a story in his *Ecclesiastical History* about a statue that he had seen with his own eyes in Caesarea Philippi. This statue, he says, represented a man stretching out his hand to heal a woman kneeling before him. Underneath the man a plant was growing up to the hem of his cloak, a plant that served as a remedy for any and all diseases. Eusebius and the people in Caesarea also knew whom the statue represented. It was Jesus, and the woman kneeling before him was the woman with a hemorrhage, whom Jesus cured (Matt.

9:20ff.; Mark 5:25ff.; Luke 8:43ff.). This woman, it turned out, had made her home in Caesarea Philippi.

But this co-opting Christian interpretation was wrong. It wasn't a statue of Christ at all; it was a pagan healer-god, probably Asclepius. But Eusebius, who saw things differently, felt flattered: "And there is nothing wonderful in the fact that those heathen, who long ago had good deeds done to them by our Savior, should have made these objects" (*Ecclesiastical History,* trans. J. E. L. Oulton, vol. II [Cambridge, MA: Harvard Univ. Press (LCL), 1980], VII, xviii, pp. 175, 177).

In their triumphal march, Christians either reconsecrated pagan statues and temples and transformed them into statues of Christ and churches or else they destroyed them. Constantine, for example, had his soldiers level a "celebrated marvel," the temple of Asclepius at Aegae in Macedonia.

Thus the cures of the sick, which in Jesus' case we can accept as having a basis in historical fact, confirm a trend that one would expect to see in the case of any famous person: the tendency of miraculous cures by others to migrate in his direction. This isn't surprising, because miraculous fairy tales are at the same time wandering fairy tales, and some of them simply migrated to Jesus. Once told about others, they are now told about Jesus; and so we find them in the New Testament. "The process whereby already existent miracle stories are transferred, like other anecdotes, to a hero (a savior or even a god) may be frequently observed in the history of both literature and religion. . . . In the *Arabian Nights* Harun al-Rashid has become the hero or supporting actor in numerous fairy tales" (Rudolf Bultmann, *Die Geschichte der synoptischen Tradition* [1961], p. 244).

Some miracles reported of Jesus are modeled on Old Testament prototypes. Take, for example, the feeding of the five thousand (or four thousand): "A man came from Baal-shal-ishah, bringing the man of God bread of the first fruits, twenty loaves of barley, and fresh ears of grain in his sack. And Elisha said, 'Give to the men, that they may eat.' But his servant said, 'How am I to set this before a hundred men?' So he repeated, 'Give them to the men, that they may eat, for thus says the Lord, "They shall eat and have some left"' So he set it before them. And they ate, and had some left, according to the word of the Lord" (2 Kings 4:42–44).

Elisha performed a number of other miracles as well. Not only did he raise the dead (2 Kings 4:34–35) and make the blind see, he also made the sighted blind (2 Kings 6:18). Fortunately, Jesus didn't imitate Elisha's harmful miracles, such as his cursing the small boys who mocked his baldness ("And two she-bears came out of the woods and tore forty-two of the boys," 2 Kings 2:24). In any event, the majority of the miracles recounted of Jesus do not derive from Jewish tradition, but from the Hellenistic milieu.

Some thirty individual miracles are ascribed to Jesus. These can be broken down into miraculous cures (the largest single category), driving out of demons, raising of the dead, and nature miracles. In the case of the miraculous cures and the related exorcisms, we can, as mentioned, accept a certain core of the narratives as historical. The medicine of Jesus' day did not distinguish carefully between sickness and diabolical possession. In the Gospels there are sick people who are labeled possessed, and possessed people who are labeled sick (Matt. 4:24; Mark 1:34). In particular, epileptics (Matt. 17:15), the dumb (Matt. 9:32; Luke 11:14), handicapped people who are both blind and dumb (Matt. 12:22), as well as those suffering from gout (Luke 13:11ff.), were looked upon as possessed by demons.

Legend picked up Jesus' cures of the sick and exorcisms of demons. In particular it seized upon the latter, amplifying and distorting them, as in the story of the demons leaving one or two men and entering a herd of swine, which immediately drowned itself (demons and all, evidently). This sort of thing can only be called fantasy jumping the rails.

We meet this story in a number of variants: Matt. 8:28ff.; Mark 5:1ff.; Luke 8:26ff. According to Mark and Luke, it was a single possessed man, whom Jesus encountered after some stormy sailing on the eastern side of Lake Gennesaret. Matthew says there were two possessed individuals, and he locates the exorcism in "the country of the Gadarenes," whereas Mark and Luke place it "in the country of the Gerasenes."

Mark tells the story this way:

And when he had come out of the boat, there met him out of the
tombs a man with an unclean spirit, who lived among the tombs;
and no one could bind him anymore, even with a chain; for he

had often been bound with fetters and chains, but the chains he wrenched apart, and the fetters he broke in pieces; and no one had the strength to subdue him. Night and day among the tombs and on the mountains he was always crying out and bruising himself with stones. And when he saw Jesus from afar, he ran and worshiped him; and crying out with a loud voice, he said, "What have you to do with me, Jesus, Son of the Most High God? I adjure you by God, do not torment me." For he had said to him, "Come out of the man, you unclean spirit!" And Jesus asked him, "What is your name?" He replied, "My name is Legion; for we are many." And he begged him eagerly not to send him out of the country. Now a great herd of swine was feeding there on the hillside; and they begged him, "Send us to the swine, let us enter them." So he let them leave. And the unclean spirits came out, and entered the swine; and the herd, numbering about two thousand, rushed down the steep bank into the sea, and were drowned in the sea.

The evil spirit, supposedly a single demon, suddenly reveals himself to be not just a plurality of spirits but a huge horde, and a military one at that. *Legion* is a word from Roman military language; at the time it meant 6,000 infantrymen, 120 cavalry, and the pertinent auxiliary forces. This was a mighty Satanic battalion that Jesus confronted in one poor maniac. Conversely, of course, Jesus also had legions at his disposal, heavenly legions, and not just one but "more than twelve" (Matt. 26:53). He didn't need them here, however, because the diabolic army surrendered voluntarily, asking only to retreat unmolested into a herd of swine. Permission was granted.

Meanwhile some features of the behavior of this demonic army seem peculiar. The demons' most obvious option would have been to run away or to hide. Instead they rush to capitulate. This demonstrates a kind of trust and faith in Jesus as the Messiah. The fact that they conjure Jesus "in the name of God" may also seem a little fishy. "In the name of God" is a formula used to get control of a demon. The demons' wish to enter a herd of swine is utterly incomprehensible. It's unworthy of intelligent creatures such as demons to desire this kind of life. And finally, the whole venture leads only to a senseless suicide by the pigs, which thereby ceased to be of any value to the demons as hosts.

Why did the demons instantly rob themselves of the very biotype they had requested? And what happened to them after that? Where did they head to? Nor do we know whether demons can swim. On the other hand, we may conjecture that demons are neither willing nor able to commit suicide.

Another disturbing thought is that with the permission amiably granted to the demons, Jesus did serious damage to the owners of the herd. All in all, this doesn't seem to have been a successful miracle. In Mark we read that after the great miracle the people come out of the city and "they began to beg Jesus to depart from their neighborhood" (Mark 5:17). This is surely a gross understatement, in view of the heavy losses in livestock and of the rage of the people. In any event, despite the massive swine-slaughter, they don't believe in Jesus. Given such poor results, we can only conclude that better methods could be devised for spreading the faith.

Incidentally, Mark and Luke present the geographical situation in a completely false light. Mark says, "They came to the other side of the sea, to the country of the Gerasenes" (Mark 5:1). Luke says: "Then they arrived at the country of the Gerasenes, which is opposite Galilee" (Luke 8:26). But Gerasa (known today as Jerash) does not lie on the shore of the Sea of Galilee; it's about sixty kilometers farther inland, as any map will show. Nor does Matthew's "country of the Gadarenes" lie on the Sea of Galilee, but about ten kilometers away. Still, to make the point of the miracle the cities had to be near the Sea of Galilee.

Upon closer inspection, this whole exorcism is merely a folktale, a droll story using the motif of deceiving the devil, which has been transferred to Jesus. The demons get from Jesus the permission they ask for, but wind up with the short end of the stick (cf. Bultmann, *Die Geschichte*, pp. 224–25).

The descriptions of Jesus' raising the dead and his nature miracles have to be seen as legends or fairy tales. There are three accounts of the dead being raised: the twelve-year-old daughter of Jairus, the president of the synagogue (Mark 5:22ff.; parallels in Matt. 9:18ff. and Luke 8:40ff.), the young man from Nain (Luke 7:11ff.), and finally Lazarus (John 11:1ff.).

A comparison of these stories reveals a point worth noticing: the tendency to heighten the element of the miraculous. When in Mark Jesus says of the daughter of Jairus, "The child is not dead, but sleeping" (Mark 5:39), it is at least theoretically conceivable that Jesus actually meant what he said, that is, that the girl wasn't dead, just unconscious. In that case, Jesus didn't resurrect a dead person, but saved someone lying in a coma.

In the story of the young man from Nain as told by Luke (who wrote after Mark), there is no longer any possibility of a merely apparent death. In this case it's clear that the dead person is really dead.

But if the raising of the young man from Nain constitutes an enhancement vis-à-vis the daughter of Jairus, the amplification in John's story is still more massive. Lazarus is not only most certainly dead, he has already been lying in the tomb for four days; he has already begun to putrefy and stink (John 11:39). As for the credibility of the miracle of Lazarus, misgivings are in order from the very fact that the other three Evangelists, who wrote before John, say nothing about the event. It's unthinkable that the writers of the Synoptics, which recount so many of Jesus' miracles, would have ignored this most staggering of wonders if they had known of it. The only possible conclusion is that they never heard of it. This means, once again, that the story didn't come into circulation until later, that it was a late-vintage fairy tale.

The story of the raising of the young man from Nain has clear echoes of 1 Kings 17, where Elijah raises the son of a widow, and where it says of Elijah, exactly as Luke says of Jesus, "[he] delivered him to his mother" (1 Kings 17:23; Luke 7:15). There is another story of the raising of a widow's son, in 2 Kings 4, but this time Elisha performs the miracle.

Rudolf Bultmann points out that raisings of the dead play a pronounced role in the ancient Hellenistic legends about philosophers. For example, Apollonius of Tyana meets the funeral bier of a bride, followed by the grieving bridegroom and the rest of the mourners, and resurrects the dead woman. "The material cited," says Bultmann, "shows the atmosphere, shows motifs and forms, and thus helps us to understand how miracle stories made their way into the Gospel tradition" (*Die Geschichte,* pp. 248ff.).

One further note about the daughter of Jairus, whom Jesus is supposed to have raised. Certain rules govern the creation of legends and fairy tales. New Testament scholarship has devoted increasing attention to the patterns of how fantasy takes over in the passing on of both oral and written tradition. One sharp observer of such patterns was David Friedrich Strauß. At the age of twenty-seven, he became the most famous theologian of the century with his *Life of Jesus* (1835). The book also earned him an official lifelong ban against any career in the Church or the academy. Strauß writes that it is a "false premise that the narrator who is more detailed and vivid is the more exact reporter, the eyewitness" (*Das Leben Jesu,* I, 784).

One might think that fantasy and imprecision go hand in hand, but it's the other way around: Fantasy and precision go together, and fantasy stands there with the air of an eyewitness. Fantasy fills in all of knowledge's gaps, and not with coarse strokes but with the fine touches of a miniaturist. Witnesses often know more about an episode twenty years later than they did immediately afterward. So whenever we find precise details, a certain amount of caution is always called for. It might be mere fantasy. The exactitude of the eyewitness and that of fantasy are hard to tell apart.

This trend of fantasy toward specificity can be observed in many passages in the New Testament. At all times fantasy has taken charge of the last words of famous people. It has always sought to clarify in them whatever was unclear; and it certainly did this with Jesus. Thus what Mark describes as Jesus' last wordless cry (Mark 15:37) is transformed by Luke (23:46) into "Father, into thy hands I commit my spirit!"

Fantasy also has a way of finding names for hitherto unknown people. We have already seen this with the three kings from the East. The same process of fantasy can be seen in the New Testament where the oldest Gospel, Mark, doesn't know names with which the more recent Gospels are quite familiar. Names that no New Testament author knows or mentions get discovered around A.D. 150, when the *Protevangelium of James* announces that Mary's parents were Joachim and Anne.

The trend to precision is almost always bound up with the trend to amplification. To fill up blanks the best-known names will be inserted. Where Mark (14:15) speaks of "disciples," Luke (22:8) says, "Peter and John." Mark 7:17's "the disciple" becomes Matthew 15:15's "Peter." Mark doesn't know that Jairus's daughter, whom Jesus raised from the dead, was "Jairus's only daughter," as Luke found out. Similarly, Mark (9:17) reports that the father brought his possessed son to Jesus. Luke (9:38) adds that it was his only son. Mark's rich man (10:22) becomes Matthew's rich young man (19:22).

Other examples: in Mark 3:1 Jesus cures a man with a withered hand. Luke (6:6) knows that it was his right hand (the more important hand for most people). Mark 9:43 and 47 speak simply of hand and eye. In Matt. 5:29–30 these become the right hand and the right eye. Whereas Luke 6:29 speaks only of a blow on the cheek, Matt. 5:39 knows that it's the right cheek. On this point Bultmann observes: "The question whether Jesus meant a blow with the palm or the back of the hand has . . . no understanding of the graphic power of popular speech" (*Die Geschichte*, p. 340). Mark reports that in the Garden of Gethsemane a servant had an ear struck off (14:47). Luke (22:50) knows more: It was the right ear. As with the right cheek, this is an amplification analogous to the one with the right hand, but of dubious significance since while most people are right-handed, they aren't right-cheeked or right-eared. The fourth Evangelist, John, has in the meantime learned the name of the disciple who sliced the ear off—Peter. John also knows the name of the servant: Malchus (John 18:10).

The so-called nature miracles are likewise fairy tales, one and all. With regard to the miraculous multiplication of the loaves, we have seen that it has Old Testament models. There are several versions of this dining miracle. In Matthew (14:13–21) "five thousand men, not counting women and children" are fed with five loaves and two fish. This is a faintly chauvinistic mode of reckoning; Mark (6:44) has simply "five thousand men"; the women and children aren't even mentioned. Luke (9:14) puts the crowd at "around five thousand men," and John (6:10) is no more polite, "about five thousand men." All the Evangelists inform us that there were twelve baskets of bread left over.

Alongside this version with the five loaves and the two fish there is yet another, added on by Mark and Matthew. This time it's seven loaves and "some" fish. In Mark 8:9 the total number of the people fed is cited as four thousand, and there are seven baskets of "broken pieces." It's the same in Matthew, except that once again women and children are not included in the total (15:38).

Many Catholic Bibles provide clear headings to distinguish the "First Multiplication of the Loaves" from the "Second Multiplication of the Loaves." But it's no good. One can write all the headings one wants; we are still left with different accounts of one and the same multiplication of loaves. There's no second miracle; and word of this is slowly getting around even among Catholic theologians.

The first signs of this shift are already visible in the Catholic *Lexikon für Theologie und Kirche*: "The exegetes, and in part Catholic exegetes as well, nowadays generally assume that both narratives are dealing with a single event" ([1958] II, 709). They are variants or doublets, whatever one wishes. But some people are still racking their brains over why in one variant the number given is five thousand and in the other it's four thousand. And these riddle-solvers even find reasons for the discrepancy, as if the whole episode were historical. But from the historical standpoint, there was neither one nor two "miraculous multiplications of loaves." There was none at all.

Nevertheless, the image of Jesus giving people bread to eat, bread in the actual or the figurative sense, is a lovely one. We need bread in both senses. We can put ourselves into this picture, even if not in the wide-screen framework of four or five thousand men, including or excluding women and children. We may imagine a much smaller but at the same time historically believable crowd, of an evening, not far from the lakeshore. We may reckon in women and children and imagine that Jesus actually sat down on the grass and ate with his listeners and supporters. And if we wish, we can sit down with them and get something to eat.

In connection with the story of the multiplication of the loaves, there are two verses that are factually untrue, although they are supposed to have been spoken by Jesus: "Do you not perceive? Do you not remember the five loaves of the five thousand, and how many baskets you gathered? Or the seven loaves of the four thousand, and how many baskets you gathered?" (Matt. 16:9–10). In this counting up of miracles, Jesus asserts the fact of the two separate multiplications of the loaves, although there was at most one, and a legendary one at that. Matthew (along with Mark) mistakenly believed that there were two, and he has Jesus share in this error as a propagandist for his own miracles. But this shows that the Evangelists do not shy away from manipulating Jesus' words and imputing to him their own arguments. This is only a small example to show that not every saying ascribed to Jesus can be viewed as actually said by him.

A further nature miracle is Mark 4:37–41 and parallel accounts, the power of Jesus to command wind and sea. No further exposition is needed for the fact that a sudden storm came up on the lake, that there was danger, that there was a fortunate rescue. But that is the whole background of this little story. There is nothing specifically Christian to theologize into it. It's a wandering fairy tale that was also told of other people. David Friedrich Strauß points to a similar power over storm and weather in Pythagoras (*Das Leben Jesu*, II, 182).

"In the Talmud the story is told that a pagan ship once sailed out on the Great Sea, and that in it there was a Jewish boy. At once a great storm arose in the sea. The pagans in the ship had pleaded to their idols, without getting any help. Then they begged the Jewish boy to call out to his God: 'And the holy One accepted his prayer, and the sea fell silent" (Johannes Weiss, in *Die Schriften des Neuen Testaments* [1917], I, 118). The passing of the Israelites through the Red Sea thanks to Moses likewise belongs in this group of sea anecdotes.

Then there's the story of Jesus walking on water. Any interpreter who follows him out onto the Sea of Galilee has lost all solid theological footing beneath him—and will be drowned in the sea of fables. And it doesn't help that similar tales are told of Buddha and others; that doesn't make it any truer. Incidentally, the holy Pope Gregory the Great (d. 604) tells of a certain Maurus, a disciple of Saint Benedict, who once walked on water, too (*Dial.* 2, 7)—or else he didn't either.

We may leave undecided the question of whether the story of the rich catch of fish (Luke 5:1–11, with the variant of John 21:1–11) should be thought of as a miracle. It may actually be about a bona fide record-breaking haul, which was then declared a miracle and worked into the context with the saying about the "fishers of men." But a fairy-tale motif may also have had some influence here.

The most eccentric of all miracles is the sad story of an innocent fig tree: "On the following day, when they came from Bethany, he was hungry. And seeing in the distance a fig tree in leaf, he went to see if he could find anything on it. When he came to it, he found nothing but leaves, for it was not the season for figs. And he said to it, 'May no one ever eat fruit from you again'" (Mark 11:12–14). And the tree withered (Mark 11:20–21).

Here a parable—something Jesus *said*—has been transformed into a miraculous *action* by Jesus, and in the process it has completely lost its point. It thus becomes the stupidest of the miraculous fairy tales. The meaning of the parable, a comparison designed to bring to their senses people who were not bearing fruits pleasing to God, is wiped out in the case of a tree that turns out to be not in the desired condition. Since the tree wasn't bearing figs because it wasn't the season for figs, that makes punishing it even more meaningless and unjust.

Here we have the human addiction to fables completely overshooting the mark. This sort of miracle doesn't make one believe in the miracle worker; at most it makes one doubt his sanity. And Jesus surely never deserved to be saddled with such miraculous doings.

Some people are troubled by the miracle stories and want to heave them overboard along with the whole New Testament. Others defend them with tooth and nail and act as if Christianity in general and the truth of Jesus' message in particular depended on everyone's believing these miracles. The Evangelists wanted to praise Jesus to the skies through their accounts of his miracles, to make him great and imposing. They wanted to show that divinity gleamed, as it were, right through his clothes. But all they did was put a pile of tiny miracles in front of the true miracle that Jesus is all about: the miracle of the love of God. The miracle stories have been used not to open up but to obstruct our view of Jesus.

CHAPTER SEVEN

Good Friday

THE STORY OF the Passion is especially revealing of the way the Evangelists manipulate historical dates and facts. But this cuts no ice with theologians, whether Catholic, Protestant, or Eastern Orthodox. If you point out to them the inaccuracies and contradictions in the Passion narratives, they'll make a few concessions; but in the final analysis they'll remain ensconced in their impregnable conviction that after all this is still the Word of God.

There is in fact no profession that can emerge so triumphantly—at least in its own eyes—from all refutations. You can practically never refute a theologian. Every now and then you think you've finally succeeded; you've gathered all the arguments of logic and historical evidence on your side. But a moment or two later you hear the words, "For that very reason . . ." or "It's precisely there that we see . . . ," and the theologian arises like the phoenix from its ashes and transforms defeat into total victory. As Rudolf Augstein says, "Every great theologian has always known how to turn . . . a deficit into riches" (*Jesus Menschensohn* [1974], p. 230). Hence, it doesn't make the least sense to tell a theologian—"to call his attention to something" would be the wrong way to put it since theologians have obviously already turned their attention to it (and to everything else)—that this or that account in the New Testament contradicts another one. The theologian will then pityingly inform you that this contradiction shows precisely what's at issue in the Scriptures. And what's not at issue, namely, whatever objection you might bring to bear against any statements in the Bible. The theologian will say something like this:

> The truth of Scripture is . . . not the correctness of the account it gives of historical facts and data. It does not consist in the certainty that everything happened the way it says in the text. That would presuppose that it was written to guarantee . . . to people the sequence of facts described therein, and to make them happy because they have at their disposal an image of the events that coincided with history as actually having happened. (Heinrich Schlier, "Rudolf Bultmann, dem Achtzigjährigen," in Besinnung auf das Neue Testament [1964], p. 53)

Schlier is a leading New Testament scholar. Raised a Protestant, he converted to Catholicism in 1953, and so he's knowledgeable about the way both Catholics and Protestants understand the Bible. Schlier continues: "It is by no means the case that I always experience the truth best in a historical account that zealously values facts, data and its own correctness. It can offer me a pile of such facts and data and guarantee the historical correctness of the narrative—yet a single anecdote can give me a better grasp of a person or an event or a situation in its true dimensions" (p. 54).

This is true. Schlier is also right to say with respect to the death of Jesus: The Evangelists were "convinced that the 'memory' of Jesus' death, which is what the Passion narrative essentially is, could take place appropriately in a form in which report and interpretation, fact and meaning, are expressed concurrently, indeed interfused together. Various means of achieving this were available, including the language of legend" (p. 55).

Putting it bluntly, a legend can sometimes reflect the truth better than a factual report. But what if the legend falsifies the facts and doesn't reflect the truth? The legend form may well be more appropriate than the bare historical data for rendering the "interpretation" and "meaning" of an event, for instance, the death of Jesus. But it also has to be said that legends can obscure the truth. Then they don't elucidate salvation history; they just make mischief, a hopeless muddle of pseudofacts that ultimately

thwart the intended message of sacred history, the "memory of the death
of Jesus." Under some circumstances, legends can sacrifice concrete history on the altar of imagination. They can even fail to notice that, in the
final analysis, by dispensing with data and facts they lessen or even abolish
the meaning of that history. In the Gospels, at all events, the historical
events of Jesus' passion have had to give way to a false interpretation of the
whole episode.

To be sure, Schlier is right again when he goes on to say about Jesus'
death:

> There is in itself . . . no more certain fact than the dying of Jesus
> on the cross on Golgatha. But what is this fact, really? From the
> standpoint of the fact itself, this must remain an absolutely open
> question. . . . It is a historical fact in itself and acquires its effec-
> tive historical meaning only when it is interpreted. But whose in-
> terpretation should count? The interpretation of history, which
> explains the unknown on the basis of what is known, with this-
> worldly–causal, . . . psychological, or sociological methods—or
> the interpretation of the Evangelists? (P. 55)

Like most Christians, Schlier naturally decides in favor of the
Evangelists.

Granted, we can perceive all facts—and not just the historical facts
of the New Testament—in their truth and meaning only as filtered
through interpretation. It is also true, and something we learn in everyday
experience, that "all human history . . . never [happens] otherwise than by
taking place in explicit or implicit understanding" (p. 42).

Suppose that a TV camera crew had filmed the crucifixion of Jesus.
The scene that appears on the screen has already been interpreted. Even
the most objective film coverage interprets by the way it is shot, uses close-
ups, or pans to show crowd reaction, by the lighting, and so forth. Without interpretation we don't understand anything. Who is the person being
executed? A murderer? A terrorist? A victim of the miscarriage of justice?
The Son of God? By whom is he being executed? By the legal organs of the
state? By the Jews? By the Romans? In this sense there is nothing objective.

We never see a naked, objective fact, only interpreted facts, and in every act of perception we never stop interpreting.

But who or what will protect us from misinterpreting the facts? Who will protect Jesus' death from a false interpretation? Who will protect us from biased distortions of the actual events? For, as Schlier rightly says, sacred Scripture is not a "heavenly book" (p. 52). It doesn't fall out of the sky in its original packaging, covered by a heavenly warranty.

Thus we can agree with the theologians that the Bible was not in fact written to "guarantee . . . to people the sequence of facts . . . and to make them happy." But it certainly couldn't have been written to make an unhappy world even unhappier by means of a misrepresented sequence of facts or to bring misery upon an entire people—as has been done in the case of the Jews.

This brings us to the political-legal side of the Passion narratives. Hitler realized that he could exploit the Oberammergau Festival (which simply retells the story of the Passion in the words of the Evangelists) to promote his anti-Semitic propaganda. In 1942,

> He said that it was one of the most important tasks to guard Germany's coming generations from the same political fate [that struck the country from 1918 to 1933], and hence to keep vigilant in them the awareness of racial danger. For this reason alone the Oberammergau Festival would absolutely have to be preserved. For hardly ever had the Jewish danger, as seen in the example of the ancient Roman empire, been so graphically illustrated as by the character of Pontius Pilate in the Festival. He appeared as a Roman whose racial and intellectual superiority is so great that he seemed a rock amid the swarming rabble of the Near East. In recognizing the enormous importance of the Festival for the enlightenment of future generations as well, he [Hitler] said he was an absolute Christian. (Rolf Hochhuth, Der Stellvertreter, historische Streiflichter [1980], p. 247)

Actually, the Gospels were able to serve as a welcome support for Hitler's hatred of the Jews because the Evangelists' picture of the Jews is negative and distorted. Whatever else it may be, the story of the Passion is a tale full of political bias. It was written to clear Christians of their reputation for hostility to the state. Hence, it flies in the face of the truth by claiming that the Jews were responsible for the whole thing. It was not Pilate, the Roman, but the Jews who killed Jesus. The Jews are the enemies of the Christians, and the Christians are not the enemies of the Romans.

The Romans had maintained that the Christians were enemies of the state. A brief glance at the political situation in Palestine will make this understandable. Born, according to Luke, in Bethlehem during the census under Emperor Augustus, Jesus was crucified under Emperor Tiberius. The census, designed for raising taxes, took place in A.D. 6 and was the occasion for the founding of the party of the Zealots in Galilee under Judas the Galilean. The anti-Roman resistance of the Zealots spread from Galilee to Judea, which was ruled by a Roman procurator, and eventually led to the Jewish War and the downfall of the country in A.D. 70 under Emperor Titus. All opposition was crushed, except in the fortress of Masada, on the west bank of the Dead Sea, where 960 Zealots were holed up, including women and children. On the last night before Masada was stormed by the Roman General Flavius Silva in A.D. 73, they committed suicide en masse. Only two women and five children survived.

The trial of Jesus was not the first time that conflict between the Galileans and Procurator Pilate had led to bloodshed. Earlier, Pilate had launched a bloodbath in Jerusalem among Galilean pilgrims whom he considered insurgents. "There were some present at that very time who told him of the Galileans whose blood Pilate had mingled with their sacrifices" (Luke 13:1). To arouse suspicion in Jerusalem in those days, one needed only to come from Galilee and to be surrounded by a swarm of Galileans. Even belonging to a group of Galileans headed by another Galilean could cause trouble. During Jesus' trial, Peter's Galilean dialect led to a confrontation between two maids, other bystanders, and Peter. In this scene one of the maids uses the word *Galilean* with the obvious implication of "anarchist." She says to Peter: " 'You also were with Jesus the Galilean.'. . . After a little while the bystanders came up and said to Peter, 'Certainly you are also one of them, for your accent betrays you' "

(Matt. 26:69ff.; cf. Luke 22:59: "Certainly this man also was with him; for he is a Galilean"). This is, of course, the famous denial scene. "And immediately the cock crowed" (Matt. 26:74; cf. Luke 22:60).

Incidentally, the Evangelists give contradictory answers to the question of how many times the cock crowed. In Matthew, Jesus predicts, apart from the threefold betrayal, a single crowing (Matt. 26:34), and that is what happens (Matt. 26:74). We find the same thing in Luke (22:34; 22:60) and John (13:38; 18:27). In Mark, however, Jesus prophesies that the cock will crow twice after the three denials (Mark 14:30). Yet in Mark the cock crows only once after all, although Mark expressly notes that this was the second crowing (Mark 14:72). We do find the first crowing at Mark 14:68 in a few manuscripts, but this passage is a later interpolation, after the copyists had noticed that one crowing was missing. The passage is thus inauthentic, and the crowing, too. We cannot determine what became of the first (authentic) crowing.

During the period of Jesus' life the whole country was a political powder keg. Pinchas Lapide says that from the time of the Maccabees (ca. 165 B.C.) to the Bar Kochba uprising (A.D. 132–35) the Jews fought sixty-two wars of independence, and sixty-one of them began in Galilee (*Er predigte in ihren Synagogen* [1987], p. 39).

The situation was comparable to one that Josephus describes. As Jewish commander of the fortress of Jotapata, he had taken part in the war against the Romans and had surrendered in 67. Concerning the time around 4 B.C., that is, some ten years before the founding of the Zealot party, Josephus writes: "And so Judea was filled with brigandage. Anyone might make himself king as the head of a band of rebels whom he fell in with" (*JA*, XVII, x, 8; LCL, p. 505). Back then, too, as Josephus goes on to tell us, there was an uprising against the Romans. The Roman legate in Syria, Varus (he would be commander-in-chief at the catastrophic defeat in the Teutoburg Forest in A.D. 9), hurried from Syria with three legions and four squadrons of cavalry, as well as all available auxiliary troops, so as to protect the Roman legion occupying Judea. He crushed the uprising, devastated Galilee, and had two thousand rebels crucified (*JA*, XVII, x, 9–10).

The chain of executions went on and on. Josephus reports of the procurator Felix (51/52–ca. 62), whom Tacitus calls a man "with the soul of a slave" (*servili ingenio, Histories*, V, ix), that "not a day passed . . . but that Felix captured and put death many of these impostors and brigands" (*JA*, XX, viii, 5; LCL, pp. 89, 91).

The Zealots who refused to pay taxes and fought in the resistance were religious freedom fighters in their own eyes, although the Roman occupying forces (and Josephus) disparagingly called them robbers. The usage passed into the New Testament, where the Zealots are often labeled robbers. Mark (15:27): "and with him they crucified two robbers, one on his right hand and one on his left." Or John (18:40): "They cried out again, 'Not this man, but Barabbas!' Now Barabbas was a robber."

Pilate's question was, "Are you the king of the Jews?" (Mark 15:2). And, according to Mark, the inscription on the cross, indicating the crime for which the criminal had been sentenced to crucifixion, read, "The King of the Jews" (15:26). Jesus was accused and condemned by Pilate as a dangerous revolutionary who aspired to political dominion.

The followers of the crucified "King of the Jews" were suspected by the Romans of being insurgents, just like the crucified Jesus. At least one of the apostles actually did belong, or had at one time belonged, to the party of the Zealots. This was Simon, who was also called the Zealot. He is mentioned in four passages of the New Testament: Mark 3:18; Matt. 10:4; Luke 6:15; and Acts 1:13. In Mark and Matthew he is called "Simon the Canaanean." This epithet has frequently been misunderstood. Commentators have variously believed that he came from the town of Cana, which became famous because of the wedding feast there, or that he was a man from "Canaan." In fact, however, the term comes from an Aramaic word meaning "fanatic" or "zealot."

Two other disciples, the brothers James and John, whom Jesus called the "sons of thunder" (Mark 3:17) may not be unequivocally classified as Zealots, but it's clear that the idea of terrorist acts of revenge was very much on their minds. When Jesus and his group were not welcomed in a village of Samaria owing to the tensions between Samaria and Judea, the brothers asked Jesus: "Lord, do you want us to bid fire come down from heaven and consume them?" (Luke 9:54). It makes no difference whether they wanted to torch the village themselves or misuse God as their arsonist.

In this context it should be remembered that some of the disciples carried arms (Luke 22:38), including Peter. When Jesus was taken prisoner, Peter tried to kill a servant of the high priest with his sword (John 18:10). But the notion that Jesus himself ordered his disciples to buy weapons— "And let him who has no sword sell his mantle and buy one" (Luke 22:36)—is a foolish misunderstanding. On the contrary, Jesus deplores and frowns on such slogans.

This passage about the "two swords," which is widely misunderstood by Christians with militaristic delusions as Jesus' call for his followers to arm themselves, reads as follows: "And he [Jesus] said to them, 'When I sent you out with no purse or bag or sandals, did you lack anything?' They said, 'Nothing.' He said to them, 'But now, let him who has a purse take it, and likewise a bag. And let him who has no sword sell his mantle and buy one.'" (Commentary: Jesus is quoting the new slogans of the disciples, who are no longer content to do without supplies and weapons. He is repeating *their* words; *his own* words come in the previous sentence.) "For I tell you that this scripture must be fulfilled in me, 'And he was reckoned with transgressors'; for what is written about me has its fulfilment.'" (Commentary: Contrary to his sermon on nonviolence, Jesus is now reckoned among the evildoers. He is looked upon as a warrior-messiah, that is, an insurgent against the Romans. He will perish amid this confusion.) "And they said, 'Look, Lord, here are two swords.' And he said to them, 'It is enough'" (Luke 22:35ff.). The phrase "It is enough," rightly argues the Catholic New Testament scholar Josef Schmidt, "refers not to the two swords they have, but to the whole discussion, which is now broken off" (*Regensburger Neues Testament: Das Evangeliumbuch nach Lukas* [1955], p. 335).

Because they were suspected of engaging in subversive agitation, the name "Christians" had the same sound to the Romans of the first three centuries that the name "Baader-Meinhof gang" has had for contemporary Germans. The most important Roman historian, Tacitus (d. A.D. 120) voices his dislike for Christians when he reports about the burning of Rome under Emperor Nero: "Therefore to scotch the rumour [that the fire had taken place by order] Nero substituted as culprits and punished with the utmost refinements of cruelty, a class of men, loathed for their vices, whom the crowd styled Christians" (*Annals,* trans. John Jackson [Cambridge, MA: Harvard Univ. Press (LCL), 1981], XV, xliv; LCL, p. 283).

The very name "Christians" had a bad sound to it: "loathed for their vices." Admittedly, they were not called Christians because they had committed crimes, any more than Baader and Meinhof bore those names because they committed acts of terrorism. But "Christians" was a name that set off alarm signals in the heads of Romans. For them "Christians" was a word that did not evoke, as it does with us today, televangelists and pious boredom, but the bloody uprisings in the Middle East that ultimately escalated into the Jewish War and were crushed by Emperor Titus in A.D. 70. Linguistically, the name "Christians" has nothing to do with "crime," but that's what it made the Romans think of.

Tacitus continues: "Christus, the founder of the name, had undergone the death penalty in the reign of Tiberius, by sentence of the procurator Pontius Pilatus, and the pernicious superstition was checked for a moment, only to break out once more, not merely in Judea, the home of the disease, but in the capital itself, where all things horrible or shameful in the world collect and find a vogue" (*Annals,* XV, xliv; LCL, p. 283).

At about this time, Pliny the Younger provides evidence that the mere name "Christians" had a baneful sound to it. In 111 he wrote in his capacity as proconsul in Bithynia to the Roman Emperor Trajan, asking for directions on how to proceed against the Christians. "For the pestilence of this superstition has spread not only in the cities, but also through the villages and across the countryside." Pliny wanted to learn from the emperor "whether the name [of Christian] alone or only the crimes connected to the name should be punished."

Pliny's problem might strike us as odd, since nowadays in the Christian West church and state have, in one way or another, allied themselves. The suspicion of being a subversive group no longer applies to Christians, but to other people. And so the following version might sound more familiar: "Is it enough to belong to the Communist party, or must it be proved in every individual case that the communists have engaged in activities designed to overthrow the Constitution?"

In any event, the mere name "Christians" worried the Romans. Early Christianity, which was now busily spreading itself through the Roman Empire, could not afford to make propaganda for a Messiah who had been executed by the Roman authorities as a political offender. Far better to present Jesus as an innocent man persecuted and betrayed by his own compatriots and fellow believers, a man in whom the Roman procurator found "no guilt" and whom this representative of Rome had even tried to set free.

And so the four Gospels—written between A.D. 70 and 95—faced a political task: to establish better preconditions for the Church's missionary activity. Specifically, they had to shift the burden of responsibility for the death of Christ from the Romans to the Jews. The Gospels carried out this assignment by means of a great anti-Jewish manipulation of history. Part of this plan was the story of the traitor Judas, the deputy and namesake of his people. From the kiss of Judas to Pilate's washing his hands stretches the arc of a twisted truth, an arc of centuries-long Christian guilt that began with the lie of the Jews as Christ-killers and that would last all the way to Auschwitz.

The four Evangelists solve the problem of shifting the blame for Jesus' death from the Romans to the Jews in various ways. They march in separate columns, so to speak, but they attack together. On the one side there are the first three Gospels, the Synoptics, Matthew, Mark, and Luke, and on the other, John. In the three older Gospels it is the Jews who (in a historical falsehood) arrest Jesus and put him on trial. John is historically correct: Here Jesus is arrested by the Romans, and no trial takes place before the Jewish High Council (Sanhedrin). Nevertheless, in John the Jews are really the guilty ones, because they stage-manage the whole operation and pull the wires. They are the malicious instigators of Jesus' death and the ones ultimately responsible for it.

Thus in the Gospels' description of Jesus' arrest, we find two versions. In Mark it involves "a crowd with swords and clubs, from the chief priests and the scribes and the elders" (Mark 14:43). Similarly in Matthew:

"Judas came, . . . and with him a great crowd with swords and clubs, from the chief priests and the elders of the people" (Matt. 26:47). Luke says simply: "There came a crowd" (Luke 22:47). According to Luke, even the high priests in person are supposed to have been present at the arrest (Luke 22:52).

In John by contrast: "So Judas, procuring a band [Greek *speira* meaning cohort] of soldiers and some officers from the chief priests and the Pharisees, went there with lanterns and torches and weapons" (John 18:3). Here the Roman state has sprung into action, but there is no mistaking the responsibility of the Jews as the power behind the scene. This is clear from the directing presence of Judas and from the emphasis given to the high priests as the masters of the servants taking part in the arrest.

The term *cohort* means a military (hence a Roman) unit. It was led by a *chiliarchos* (John 18:12). A chiliarchos (literally, the leader of one thousand men) was a *tribunus militum,* a commander of a cohort. This was the tenth part of a Roman legion and amounted to six hundred soldiers. There actually was a Roman cohort in Jerusalem, permanently stationed in the Antonia Fortress (Josephus, *JW,* V, v, 8; LCL, pp. 275, 277). But the idea that this whole cohort was mustered out to arrest a single man is absurd. The large number of Roman soldiers is supposed to document the great influence that the Jews had on the Romans throughout the trial.

According to the Synoptics, Jesus' arrest is followed by a trial before the Jewish High Council, in which he is condemned to death. In Matthew and Mark there are two sessions of the Sanhedrin, once immediately after Jesus' arrest and the second time early the next morning. In both sessions Jesus is brought before his judges. Luke says that there was only one session, early in the morning (Luke 22:66).

Finally, according to John, the Sanhedrin never meets at all. There is simply a hearing at the house of Annas. Annas then dispatches him to Caiaphas, who ultimately sends Jesus over to Pilate. John never mentions a Jewish trial. Now, the author of John has a pronounced and ubiquitous hostility to the Jews (the expression "the Jews" occurs seventy times in the Gospel of John; in half of these [thirty-four] the phrase has the clear connotation of "the enemies" of Jesus). So John would never have missed the

opportunity of unleashing a proper denunciation of the Jews—if such a
trial had ever taken place.

We can no longer reconstruct the actual course of events in the condemnation and execution of Jesus. But one thing remains clear: No Jewish
trial before the Jewish High Council, as recounted in the Synoptics, ever
took place. That would have constituted a massive violation of Jewish
law. There is no time here to go into the detailed legal reasons why this
is so. Let me simply refer the reader to Weddig Fricke's book *Standrecht-
lich gekreuzigt: Person und Prozeß des Jesu aus Galiläa* (1988). Fricke has
brought together all the reasons why the Gospel scenario of the trial of
Jesus before the Sanhedrin is simply impossible. Beyond that, I suggest the
already mentioned book by Pinchas Lapide, *Wer war schuld an Jesu Tod?*
(1987), and finally the standard work of Hermann Strack and Paul Billerbeck, *Kommentar zum Neuen Testament aus Talmud und Midrash* ([1965]
I, 1024).

Here is a brief summary of why the whole episode is impossible, in
the words of the Jewish philosopher of religion Schalom Ben-Chorin:

> *Jesus celebrates the seder-night (that is, the Passover meal) with
> his disciples. If he was to be arrested by the Jewish authorities on
> this night, after the solemnities, it would be unthinkable for the
> hearing to have taken place in the house of the high priest Ca-
> iaphas on this most holy of nights. Unthinkable too that Jesus
> would be handed over to Pilate on the morning of the feast, and
> crucified on the first day of Passover. . . . Anyone familiar with
> Jewish law and customs immediately senses here that the whole
> thing simply couldn't have happened. If Jesus had been arrested
> on the seder night, then he would have been kept in custody until
> after Passover, and everything else would have been played out
> afterwards.* (Bruder Jesus [1987], pp. 131-32)

While the trial before the Sanhedrin never actually took place, the
trial before Pilate certainly did. But this doesn't mean that Pilate personally took charge of the case (which was only one of many). None of
the Evangelists can erase the fact that the Roman trial actually occurred.

But all four Evangelists take pains to whitewash Pontius Pilate as far as possible.

Over the years from 70 to 95, we can watch the process from Mark to Matthew and Luke (the latter two are dependent on Mark), all the way to John, the last of the four Gospels. The bottom line is that Pilate is increasingly excused, while the guilt of the Jews is depicted in ever more glaring colors. In his Gospel Luke largely borrows the text of Mark but adds a series of statements designed to make the guilt of the Jews more vivid. Luke has the Jews charge Jesus in the presence of Pilate: "We found this man perverting our nation, and forbidding us to give tribute to Caesar, and saying that he himself is Christ, a king" (Luke 23:2). And then: "But they were urgent, saying, 'He stirs up the people, teaching throughout all Judea, from Galilee even to this place'" (Luke 23:5). Galilee was a name guaranteed to cause uneasiness in the mind of the occupying power.

Luke has Pilate emphasize three times that Jesus is innocent: "I find no crime in this man" (Luke 23:4). "You brought me this man as one who was perverting the people; and after examining him before you, behold, I did not find this man guilty of any of your charges against him" (Luke 23:14). Finally: "Why, what evil has he done? I have found in him no crime deserving death" (Luke 23:22).

Three times Luke has Pilate stress the fact that he finds no guilt in Jesus, that he wants to let Jesus "go free" (Luke 23:16, 20, 22). And while Mark and even Matthew write that it was Pilate who had Jesus crucified (Mark 15:15; Matt. 27:26), Luke writes: "But Jesus he delivered up to their [the Jews'] will" (Luke 23:25).

Like Luke, Matthew largely borrows the text of Mark; and he, too, inserts features that illustrate how guilt has been shifted from Pilate to the Jews. These amplifications, by the way, are found nowhere else in the four Gospels: "Besides, while he was sitting on the judgment seat, his wife sent word to him, 'Have nothing to do with that righteous man, for I have suffered much over him today in a dream'" (Matt. 27:19). There follows the scene in which Pilate has water brought out and washes his hands in innocence: "I am innocent of this man's blood; see to it yourselves" (Matt. 27:24). "And all the people answered, 'His blood be on us and on our children!'" (Matt. 27:25).

The Jewish New Testament scholar Pinchas Lapide remarks on this passage: "the Greek text . . . leaves no doubt that here the entire nation of the Jews is taking the guilt upon themselves, although in the previous verse mention was made only of a crowd on the verge of riot (Matt. 27:24). This is a demographic surge from at most three thousand souls to around five million people, and all in the space of two lines" (Lapide, *Wer war schuld*, p. 88).

The Pilate described by the Gospels is not a historical figure. That picture is a malicious anti-Judaic legend. As the Evangelists see it, by recognizing and declaring Jesus' innocence, Pilate makes the infamy of the Jews obvious. In their blind fanaticism they have no scruples about shedding innocent blood—indeed royal and divine blood. Pilate may wash his hands to protest his innocence, but the Jews cannot. That is the meaning of this story: The blood of the Redeemer sticks to their hands. By washing his hands, Pilate exposes the fact that they are a pack of murderers, unconcerned with justice but keen to satisfy their hatred. In so doing, he lays the foundation for the long and bloody history of the persecution of the Jews as the murderers of Christ.

This story stretches all the way to Auschwitz. In the second part of *Shoah*, the powerful film by Claude Lanzmann, we see a group of people in front of a church in Chelmno (Poland). At one time during World War II, Jews were gathered together in this church, to be taken away in specially equipped vans, gassed during the trip, and buried in the forest. One of the Poles tells the following story: An eyewitness reported to him that when the Jews were driven together in a square to be evacuated, a rabbi asked the SS man for permission to say a final word to the Jews. The SS man gave his OK. Then the rabbi said: "Two thousand years ago we killed Jesus, who was innocent. We said that his blood should be on us. And now this is happening to us; his blood is upon us."

Other bystanders in this scene pick up the story: "Yes, Pilate wanted to let him go. He washed his hands in innocence [the Pole who told the story about the rabbi makes the gesture of washing his hands], but the Jews said, 'His blood be on us.'" These Christians have taken the supposed Jewish self-cursing and so thoroughly internalized it that they actually believe that a Jew, a rabbi, would deliver this Christian speech. And they actually heard that speech with their own ears, or at least heard it from someone else who had heard it.

The Christian canonization of Pilate in the New Testament reaches its zenith in the fourth Gospel. While Mark and Matthew report that Jesus gave Pilate no answer—"But he gave him no answer, not even to a single charge; so that the governor wondered greatly" (Matt. 27:14; cf. Mark 15:15)—in John Pilate and Jesus almost engage in a friendly conversation. In the course of this discussion Jesus explains the nature of his kingdom as the reign of truth, and Pilate raises himself to philosophical heights with the question, "'What is truth?'" (John 18:38). As a result of this exchange, Pilate says three times that he finds no guilt in Jesus (John 18:38; 19:4, 6).

John may not be able to cancel the historical fact that Jesus was executed by the Roman procurator, suffering capital punishment in the Roman style, by crucifixion. But he brings a factor into play that is designed to prove that the crucifixion took place entirely against Pilate's will. According to John, Pilate was blackmailed by the Jews, who threatened his career: "'If you release this man, you are not Caesar's friend'; . . . when he heard these words, he brought Jesus out" (John 19:12–13). What John wants to say is that, practically speaking, Jesus was crucified "under" Pontius Pilate, but not *by* him. "Under Pontius Pilate," as if merely citing a date, is the Nicene creed's way of downplaying Pilate's importance. But Pilate had Jesus executed, in the Roman, not the Jewish, fashion.

In this respect Tacitus is an unbiased reporter when he correctly says, "Christus Tiberio imperitante per procuratorem Pontium Pilatum supplicio adfectus erat" (Christ . . . had undergone the death penalty in the reign of Tiberius, by sentence of the procurator Pontius Pilate [*Annals* XV, xliv; LCL, p. 283]).

Thus the Christian judgment of Pilate grew more and more favorable from Gospel to Gospel. Bad as the development of the legend of Pilate has been for the Jews, Pilate later came off very well with the Christians. In the period after the New Testament, he continued his Christian career. Pious apocryphal writings were composed in his name, for example, a letter to Emperor Claudius and a correspondence with Herod. His wife acquired even greater prestige, since in Matthew's Gospel she had sent word to him, "Have nothing to do with that righteous man, for I have suffered much over him today in a dream" (Matt. 27:19). Origen (d. 253) says that she converted to Christianity (*Comm. in Matth.*, n. 122). In the so-called Paradosis, the "tradition" of Pilate (5th century), which describes how Pilate, too, came to believe in Christ and was beheaded for his faith by order of the emperor, we even learn her name: Prokla in Greek, Procula in Latin (cf. Chapter Fourteen, "The Apocrypha"). And, to bring this tale to a happy ending, both Pilate and his wife were honored as saints (on 19 or 25 June) in the Ethiopian calendar (Heinrich Joseph Wetzer and Benedikt Welte, *Kirchenlexikon*, X, 4).

The Gospels' story of Pilate proclaims no "good news"; it sows the seed of hatred. Almost two thousand years after the fact, people can still quote the Jews as saying that their persecution by Christians and their annihilation in the gas chambers was a fate they deserved. That such a statement is even possible shows the maliciousness of a bias (evident back in New Testament times) that claims to be representing the cause of Christ but that constitutes its perversion: The calumny against the Jews in the New Testament became the Christian legal title to their persecution and destruction.

In *Faith and Fratricide: The Theological Roots of Anti-Semitism* (1974), the American theologian, Rosemary Radford Ruether, correctly points out that these anti-Jewish trends were not an accidental excess of later Christian generations. They did not derive from later developments; they were present in the Gospels from the very beginning. In fact, they lie at the core of the New Testament's preaching.

The Passion narratives of the four Gospels paint a legendary, historically false picture, not just because of their pro-Roman, anti-Jewish orientation, but for another reason as well. In distorting the truth, the legend championed not just the culprits, but their victim as well. Along with their fateful political tendency to blame the Jews, the Gospels also develop false theological interpretations of the death of Christ and of the events preceding his death. Once again the standpoint of the Synoptics differs from that of John. But in both the Passover meal plays a crucial role.

According to the Synoptics, just before his death Jesus celebrated the Passover seder with his disciples, and during this meal he instituted the Eucharist. The latter, on the one hand, belongs to the tradition of the seder, but on the other, as the meal of the "new covenant," is meant to replace the Passover meal of the "old covenant." The Passover meal is seen by the Synoptics (as it already had been in Paul, in 1 Corinthians 11) in a new (false) interpretation: Jesus gives himself, his flesh and blood, as a meal.

The eucharistic words of Jesus, which portend his death before it happens ("This is my body," "This is my blood") were not put into his mouth until after he died. (On the false reading of Jesus' death, see Chapter Eighteen, "Redemption by Execution.") Students of religion call this sort of episode a cult legend. It serves to explain a cultic action practiced in the community. Concretely, this means that the Christian eucharistic meal (in memory of Jesus) came first, with the words establishing the sacrament being added on later. In the period that followed, Jesus' words were understood in an ever more weighty and pregnant sense. Eventually Christians fought bloody battles over whether the bread really "is" the body of Christ or only "means" it, and whether the wine really "is" the blood of Christ or only "means" it. In any event, all this led Christians to maintain a vivid recollection of Jesus' death.

According to John, on the other hand, Jesus never spoke the words instituting the Eucharist before his death. Rather, Jesus himself is the slaughtered paschal lamb. Jesus could not celebrate the Passover seder as the Last Supper, because by that time he was already dead. In view of these two conflicting interpretations and the differing Gospel narratives based on them, it is no longer possible to ascertain the objective historical facts. The Evangelists don't orient their interpretations to actual events; they allow their interpretations to dictate the events. For this reason factual history comes apart at the seams.

Thus for all four Evangelists the feast of Passover is the key to understanding the death of Jesus—for the Synoptics because Jesus spoke the eucharistic words at a Passover seder by way of interpreting his death, for John because Jesus is the paschal lamb.

Passover is an ancient Jewish feast, but its origins are unknown. It was one of the three greatest Jewish festivals, the so-called pilgrimage festivals, namely, Passover, Shavuoth (Pentecost, fifty days after Passover), and Succoth, the feast of Tabernacles (first half of October).

Passover was celebrated among the Jews in memory of their divine rescue during the exodus from Egypt (Exodus 12). God spared every house whose doorposts were marked with the blood of a lamb. In all other houses he killed the first-born, both of humans and of animals: "At midnight the Lord smote all the first-born in the land of Egypt, from the first-born of Pharaoh who sits on his throne to the first-born of the captive who was in the dungeon, and all the first-born of the cattle; and there was a great cry in Egypt, for there was not a house where one was not dead" (Exod. 12:29–30). Thus blood protected man and beast from being killed. Blood has a redemptive effect. Christianity presses this macabre thought to its macabre limit with the theological interpretation of Jesus' death.

Passover was celebrated on the 14th and 15th of Nisan, the month when spring began and the first month of the Jewish year. The months began with the new moon. The first day after the evening when, following the new moon, a bit of the crescent moon was visible once again was the first day of the month. Thus Passover was always celebrated under a full moon. Right after the feast of Passover came the feast of unleavened bread, from the evening of the 15th of Nisan till the 21st of Nisan.

The Jewish day began, not as it does with us, at midnight, but in the evening, at dusk. The new day was there when the first stars could be seen. This new day was said to have "shone forth." Hence, Passover, too, lasted from evening to evening. By our system of reckoning, which measures days from midnight to midnight, the Passover meal took place on the "eve" of Passover. For the Jews, however, this was the beginning of the day on which the festival was celebrated. Incidentally, the bright time of the day, the "half" when it was light, began with sunrise and ended with sunset. Both day and night were divided into twelve hours. The length of these hours varied with the season. Around the summer solstice the light time of day lasted fourteen hours and twelve minutes, while at the winter solstice it was only nine hours and forty-eight minutes long (Strack and Billerbeck, *Kommentar*, II, 543). Thus the hours varied in length from forty-nine to seventy-one minutes. The first hour of the day began at 6:00 A.M. (our time) only at the vernal and autumnal equinox. The Passion of Jesus occurred in the spring, hence around the time of the equinox.

Thus in the Synoptics Jesus celebrates the Last Supper with his disciples on the evening of the 14th of Nisan, on the same evening that the Jews held their Passover seder. According to the first three Evangelists, Jesus had given an order for the Passover meal to be prepared. Part of such preparations was to secure a sufficiently big room—a seder could be celebrated with a minimum of ten persons (Strack and Billerbeck, *Kommentar*, IV, 42)—and a ritually correct sacrificial lamb. This had to be a one-year-old male lamb or kid (Strack and Billerbeck, *Kommentar*, IV, 43). Either the organizer of the seder or someone assigned by him brought the animal to the Temple and slaughtered it there in the forecourt. For Passover the animal was not dismembered but roasted whole on a fire, not on a metal, but a wooden, spit and not, of course, in the festival hall itself but in the courtyard of the house. Which one of the disciples brought the sacrificial lamb to the Temple and slaughtered it is not mentioned in the Gospels. The seder could not begin until after the onset of darkness on the 14th of Nisan. By Jewish reckoning it was now already the 15th of Nisan. The meal had to end before morning (Strack and Billerbeck, *Kommentar*, IV, 54), but it usually ended before midnight. Women took part in their husbands' seder (Strack and Billerbeck, *Kommentar*, IV, 45). Contrary to the generally accepted Christian notion that sees Jesus in an exclusively male gathering, it is more reasonable to assume that women were there, too. That fact that women are not mentioned cannot be taken to mean that they weren't on hand. The four male Evangelists frequently fail to count them in or even mention their existence, as we have seen, for example, in the miraculous multiplication of the loaves and fishes.

As has been already pointed out, the fourth Evangelist, John, takes a somewhat different theological position in his presentation of Jesus' death. According to John, Jesus did not celebrate the seder with his disciples, nor during the course of it did he refer to his imminent death with the words "This is my body. . . . This is my blood." Rather, John says, Jesus had already died by then and was himself the slaughtered paschal lamb. This becomes clear, for instance, when the Roman soldiers come to break the legs of Jesus, as they did to the two men crucified with him, and they find Jesus already dead. John sees in this a fulfillment of an Old Testament commandment (Exod. 12:46): "For these things took place that the scripture might be fulfilled, 'Not a bone of him [i.e., the paschal lamb] shall be broken'" (John 19:36).

John's version of the Passion aims to show that Jesus is the true paschal lamb. One may take this notion as profound or just an obsession: It isn't really clear what John was trying to say with it. The idea of seeing a human being as a sacrificial animal and the execution of that human being as a redemptive slaughtering is, any way you look at it, a theology for butchers.

In accordance with this prehistoric barbarism, the fourth Gospel has straightened out the sequence of events. According to John, Jesus was condemned at noon and crucified in the afternoon, at the same time that the paschal lambs were being slaughtered. This is important to John, who, like the other three Evangelists, was more concerned with theology than with historical facts. He wants to present Jesus as the true paschal lamb, and so he chooses to have Jesus killed just when the paschal lamb was being killed—on the afternoon before the feast of Passover.

But this theological profundity gives rise to historical nonsense. The crucifixion in this scheme would have occurred at a point in time immediately before Passover and the Sabbath (which in John take place on the same day), when the presence of dead bodies on the cross would have rendered the whole country unclean. According to the law (Deut. 21:23), the bodies had to be not just taken down but buried before sunset. And obviously the condemned men had to have already died. But there simply wasn't enough time for all that in the brief period between the crucifixion at noon and sunset not many hours later. The agony of crucified prisoners often lasted for several days.

Even the breaking of the legs (*crurifragium*), which the Jews requested in order to keep the purity of the Sabbath, would have been useless: "Since it was the day of Preparation, in order to prevent the bodies from remaining on the cross on the sabbath (for that sabbath was a high day) the Jews asked Pilate that their legs might be broken, and they might be taken away" (John 19:31).

Thus John's report of Jesus' death on Good Friday is no more credible than the Synoptics' story of the supposed trial before the Sanhedrin during Passover. The Good Friday afternoon before Passover becomes a mystery play directed by the Evangelist without regard for the real fate of Jesus the human being. John's evaluation of Christ's death is in fact a degradation of Jesus' concrete death, which can't have happened as the Evangelist describes. Thanks to this manipulative directorial fantasy of death, based on a model from some religious Stone Age, we have been denied any chance of knowing the time when the real, historical death of Jesus took place.

The contradictions between the Synoptics and John are plain to see: Admittedly, the day Jesus died is the same in all four Evangelists, namely Friday. But these Fridays bear different dates. In John it's the 14th of Nisan, in the Synoptics it's the 15th of Nisan. These Fridays differ in other ways as well. In John Friday is the day before Passover (Jesus the paschal lamb is slaughtered the day before), and in John the Saturday following this Friday is both Passover as well as, naturally, the Sabbath. In the Synoptics, Friday itself is Passover and the next day is naturally the Sabbath, but not Passover. Obviously these two configurations of the feast could not occur in one and the same year.

Thus we have no idea what year Jesus died in. It seems strange that the Evangelists cite no date for this, not even a false one. Even Luke, who supplies the birth of Jesus and the beginning of John the Baptist's career with a downright pompous listing of dates, is silent here. By the way, putting aside for the moment all the inconsistencies, if the execution of Jesus actually did take place on the 14th of Nisan, as John claims, then according to the very complicated calculations of some historians, the day of his death would have been either 7 April in the year 30 or 3 April in the year 33 (cf. Bo Reicke and Leonhard Rost, *Biblisch-Historisches Handbuch* [1966], III, 2223).

All in all, we have to say that both the day and the hour that Jesus died are unknown. The accounts of the Synoptics and John are mutually exclusive; furthermore, there are serious inconsistencies even within the accounts of the individual Evangelists. And even though all four Evangelists say that Jesus died on a Friday, we are by no means sure that this is the case. Other days of the week are conceivable. The brief interval between the Last Supper, whether this was a seder (the Synoptics) or not (John), and the crucifixion is impossible. The likely historical truth is that all the events of the Passion were distributed over the course of several days.

For this reason some recent theologians argue that an early chronology of the Passion, which dates from the 3rd century (*Didaskalia* 21) and is based on a longer time frame, might just be correct (*LThK*, II, 423). They consider the following possibility: "The hypothesis that Jesus might have followed the calendar of Qumran and celebrated the Passover on Tuesday evening without a ritually slaughtered lamb very much deserves to be taken seriously" (*LThK*, VIII, 136). And in the *Enzyklopädie zur Heiligen Schrift, Die Bibel und ihre Welt*, we read: "In general, scholars believe that the Last Supper was celebrated on Thursday, the night before the crucifixion. But another theory, supported by the Qumran scriptures, maintains that the Last Supper was celebrated on Tuesday night before the crucifixion" (1969, p. 804).

But then, along with all the other unbelievable statements of the Evangelists in the Passion narrative, the disciples' questions about the slaughter of the paschal lamb (Matt. 26:17; Mark 14:12; Luke 22:7–8) would likewise have to be considered a fiction. All the theories and critical studies of an alternative date for the events of Passover simply show how little historical credibility attaches to the Gospel accounts of Jesus' Passion.

One more point on the burial of Jesus as described by John. It should be noted in advance that the name Golgatha (Place of the Skull) used to label the place of execution is found nowhere else, so it's most likely legendary. John reports of a certain Joseph of Arimathea that he took the corpse of Jesus down from the cross and with the help of Nicodemus, who had brought along a mixture of a "hundred pounds" (1 pound equals 1 Greek "litra," which is 327.45 grams) of myrrh and aloes (John 19:39). The two men supposedly wrapped the body of Jesus in linen cloths, along with this enormous amount of spices, and buried it in a new tomb in a garden near the place of execution. "So because of the Jewish day of Preparation, as the tomb was close at hand, they laid Jesus there" (John 19:42). This description speaks, on the one hand, of a hasty burial and so conveys the impression that the tomb was only provisional. On the other hand, such an expensive, large-scale burial takes time. These two aspects don't fit together, just as the whole time frame in John doesn't fit, as already mentioned: On a single afternoon the crucifixion, death, and burial were over by 6:00 P.M., when both the Sabbath and Passover began. Jesus had no time to die. In the other Evangelists, however, Jesus takes six hours to die, from 9 A.M. to 3 P.M.

But this Joseph of Arimathea is not a real person. He is a fictional character, though an ideal combination for the burial John describes: He is at once a disciple of Jesus and a member of the High Council, as well as someone who is on good terms with Pilate (John 19:38). (As we know already, Pilate was especially well disposed toward Jesus.) Finally, he is rich (Matt. 27:57). This sort of combination is practically unthinkable. Hence, in his commentary on John, Bultmann designates the entire scene (John 19:38–42) an "edifying-legendary formation." And, of course, "in the place where Jesus was crucified" (John 19:41) there was no tomb of a rich man in a garden. There were tombs in the neighborhood of a place of execution. These, however, were presumably mass graves for the executed prisoners, which the Romans didn't bury in a kind of boneyard but hastily dumped together.

Jesus was executed with two others, the so-called robbers, who presumably were executed, like Jesus, for political reasons. Hence, we may assume, first, that all three were condemned in one and the same trial, and that, second, all three were buried in the same mass grave. It is characteristic that according to all four Gospels, Jesus was buried neither by his family nor by his disciples (though in the Synoptics a few women witness his burial: Matt. 27:61; Mark 15:47; Luke 23:55). Instead he was buried by a third party, a point that the description of the burial still clearly remembers. But it wasn't two rich and pious men who buried him—why should his family and his friends have stayed away from the burial? It was the Romans who buried him in a mass grave. And with the large number of the graves, which were immediately flattened, no one could say anymore where it was.

There was no splendor and glory hovering over Jesus' burial. There were no hundred pounds of myrrh and aloes. After the most wretched and ignominious of all deaths, it was presumably the most miserable and wretched of all burials.

Appendix 1

The cross of Christ was rediscovered: According to the Missale Romanum on 3 May A.D. 320, according to the *Lexikon für Theologie und Kirche* on 14 September 320. "The fact that before the year 350 the Holy Cross was rediscovered [is] historically unassailable," says the Wetzer and Welte *Kirchenlexikon* ([1891] VIII, 1098). It was the emperor's mother, Helena, in person who, on orders from her son, the Emperor Constantine, undertook the difficult but ultimately successful search. She had pagan temples demolished (some sources maintain that a temple to Venus had stood on the spot) and sent statues of the gods crashing to the ground; and she dug under the rubble until she finally and fortunately struck the burial cave. Not far from there the cross (of cedar) was found, more precisely three crosses were found, which was logical. The problem of which cross was the authentic one was solved by taking all three to a mortally ill woman, who was made well by touching the true Cross. On that occasion another dead person on whom the cross was laid came back to life again.

In addition, the holy nails were found. One of these Constantine had forged into his helmet, another into his horse's bit. At the site where it was found, the emperor had a church of the resurrection and a church of the cross erected. In the latter was preserved a portion of the cross, but Constantine immediately took the largest piece back to Constantinople with him. It was first kept in the church of Hagia Sophia but later brought to the Imperial Treasury. In 614 the Jerusalem piece was taken away to Persia by the Persian King Khosrau or Khosroes II, but Emperor Heraklios luckily managed to get it back, on 3 May 628, according to the *Lexikon für Theologie und Kirche,* or on 14 September 628, according to the Missale Romanum. But in 1187 it was lost, and "this time for good, in a battle at Hastin in Galilee, after the Bishop of Bethlehem had worn it in the battle" (*LThK*, VI, 614). Fortunately, right after the discovery of the cross in 320, bigger and smaller pieces had been cut or sawn off Christ's cross. There is testimony to this effect from the Church Fathers, such as Cyril of Jerusalem (d. 386) and John Chrysostom (d. 407). Particles of these parts went all over the world, going to emperors and kings and patriarchs and bishops and monasteries and so forth. Finally they even came to simple believers. The author of this book considers herself fortunate to possess a little particle of wood, set in a silver medallion, that comes from the cross of Christ. (Or, then again, maybe it doesn't.)

Appendix 2

In Toulouse during the Middle Ages there was a Christian festival custom that every year on Christmas, on Good Friday, and on Ascension Day in front of the church door, a Jew, specially chosen for the occasion, was given a sound box on the ears. On account of such mistreatment, a group of Jews, as the biography of Archbishop Theodard of Narbonne informs us, turned to the Frankish King Carlmann, who thereupon convoked the Synod of Toulouse in the year 884. The Jews might have spared their faith in Christian justice. At the Synod Archbishop Ricard labeled the Jews' complaint to the king a calumny of Christ and of Christians. He ordained that "the Jew chosen to be struck on the ear must cry out three times: 'It is just that the Jews must bend their necks beneath the blows of the Christians, because they were not willing to submit to Christ'" (Joseph von Hefele, *Konziliengeschichte* [1860], IV, 523–24).

CHAPTER EIGHT

The Fairy Tale
of Judas the Traitor

THE IMAGE OF Jesus is bound up with the existence of Judas. On the one hand, Jesus promised Judas, as he did to all the disciples, "You who have followed me will also sit on twelve thrones, judging the twelve tribes of Israel" (Matt. 19:28). On the other hand, he knew "from the first" (John 6:64) that Judas would betray him. It's puzzling that Jesus could nonetheless promise him a throne in heaven and, above all, that he could entrust the common purse to him. Judas was a thief (John 12:6). Perhaps he always had been a thief, or perhaps only his experience as cashier turned him into one. In any event, the fact that Jesus selected him for this job can't be called his most fortunate move, either financially or psychologically.

Happily for all concerned, Judas the traitor is a figure out of a religious fairy tale, not a historical person but a fictional character—though an effective one. But then a figure of darkness next to a figure of light is always fascinating, especially when we see evil personified alongside a divine person. The Judas presented in the Gospels as the quintessence of all wickedness never existed. Moreover, even if we grant that he did, he never betrayed Jesus, because he had an alibi.

He gets it from the majority of his accusers, three of the four Evangelists: The Synoptics have him present all during the Last Supper; or at least they never say that he left. Had he gone off, that certainly would have been worth mentioning. Thus their silence on the subject is evidence enough. Luke, in fact, explicitly refers to his presence at the end of the seder (Luke 22:21), after the institution of the Eucharist (Luke 22:14–20). After that, the only thing that happened was a quarrel among the disciples over which one of them would be ranked as the greatest, and in the course of this episode Jesus makes no exception for Judas when he says to them, "I assign to you . . . a kingdom, that you may eat and drink at my table in my kingdom, and sit on thrones judging the twelve tribes of Israel" (Luke 22:30). After that, Jesus goes with the disciples to Gethsemane, as Mark and Matthew report. Luke speaks merely of the Mount of Olives: "and the disciples followed him" (Luke 22:39), evidently meaning all twelve.

Then Judas suddenly shows up with an armed troop and "betrays" Jesus. But that makes no sense; everything can't be organized so quickly. Furthermore, when treachery is suspected, a hiding place can be easily changed. And should we wish to assume that Judas had first treacherously gotten together with Jesus' persecutors, that would mean that Jesus' hiding place (if such it was) was known even without Judas's help. In that case, no one was needed to identify Jesus. Jesus himself makes it clear that his enemies had long known who he was.

John has Judas leave the room in which Jesus is eating the Last Supper with his disciples. (Once again, for John this was not a Passover seder, but a different meal on a different day.) John has obviously noticed that an account in which Judas is present all through the meal leaves no time for the betrayal to take place. He corrects this by making Judas leave. But the fact remains that the Synoptics contradict him, and since the witnesses disagree, Judas should at least be given the benefit of the doubt.

It is completely unclear why Judas actually betrayed Jesus. Money alone can hardly have been a sufficient motive. In that case, Judas would have done better to abscond with the common purse. We also don't know at what point in time, as the Gospels report, the devil entered Judas. John assigns this event to the Last Supper (John 13:27), while the Synoptics place it several days before this (Mark 14:10–11; Matt. 26:14–16; Luke 23:3–4). Trying to resolve this problem by assuming that the devil entered Judas twice only leads to new difficulties: The Synoptics report that Judas had already discussed the betrayal with the high priests after the devil had first entered his heart, so that the second diabolical visitation seems superfluous. It's also strange that Judas, as if to spite the devil, does not immediately run off like a man possessed, but first needs to be charged by Jesus to commit his treachery "quickly" (John 13:27). Only in the wake of this double impulse, from the devil and from Jesus himself, does he head off into the night.

The whole situation at the Last Supper has a few other remarkable features as well. After Jesus declares, "One of you will betray me" (John 13:21), the only reaction from the disciples is Peter's desire to know who it will be. Evidently he considers anything possible and everyone there a conceivable suspect. But after his curiosity is satisfied when Jesus identifies the traitor, nothing happens. It seems as if the disciples have accepted the announcement of the betrayal with indifference. While in John, Jesus is "troubled in spirit" (John 13:21) as he announces the betrayal, here they make no response. Evidently they return to their eating and drinking. In any event, none of them does anything to prevent the betrayal of Jesus and the threat of his death, thereby becoming, one and all, accomplices of the traitor.

In Luke the reaction of the disciples to Jesus' statement that one of them will betray him is still more incomprehensible. After they puzzle over who it might be, they proceed to their dispute over the pecking order ("which of them was to be regarded as the greatest," Luke 22:23–24).

The disciples here present an image of emotional impoverishment. This fits in with Jesus' being "sorrowful and troubled" later in Gethsemane (Matt: 26:37; Mark 14:33), with his sweat becoming "like drops of blood" (Luke 22:44), and with the disciples' repeatedly falling asleep, even though he had asked them to watch with him. This can't have been due simply to the fact that they have drunk several cups of wine. It shows, rather, how unconcerned they were.

The whole image of the disciples in connection with Jesus' Passion is strange and actually quite pitiful. Not only are they passive in the face of the threatened betrayal; not only do they sleep while he suffers; they don't even try to rescue him. Instead of acknowledging Jesus, Peter denies him. And at the death of their Lord, the disciples, except for the so-called beloved (but legendary) disciple, are not present and thereby deny him again. They do not witness his dying, not even "from a distance," as it says of the women who accompany him. Nor do they bury him.

But the questionable behavior of the disciples, their indifference to the betrayal, is of no consequence; because there was no betrayal and thus no traitor: Judas is a creation of fantasy. He is made up mostly of Old Testament quotations and hence is a personified anthology.

The motif of the traitor is common enough and can be found elsewhere in the Bible. It was available for use in the story of the Passion since the Evangelists saw Jesus' fate prefigured in the Old Testament. David was betrayed by his adviser Ahithophel from Giloh, when the latter joined the conspiracy led by David's son Absalom (2 Sam. 15:12). Judas had to kiss Jesus, as Joab, David's general, kissed Amasa, the ex-commander of Absalom's troops, as he stabbed him to death (2 Sam. 20:9–10).

The dramatically effective figure of Judas is indebted above all to a verse in the Psalms (attributed to David): "Even my bosom friend, in whom I trusted, who ate of my bread, has lifted his heel against me" (Ps. 41:10, quoted in John 13:18). In his montage of material in Jesus' address to Judas, Matthew borrows another detail from the same psalm: When Jesus is arrested, he says to Judas, "my friend" (Matt. 26:50).

It's interesting that the Qumran sect, which will be discussed later, had one or more traitors in the group surrounding the "Teacher of Righteousness," and the same verse is used in this context. It appears in a hymn ascribed to the Teacher of Righteousness, who lived a long time before Jesus (1QH V:22–24; *TEWFQ*, p. 364).

The scene of the thirty pieces of silver that Judas flings into the Temple and of the subsequent purchase of the potter's field with the money is described with an explicit evocation of the Old Testament: "Then was fulfilled what had been spoken by the prophet Jeremiah, saying, 'And they took the thirty pieces of silver, the price of him on whom a price had been set by some of the sons of Israel, and they gave them for the potter's field, as the Lord directed me'" (Matt. 27:9–10).

But actually this isn't in Jeremiah. The passage (Jer. 32:6–9) does mention the purchase of a field, but not a potter's field, and not for thirty pieces of silver but for seventeen. Matthew has mixed something up here. He evidently has another passage in mind, namely, Zech. 11:12–13: "And they weighed out as my wages thirty shekels of silver. Then the Lord said to me, 'Cast it into the treasury'—the lordly price at which I was paid off by them. So I took the thirty shekels of silver and cast them into the treasury in the house of the Lord."

After confusing Zechariah for Jeremiah, Matthew makes a second mistake with the thirty pieces of silver that the high priests literally "weighed out to him" (Matt. 26:14). As Pinchas Lapide points out:

> In Jesus' day there were gold and silver denarii, the double as (a Roman coin), three-as pieces, minai, lepta, selas, drachmas, and double-drachmas—but no coin or currency known as "pieces of silver." These had gone out of circulation around 300 years before. Equally anachronistic is the "weighed out." This was customary in Zechariah's time, but by Jesus' day had long been replaced by minted silver coins. (Wer war schuld an Jesu Tod? [1987], pp. 23-24)

For whatever reason, Judas betrayed his lord, and whatever he may have betrayed, it has been known from time immemorial that traitors deserve death. And so Judas dies a double death. Matthew reports the first, Acts of the Apostles the second. Matthew sees the death of the traitor Judas prefigured in the death of Ahithophel, who went and hanged himself (2 Sam. 17:23). Matthew 27:5 says: "And throwing down the pieces of silver in the temple, he departed; and he went and hanged himself."

In Acts of the Apostles, Peter describes the death of Judas to the assembled community in a different way:

> Brethren, the scripture had to be fulfilled which the Holy Spirit spoke beforehand by the mouth of David, concerning Judas who was guide to those who arrested Jesus. For he was numbered among us, and was allotted his share in this ministry. Now this man bought a field with the reward of his wickedness; and falling headlong he burst open in the middle, and all his bowels gushed

out. And it became known to all the inhabitants of Jerusalem, so that the field was called in their language Akeldama, that is, Field of Blood. (Acts 1:16-19)

In Matthew, Judas repents of his betrayal before his death; in Acts, he does not. In Matthew, it is the high priests who buy the field—a potter's field; in Peter's version, it is Judas who buys a field. In both Matthew and Acts, the field is called "the field of blood" but in Matthew this is because the field was bought with "blood money"; in Acts, because of Judas's bursting open.

A few theologians have succeeded in fitting the two New Testament deaths into a single unified death: "There is no pressing reason to assume that we have two quite different traditions here. It is altogether possible that what Peter describes happened to the corpse of the hanged man" (Heinrich Joseph Wetzer and Benedikt Welte, *Kirchenlexikon* [1889], VI, 1925).

In reality, the one mode of Judas's death excludes the other. Perhaps that is why Papias, a bishop of Hierapolis in Phrygia (d. A.D. 120/130), later described a third death. This death, in keeping with the law of amplification in legend formation, is the most terrible of all. Papias reports that Judas was so monstrously bloated that "he could no longer come through where a vehicle could pass easily," not even with his head. "Finally his belly burst asunder and his bowels were scattered." But previously he had to endure still more horrors. His rotting body emitted pus and worms; his penis got extremely swollen; and the place where he died after nameless torments remained desolate and uninhabited. Till Papias's own day, more than a century afterward, nobody could pass it by without holding his nose, "so strong was the ensuing discharge from his flesh" (*NTA*, II, 64; Karlheinz Deschner, *Abermals krähte der Hahn* [1987], p. 121).

There is further evidence that the stories of Judas's betrayal are fairy tales. In 1 Corinthians, Paul reports that Jesus "appeared to Cephas, then to the twelve" (1 Cor. 15:5). Judas was one of those twelve. (In Mark 14:20 it says: "One of you will betray me. . . . It is one of the twelve.") Thus, according to Paul, the group of twelve apostles was still intact after Jesus' resurrection. A few later manuscript copyists have, it is true, corrected Paul and changed "twelve" to "eleven." And the Vulgate—the Latin translation of the Bible, which is in common use in the Catholic Church—translates Paul's Greek "twelve" with a Latin "eleven." But there is no doubt that Paul speaks of "the twelve" to whom the resurrected Jesus appeared. However one wishes to interpret these appearances, the important thing in this context is that the twelve were all still there.

The figure of Judas belongs to the anti-Jewish biased reporting that we have already seen in the description of the events of the Passion. By his very name Judas (which means "Jew" in Hebrew) is labeled a representative of the Jews. Even if Judas the traitor never existed, there was always the Christian hatred directed not only at this man but at his whole people. And that real hatred is the bad side of this completely invented story.

Appendix

In his *Divine Comedy* Dante banishes Judas to the lowest section of the ninth and last circle of Hell, the Giudecca, the circle of Judas. This is the residence of Satan, the deepest point in Hell, the center of the earth and the world. Lucifer is fixed in the ice of a frozen lake. The three giant pairs of wings that he beats, trying to free himself, blow a cold wind that freezes over everything in its path. Only the upper half of Lucifer's body towers out of the ice, and in the central mouth of his three heads he has Judas between his teeth (Brutus and Cassius are in the other two mouths). Continually crunching the doomed apostle between his jaws, he shreds Judas's back with his claws. The three heads of Satan are the perverse counterpart to the heavenly Trinity. Judas has plunged from the grace of the triune God as far down as possible, directly into Satan's maw.

The 34th canto of Dante's *Inferno,* in which this scene occurs, begins with the opening verse of a pious Catholic hymn sung on Good Friday, "Vexilla regis prodeunt" (the banners of the king go forth). But the king meant here is the king of Hell, and he has as little compassion for Judas as God, the king of Heaven, had. Lucifer is crying: "Six eyes wept tears that, mixed with blood and slaver, flowed down three chins" (xxxiv, 53–54), and, weeping, he bites about the body of Judas—"Judas, who has his head inside, and outside wriggles his legs."

But let's leave this place of horror and end instead with the last verse of the 34th canto, when Dante once again arrives on the surface of the earth and notes with a sigh of relief, "e quindi uscimmo a riveder le stelle" (and from there we came forth to see the stars once more).

CHAPTER NINE

Easter

ONE OF THE loveliest stories in the New Testament is the scene that takes place at the empty tomb. It's the story of Mary Magdalen, who goes to the sepulcher of Jesus on Easter morning. She goes there alone, and it's still dark, but her fear of the lonely darkness doesn't hold her back. John the Evangelist doesn't say why she went. But then what man could tell a woman's reasons for going alone at night to a tomb? She went there to cry.

It is still dark when she arrives at the tomb. But as she stretches out her hand to touch the heavy stone door, she gets a terrible shock. The stone has been rolled aside, and nobody else is there. She turns around, and, beside herself with excitement and grief, she runs back into the city, to Peter and the "beloved disciple," so as not to be alone at this moment, and to tell them what has happened. Now the two men run to the tomb and enter it, but it's empty, with only the shrouds lying there. The men have seen enough, and they return home.

Mary Magdalen remains on the scene, at first standing outside. Then she bends down, weeping, into the tomb and suddenly sees two angels there, who ask her why she is crying: "Because they have taken away my Lord, and I do not know where they have laid him" (John 20:13). The men say nothing. Then she walks out of the tomb and sees someone standing there whom she takes to be the gardener; he, too, asks her why she is crying. She says, "Sir, if you have carried him away, tell me where you have laid him, and I will take him away." The stranger looks at her and calls her name, "Mary." Then she recognizes him and says only one word, "Rabboni" (teacher).

One can twist and turn it any way one likes, but this is a love story, even if it's only a fairy tale. However, we can also view it the other way around: It's only a fairy tale, but a true one nonetheless.

The empty tomb on Easter Sunday morning is a legend. This is shown by the simple fact that the apostle Paul, the most crucial preacher of Christ's resurrection, and the earliest New Testament writer besides, says nothing about it. As far as Paul is concerned, it doesn't exist. Thus it also means nothing to him, that is, an empty tomb has no significance for the truth of the resurrection, which he so emphatically proclaims. Granted, for Paul all of Christianity depends upon the resurrection of Christ—"If Christ has not been raised, then our preaching is in vain and your faith is in vain" (1 Cor. 15:14). But in Paul's view, that has nothing to do with an empty tomb. He manifestly has no idea of any such thing. If Paul had ever heard of the empty tomb, he would never have passed over it in silence. Since he gathers together and cites all the evidence for Jesus' resurrection that has been handed down to him (1 Corinthians 15), he certainly would have found the empty tomb worth mentioning. That he doesn't proves that it never existed and hence the accounts of it must not have arisen until later.

This is the position taken by the most important Catholic theologian of this century, the Jesuit Karl Rahner: "The 'empty tomb' is rather to be judged an expression of a conviction that had already become widespread for other reasons" (Schriften zur Theologie [1975], XII, 348). The belief in the Resurrection is older than the belief in the empty tomb. The faith of Easter was not the result of the empty tomb; rather, the legend of the empty tomb grew out of the faith of Easter. It is a pious embroidery on an event that people wanted to imagine in a concrete sense.

Paul, the great preacher of the resurrection, bases his faith on something other than the empty tomb. We learn what converted him to faith in Christ from a clause in his letter to the Galatians: "You have heard of my former life in Judaism, how I persecuted the church of God violently and tried to destroy it; and I advanced in Judaism beyond many of my own age among my people, so extremely zealous was I for the traditions of my fathers. But when he [God] . . . was pleased to reveal his Son to me, in order that I might preach him among the Gentiles . . ." (Gal. 1:13–16). But we never learn how this conversion occurred, or how we should classify it psychologically.

Later his conversion is given legendary amplification in chapters 9, 22, and 26 of Acts of the Apostles in partially contradictory versions. But Paul himself didn't want to describe or discuss the manner of the "revelation." So let's leave it at that, but we can say this: On the basis of personal experience, Paul was convinced that the resurrected Christ had met him in order to commission him as the Apostle to the Gentiles. He mentions this personal encounter in 1 Corinthians (9:1 and 15:8). The latter is the passage in which he cites all the evidence that in his eyes attests to the resurrection of Jesus.

There is another reason why the empty tomb, which Paul has obviously never heard about, couldn't play any role for him: because he understands Jesus' risen body as a "spiritual body." The question of what became of the corpse laid in the tomb has no meaning for him:

> But someone will ask, "How are the dead raised? With what kind of body do they come?" You foolish man! What you sow does not come to life unless it dies. And what you sow is not the body which is to be, but a bare kernel, perhaps of wheat or of some other grain. But God gives it a body as he has chosen, and to each kind of seed its own body. . . . So it is with the resurrection of the dead. What is sown is perishable, what is raised is imperishable. . . . It is sown a physical body, it is raised a spiritual body. . . . I tell you this, brethren, flesh and blood cannot inherit the kingdom of God, nor does the perishable inherit the imperishable. (1 Cor. 15:35–50)

Here is still more proof that Jesus' empty tomb has no significance for belief in the resurrection: Christianity was not the first religion to teach the resurrection of the body. Before his conversion, Paul was a Pharisee (Phil. 3:5). And the Pharisees, as well as the great majority of the

Jewish people in Jesus' day, believed in the resurrection. Only the Sadducees did not. In Acts 23:8 we find a brief note about this: "For the Sadducees say that there is no resurrection, nor angels, nor spirit; but the Pharisees acknowledge them all."

The Sadducees based their skepticism about the resurrection on the fact that the Pentateuch (the core of the Bible for them) says nothing about it. They are right. Actually, belief in the resurrection did not penetrate Judaism until the 2nd century B.C., as the result of Greek and Persian influences. There is no clear testimony to faith in the resurrection until the very latest book in the Old Testament, the Book of Daniel, which was composed around 165 B.C. (see Chapter Sixteen, on Hell).

It's not easy to understand what dying means, and the significance of death itself has yet to be discovered. Hence it comes as no surprise that death doesn't mean the same thing to everyone. This is not the place to go into the differences or interactions between the Greek idea of the immortality of the soul and the Jewish idea of the resurrection of the body. In the face of death, all claims to superior knowledge are signs of total ignorance.

Thus well before Jesus arrived on the scene, the Jews, except for the Sadducees, believed in the resurrection. "And Sadducees came to him, who say there is no resurrection; and they asked him a question, saying, 'Teacher, Moses wrote for us . . .'" They cite the example of a woman who has been widowed seven times and the chaos that must arise after the resurrection in sorting out whose wife she would be. In his answer ("Is not this why you are wrong, that you know neither the scriptures nor the power of God?" etc. [Mark 12:18–27]), Jesus challenges the Sadducees, arguing that the resurrection is attested to by Moses, thereby inclining to the Pharisees' reading of Scripture.

Most of his Jewish contemporaries likewise shared this faith. When Jesus says to Martha after Lazarus had died, "Your brother will rise again," Martha sadly replies, "I know that he will rise again in the resurrection on the last day" (John 11:23–24). Martha didn't believe in an empty tomb. Only legend has the corpse of her brother, Lazarus, running about again for a while (until his next burial). So Martha was left with only the belief in the real resurrection, which has nothing to do with empty tombs and ambulatory dead people.

The Christians have misunderstood the resurrection of Christ pretty much from the very beginning. Equating the empty tomb with his resurrection, they mistook the one for the other. They looked on the empty tomb as a sort of consequence of the resurrection, and then they classified it as proof of the resurrection. But an empty tomb can be empty for the most varied reasons, and it never proves that any resurrection occurred. Conversely, a dead man may certainly lie in a tomb: Such a fact is no obstacle to faith in his resurrection, because resurrection is something different from a dead man's coming back to life.

The Jesuit Karl Rahner, a reflective theologian who wasn't content with the prevailing primitive Catholic theology, once said: "If we were to orient ourselves . . . to the idea of reviving a physical-material body, then we would a priori miss not only the general sense of 'resurrection,' but also that of the resurrection of Christ" (*Schriften zur Theologie,* p. 349). Resurrection does not mean reviving a corpse.

In a certain sense the belief in an empty grave hinders a proper understanding of the resurrection of Christ. It creates the impression that the resurrection of Christ occurred at some point "afterwards," that is, on the third day after his death, and that Jesus was simply dead during the interval or suspended in some nebulous locale between here and nowhere. All that isn't Christ's resurrection or anyone else's.

That was the viewpoint of another thoughtful theologian, Rudolf Bultmann, who was so reviled by the pious legend-addicts for his "demythologization" of Christianity: "If God is the God who is always to come, then our faith is the faith in the God who comes to us in our death" (letter to author, 18 February 1962).

The action of God that takes place in death cannot be compressed, as if it were a three-act play, into the course of time or into assigned locations. This can't be done even if people like to imagine it that way, nor just because the Gospels present it in separate stages of a temporal and spatial sequence. All this is legendary illustration. The death and Resurrection and Ascension of Jesus happened in a single instant.

People like to picture things. But in the Gospels' version of events on Easter morning (or Saturday evening, as we shall see) the human delight in telling tales has allowed itself a great deal of free play. So much free play,

in fact, that a brief look at these texts is enough to classify all the Evangelists as pious tellers of fairy tales. If we took them at their word, each
would give the lie to the other three. Each would find the others guilty of
falsehood.

Some thinkers have been led by the faultiness of the proofs served up
in the Gospels to reject any faith in the resurrection of Jesus or anyone
else. In his *Apologie oder Schutzschrift für die vernünftigen Verehrer Gottes*
(Apologia for the Rational Worshipers of God), seven parts of which were
published beginning in 1784 by Gotthold Ephraim Lessing (d. 1781) under
the title *Fragmente eines Wolfenbüttelschen Ungenannten* (The Wolfenbüttel Fragments), Hermann Samuel Reimarus (d. 1768) stresses that "the
proof of the resurrection of Jesus from Scripture cannot endure to all eternity before the judgment seat of reason." From Lessing's time until ours,
the "Wolfenbüttel Fragments" have been a continual cause of unrest in the
pious herd of obedient sheep. In fact, the complete text of Reimarus
couldn't be published in Germany till 1972. Reimarus specifically skewers
"ten contradictions" in the Gospel accounts of the resurrection. Yet what
about people who can't prove the resurrection and who are unwilling to
have proofs imposed upon them by some old, long-dead "eyewitnesses,"
on the basis of prophecies from some old books? Is there nothing at all for
such doubters, nothing that could convince them of a resurrection or at
least could let them hope for one? This question shouldn't be answered
too hastily in the negative.

And now to some of the contradictions in the accounts of the empty
tomb. Different times are cited for the visit to the tomb (Saturday evening
or Sunday morning). Different visitors are mentioned (two women in
Matthew, three women in Mark, at least five women in Luke, only Mary
Magdalen in John). In particular, Mark says: "And when the Sabbath was
past, Mary Magdalen, and Mary the mother of Salome, and Salome,
bought spices, so that they might go and anoint him. And very early on
the first day of the week they went to the tomb when the sun had risen"
(Mark 16:1–2).

Matthew has only two visitors, "Mary Magdalen and the other
Mary" (Matt. 28:1). In addition, the visit has already taken place on Saturday evening. That is how the passage "Now after the sabbath, toward the

shining forth of the first day of the week, Mary Magdalen and the other Mary went to see the sepulcher" (Matt. 28:1) should be understood, and not, as it usually is, taken to refer to Sunday morning in our sense.

As it was understood back then, the day after the Sabbath, the first day of the week, began immediately after the end of the Sabbath; and the Sabbath ended at sundown on Saturday evening. The new day was said to "shine forth," not with the dawn but when the first stars could be seen.

Matthew uses the same verb for "shine forth" (*epiphoskein*) that Luke uses at the end of his description of the taking down of Jesus' body from the cross: "It was the day of Preparation, and the sabbath was beginning" (Luke 23:54). The Sabbath began or "shone forth" not on the next morning, but immediately after the day of Preparation, which in turn ended with nightfall. No one would claim here that the Sabbath did not begin until the next morning, and that Jesus must not have been taken down from the cross until the next morning.

Jerome understood Matt. 28:1 correctly and translated it in the Vulgate, "Vespere autem sabbati" (on the eve of the Sabbath), but today the passage is falsely translated almost everywhere else as "Now after the sabbath, toward the dawn of the first day of the week, Mary Magdalen and the other Mary went to see the sepulcher." In the original Greek text, however, there is not the least mention of dawn.

In Luke it is the women disciples who had come with Jesus from Galilee who go to the tomb. The text says of them, "But on the first day of the week, at early dawn, they went to the tomb" (Luke 24:1). This is Sunday morning in our sense. Several names are given in verse 10: "Now it was Mary Magdalen and Joanna and Mary the mother of James and the other women with them who told this to the apostles" (Luke 24:1). So there were at least five women, but the group was probably larger than that.

In John, Mary Magdalen goes to the tomb on Easter morning all by herself. She is the only visitor to the tomb who is mentioned in all four accounts. She is the fixed point among a series of varying figures. She obviously played a leading role in the group of the disciples.

The fact that she lived is not in doubt. But with regard to her image in the early Church and still more in later times, Mary Magdalen is a figure with legendary features. Not much is reported about her in the

New Testament. Her name tells us simply that she came from Magdala, a town on the Sea of Galilee. We hear from Mark (15:40–41) that there were women among Jesus' disciples "who, when he was in Galilee, followed him, and ministered to him." The passage doesn't say what "ministering" means; in any case, it primarily referred to financial arrangements. Among these evidently well-off women, Mary Magdalen is the first to be named.

Luke speaks expressly of financial help given to Jesus and the twelve by women, "who provided for them out of their means."

Here, too, Mary Magdalen is the first to be cited in the list of women (Luke 8:2). Meanwhile, she has been demoted from her status as an emancipated sponsor of Jesus: In many Bible translations we find Mary Magdalen included under the sexist heading of "The Serving Women." According to the Gospel of John (19:25) Mary Magdalen stood beneath the cross. Luke (8:2) mentions that "seven demons had gone out from her." Luke tells us that other women had been possessed by evil spirits, but such a massive exorcism is reported only of Mary Magdalen. Yet whether there were seven demons or perhaps only six or even eight, we can banish them one and all (along with the demons in the other women) into the fantasy realm of whoever wrote the Gospel of Luke. Luke is the only Evangelist who pins all these demons on Mary Magdalen. The other Evangelists know nothing about this, and the conclusion to Mark (16:9–20), in which Mary Magdalen's demons also appear, is not genuine.

But the later Christian community of readers was fascinated by Mary Magdalen's demons. Early on she was identified with the so-called great sinner who bathed the feet of Jesus with her tears, dried them with her hair, and then kissed and anointed them (Luke 7:38). This is the woman about whom Jesus said that many sins had been forgiven her because she had loved much (Luke 7:47). The process of an otherwise unknown person's receiving a familiar name through someone's authorial fantasy is frequently met with. We have already mentioned it as one of the regular elements of legend formation.

The great sinner and Mary Magdalen, therefore, are not to be viewed as one and the same person. Nevertheless, Tertullian (d. after 220) did it (*De pudic.*, 11). Jerome (d. 420) did it (*Praef. in Os.*). Ambrose (d. 397) did it (*lib. 6 in Luc.*, n. 14). Augustine (d. 430) did it (*De conserv. Evang.*, 79). Pope Gregory the Great (d. 604) did it (*In. ev. hom.*, 25, 1,10; 33,1). None of this lessened the interest in Mary Magdalen. Quite the contrary. She even found a place in the Roman Missal as a holy sinner and sinful saint (officially a "penitent"); her feast is on 22 July. When Faber Stapulensis (d. 1536) dared to doubt whether the Church's case for identifying the two women could stand up, his work was forbidden by the Sorbonne and put on the Index. Nowadays the idea that Mary Magdalen and the great sinner are one and the same "may be characterized as the firm conviction of the Catholic Church" (Heinrich Joseph Wetzer and Benedikt Welte, *Kirchenlexicon* [1893], VIII, 738).

Catholic conviction has a number of other things to report about her—for example, that she was first buried in Sainte Baume, in southern France, and later definitively buried in the Dominican abbey of St. Maximin at Aix-en-Provence. On the other hand, other people know that she was buried in Ephesus, whence Emperor Leon VI had her brought to Constantinople. Finally, ever since the 11th century the monks of Vézelay have also known that she lies buried in *their* monastery. In her name there are a number of religious associations "for the betterment of fallen girls."

Now to the various encounters that the women had: In Mark they see a young man in a white garment: "And looking up, they saw that the stone was rolled back—it was very large. And entering the tomb, they saw a young man sitting on the right side" (Mark 16:4–5). He charges the women to tell "Peter and the disciples" that the resurrected Jesus is going before them to Galilee and will show himself to them there. But the women flee in fear, and likewise out of fear they don't tell anyone anything, contrary to the young man's order. With that the Gospel of Mark comes to an end. Most translations of the New Testament contain an appendix describing the appearance of Jesus to Mary Magdalen and his global commission to preach the Gospel ("Go into all the world . . ."), as well as a brief account of the ascension. But theologians are by now in practically unanimous agreement that this section is a later interpolation.

In Matthew a single angel appears to the women. At first the angel isn't there, only a detachment assigned by Pilate to guard the tomb, and the stone has not yet been rolled away. When the angel comes down from

heaven, he causes a major earthquake. We aren't told whether this was deliberate or inadvertent, nor are we informed of the damage and the possible victims. In any event, the angel rolls the gravestone aside and sits
down on top of it, perhaps exhausted by the effort. "His appearance was
like lightning," and his clothes are, as usual with angels, white as snow.
The terrified guards all become "like dead men" (Matt. 28:2ff.).

The angel gives the women the same charge as the young man in
Mark does, but this time they obey him, though not right away, because
while they are running to spread the word, they are met by Jesus himself.
Incidentally, here the women are allowed to embrace Jesus' feet, while in
John Jesus doesn't let Mary Magdalen do this (John 20:17). Jesus then gives
them the same command they have already gotten from the angel—
namely, to tell the disciples to go to Galilee, where Jesus will show himself
to them. And that's how it happens: "Now the eleven disciples went to
Galilee . . . and when they saw him, they worshiped him" (Matt. 28:16ff.).

In Luke it's not a single young man, as in Mark, nor a single angel, as
in Matthew, but two men, though once again wearing white garments
(Luke 24:4). In addition, the story is a little different from the one we're familiar with. There is no mention of guards or of an earthquake. The stone
has already been rolled away, and the men don't come until the women
have puzzled over the situation for a while. Instead of getting orders from
the men, they act on their own initiative and report everything to the
apostles. But they might have spared themselves the trouble, because
the apostles take the whole account to be nonsense and don't believe a
single word the women tell them (Luke 24:11). The extra verse that one
finds in Catholic translations, "But Peter rose and ran to the tomb; stoop-
ing and looking in, he saw the linen cloths by themselves; and he went
home wondering what had happened" (Luke 24:12), is a fabrication, designed to gloss over the previous scene and rescue Peter's honor.

The business with Galilee as Luke tells it is altogether different from
Matthew's and Mark's version. Here Jesus appears to the disciples not in
Galilee but in Jerusalem (Luke 24:36ff.), and he expressly bids them not to
leave Jerusalem, but to wait there for the Holy Spirit (Acts 1:4). According
to Luke, if they had gone to Galilee, due to contradictory instructions
from Jesus or the angels, they would have completely missed Jesus.

Thus the angels differ not only in their orders as to where the disciples should go in order to see Jesus, but also in their numbers and appearance. In Mark there is a single young man. Since one might not immediately guess what lies behind this, he wears a white garment to identify himself as an angel. In Matthew there is a single angel, but this time he looks like a bolt of lightning, and not like a young man. In Luke there are two men. In contrast to the scene in Mark, they are somewhat older angel-men, but they, too, are dressed in white, which seems to be a sort of angelic uniform. Finally, in John there are two angels, but they look neither like young men nor like lightning, but simply like ordinary angels.

The reader can't help noticing that at Jesus' resurrection we don't have a great and important angel making an appearance as in the annunciation scenes when the angel Gabriel, who otherwise stands in the presence of God, comes to Mary and Zechariah. But Jesus' resurrection was at least as important as the birth of John the Baptist. Maybe the angel who looked like lightning was a somewhat higher-ranking angel. He must have been more powerful than the others, since he unleashed the earthquake. But apart from this angel, they were all angels just like you and me.

In addition, the angels in John are rather taciturn. John's Gospel differs from the Synoptics in that the angels at the tomb do not announce Christ's resurrection, but simply ask Mary Magdalen why she is crying. After she explains the reason, they have no reaction and give no explanation for the disappearance of the corpse. And so we're back again in the scene where this chapter began. Thus the story ends well after all, not with a woman's deep, hopeless perplexity, because now she sees Jesus standing there. He, too, asks why she is crying and calls her by name. And he, too, explains nothing—but now no explanation is needed.

CHAPTER TEN

The Ascension

And while eating with them he charged them not to depart from Jerusalem, but to wait for the promise of the Father, which, he said, "You heard from me, for John baptized with water, but before many days you shall be baptized with the Holy Spirit." So when they had come together, they asked him, "Lord, will you at this time restore the kingdom to Israel?" He said to them, "It is not for you to know times or seasons which the Father has fixed by his own authority. But you shall receive power when the Holy Spirit has come upon you; and you shall be my witnesses in Jerusalem and in all Judea and Samaria and to the end of the earth." And when he had said this, as they were looking on, he was lifted up, and a cloud took him out of their sight. (Acts 1:4–9)

This is the complete description of Jesus' Ascension in Acts of the Apostles. The rendering of Jesus' speech is somewhat confused. Direct and indirect discourse blend together. Thematically, too, it's somewhat disordered: In between the baptism with the Holy Spirit and the power of the Spirit, a discussion has been worked in about the deadline for the establishment of the Kingdom of God in Israel. One wonders why so gifted a narrator as the author of Luke has pieced together the whole passage with so little care.

Presumably Luke is using the Ascension as a literary device, as a sort of prologue to the events he will later describe. It serves him as an introduction and transition to the deeds of the apostles, beginning with the events of Pentecost. Here Jesus is merely a sort of announcer of the miracle of Pentecost in the following chapter. The "forty days" (Acts 1:3) simply provide material to fill up the time after Easter. Though he considers Jesus' role as announcer important, Luke wants to dispatch him quickly to heaven, so as to turn to the coming Holy Spirit and events on earth and in the Church. Jesus' history is over; the Church's history is just now beginning.

But in any case, in the middle of dinner Jesus has gone up into heaven. He really ought to have at least finished the meal. We who stand down on the earth and gaze after him are slightly perplexed at such a daring ascent. That sort of trip is tiresome, even if Jesus did have a little something before, and time consuming. We don't know how fast Jesus traveled or flew, and whether he accelerated as he went along. But even if he zoomed at the speed of light, the next heaven is at least a billion light years away. So, whatever the case, the Catholic New Testament scholar, Gerhard Lohfink, had a point in his fine little book *Die Himmelfahrt Jesu: Erfindung oder Erfahrung?* (Jesus' Ascension: Fact or Fiction? 1972) when he jokingly entitled one of his chapters "And He's Still Flying Now."

Incidentally, Luke's account leads us to conclude that the last meal that Jesus had before taking off for heaven took place out of doors. Not that Jesus couldn't have flown out of the room up through the roof, but then it would have been harder for the disciples to train their eyes on their ascending master.

Commenting on the whole account of the Ascension, David Friedrich Strauß notes with biting accuracy:

> *We know that anyone who wants to go to God and the precincts*
> *of the Blessed is taking a needless detour, if he thinks this means*
> *he has to soar into the upper levels of the air. Surely Jesus . . .*

would not have taken such a superfluous journey, nor would God have made him take it. Thus one would have to assume something like a divine accommodation to the world-picture people had back then, and say: In order to convince the disciples of Jesus' return to the higher world, even though in fact this world was by no means to be sought in the upper atmosphere, God nevertheless staged the spectacle of this sort of elevation. But this would be turning God into a sleight-of-hand artist. (Das Leben Jesu [1837], II, 678-79)

In Acts of the Apostles, after Jesus' Ascension into heaven, two men suddenly appear in the familiar white garments. By now we are used to this sort of sight. But only respect for the angels prevents the reader from thinking the angels stupid for asking: "Men of Galilee, why do you stand looking into heaven?" Even angels might have known that an ascent into heaven was reason enough to be looking in that direction. And there's no reason for the rebuke implied in the angels' question. That is why the men of Galilee don't even bother to answer them.

The Ascension, like Pentecost, was a wholly male affair. There were no women on hand. Even the angels, who appear on Jesus' launching pad, are expressly described as "men." Discrimination against women in the Church was in full swing: Women may have been witnesses to the Resurrection, but not to the Ascension.

Meanwhile, a "sabbath day's journey" (which was a little over half a mile) away from Olivet, the mother of Jesus sat "with the women" in a room on the ground floor of a house in Jerusalem (Acts 1:12–14). After the Ascension the men returned to this house. Perhaps Mary would have liked to share her son's last meal and to wave good-bye for the very last time, but she never got to.

Fortunately, the women were so coldly ignored only by the reporters of the event, not by Jesus himself. That is because the account of Christ's Ascension after forty days is a mere legend.

There were ascents into heaven made long before and quite apart from Jesus. Gerhard Lohfink points to the ascension, described by the

Roman historian Livy, of Romulus, the founder of the city of Rome, who came to be venerated as a god: "One day Romulus held an assembly of the people before the city walls to review the army. Suddenly a thunderstorm broke out, wrapping the king in a thick cloud. When the cloud lifted Romulus was no longer on earth. He had gone up into heaven" (*Die Himmelfahrt Jesu*, p. 9).

Lohfink cites still more ascents into heaven:

> *Similar stories were also told in antiquity about other famous men, for example, Heracles, Empedocles, Alexander the Great, and Apollonius of Tyana. Characteristically the scene is set with spectators and witnesses, before whose eyes the person in question disappears. Often he is borne aloft by a cloud or shrouded in darkness that takes him from the eyes of the people. Not infrequently the whole business takes place on a mountain or hill.* (pp. 7-8)

From this standpoint, Jesus' Ascension was nothing out of the ordinary. Jesus, too, disembarked from a mountain, the Mount of Olives, for heaven. The point is that from a mountain it's not quite as far to heaven.

In the primitive Church the legend of the Ascension did not emerge until relatively late, and then as the conclusion to the legend of the dead Jesus' walking the earth. Paul, who knows nothing about an empty tomb, likewise knows nothing about the Ascension. For him, resurrection and ascension are one and the same. Romans 1:4 says: "designated Son of God in power . . . by his resurrection from the dead." In his essay "Der historische Ansatz der Himmelfahrt Christi" (The Historical Trace of Christ's Ascension), Lohfink rightly finds that "there is no vestige in Paul of a particular ascension taking place in view of the disciples after the resurrection has already been completed" (*Catholica* [1963], pp. 1, 49).

Even the four Gospels fail to mention Jesus' ascent into heaven. The account in Mark that does is part of the spurious conclusion added on later. The authentic text (Mark 16:8) ends with the frightened women fleeing from the tomb. In Matthew the risen Jesus says during his appearance in Galilee: "All authority on heaven and on earth has been given to me" (Matt. 28:8). This means that the risen Christ has already been exalted into

(Matt. 28:8). This means that the risen Christ has already been exalted into heaven. With this appearance Matthew's Gospel ends.

In John the death of Jesus on the cross is seen as that exaltation: "'And I, when I am lifted up from the earth, will draw all men to myself.' He said this to show by what death he was to die" (John 12:32–33; cf. 3:14, 8:28). John's Gospel ends with the last meeting of the disciples with the risen Jesus at the Sea of Galilee. This really doesn't fit the Johannine notion that death already means exaltation. But in any event, John knows nothing about an Ascension.

The account of the Ascension in Luke is spurious. The phrases "was carried up into heaven" and "worshiped him, and" (Luke 24:51–52) are lacking in essential ancient manuscripts, and hence are not printed in Nestle's standard edition of the original Greek text of the New Testament. The Ascension also does not fit in with the rest of the Gospel of Luke. In it the crucified Jesus says to the "good thief," "Truly I say to you, today you will be with me in Paradise" (Luke 23:43). And in Luke 24:26 the risen Jesus says to the disciples at Emmaus: "Was it not necessary that the Christ should suffer such things and enter into his glory?" This means that the resurrected Jesus has already gone to heaven as the Exalted One.

Nonetheless, the interpolated phrases (Luke 24:51–52) are firmly anchored in both Catholic and Protestant translations. But even if we were to look on this passage as authentic—and Lohfink thinks it is—we would still be left with one and the same reporter, author of both the Gospel of Luke and Acts of the Apostles. Then Luke would contradict his own testimony, since in Luke 24:50–51, the Ascension occurs at a different time and in a different place than in Acts, that is, on the same day as the resurrection, not after forty days, and in Bethany rather than on the Mount of Olives.

True, we don't know exactly where Bethany was, but according to the Gospel of John (11:18), the distance between Bethany and Jerusalem amounted to fifteen stadia. Josephus says that the distance from Jerusalem to Olivet was five stadia (JA, XX, viii, 6; LCL, p. 93). That would put Bethany 2,664 meters from Jerusalem, whereas it was only 880 meters from the Mount of Olives to Jerusalem. (The "sabbath day's journey" mentioned in Acts 1:12 was the distance that a Jew could travel on the Sabbath without breaking the Third Commandment: 2000 ells or around 880 meters.)

We cannot take the silence of Paul and the Gospels (at least three of them) to be a deliberate silencing. So it seems obvious to infer that the Ascension was unknown to them and that not until Acts, composed around the end of the 1st century, did this legend come into vogue. In the narrative of the Ascension, as we have already seen, one legend drew another after it: The legend of the empty tomb, which told of Jesus' walking the earth again in the flesh, had to be brought to a conclusion, because Jesus could not spend the next two thousand years among us as another wandering Jew.

The Protestant New Testament scholar Georg Kümmel writes:

> While the oldest early Christian tradition understands the resurrection as a raising up to God, the narrative of the Lucan scriptures about Christ's ascension presupposes the return of the resurrected Jesus into earthly life, which ends with the ascension. . . . The tale of the ascension is . . . , by comparison with the belief in the resurrection, a late, secondary legend. It is at odds with the central early Christian belief in the resurrection and exaltation of Christ, and as a materialization of this belief it must be subjected to myth-criticism. (Religion in Geschichte und Gegenwart [1959], pp. 3, 335)

The author of Acts, as commentators generally agree, may well have understood "forty days" in a symbolic rather than a literal sense. But as long as one understands the forty days as any period of time, however long or short, one has misunderstood the Resurrection or Ascension. Just as the resurrection of Christ did not mean an event that occurred at some point after his death ("on the third day"), but took place immediately *in* his death, so the lifting up of Christ likewise took place immediately *in* his death. The word *ascension* should be used only as the label for a legendary event. The true exaltation of Christ is no "ascent into heaven"; and the death, Resurrection, and exaltation of Christ are one single event, a single instant.

The Ascension of Christ means something different from, and more than, a movement from one place to another, whether up or down, right or left. The Ascension is not a rocketlike launch through the universe, leading to a location where, perhaps beyond this world, some heavenly place might lie. The Ascension doesn't mean the Beyond (beyond this world), but, just like the Resurrection, the definitive openness of a future. Ascension can't be described as a change of place, and it can't be fixed in time as an event at some point after death and resurrection. It is not an event in time and space; and with the "ascension" the risen Christ didn't go away or drive away or fly away. Instead he became once and for all the One who is close to us.

How are Christ's Resurrection and Ascension to be untangled from the mind-set that flatly dates and naively localizes them, as we see in official preaching and the Church's liturgy? The problem is unsolvable, so long as the hierarchy, out of ignorance or fear of thinking, makes no effort to get a deeper understanding of what Christianity is and wants. But in the long run, even so-called simple Bible readers will not be soothed with the old tranquilizers, even though other Bible readers are trying to do just that.

Catholic theologian Franz Joseph Schierse aptly describes the difficulties that a religion teacher has with Bible readers, even though his conclusions are false. He writes:

> You can't begin to understand the text, the message . . . of Acts of the Apostles, until you go beyond the level on which the historico-critical method frames the problem. . . . Ever since the rise of the historico-critical approach, in other words over the last 200 years, even simple Bible readers have increasingly allowed the "law of thinking" to be shoved down their throat by a notoriously rationalistic scholarly discipline. This is the only way to explain the fact that in both Bible discussion groups and religious instruction people are generally stuck on the question: What happened, and how did it happen? How did the narrative actually take place? Bible readers are not mollified until they have been credibly assured that the text at issue, this or that story, is really reporting

about historical facts. For example, if they were to be told that it's
highly doubtful that the Apostles saw with their own eyes the
risen Jesus swept up to heaven (Acts 1:9–10), they would get very
restless. The speaker or religion teacher would have to put up with
being blamed for a lack of faith. ("Geschichte und Geschichten,"
in Bibel und Kirche *[1972], pp. 6, 35)*

Schierse's view is only half right. He sees the fault in the historico-critical interpretation. In his eyes it's a straitjacket, and the "simple Bible readers" who are caught in it let things "be shoved down their throat," insofar as it confines their view to the question, Did the things happen this way or not? Schierse doesn't realize that historico-critical research can liberate Bible readers from the coercion to understand the biblical text in the literal sense. Schierse is right to see historico-critical scholarship as only the first step on the lower level of understanding. But it's still a step in the right direction toward "understanding the text," after one has transcended "the level on which the historico-critical method frames the problem." But in fact, it never gets to this point, because the simple Bible reader is not permitted even to set foot on that level. The official Catholic-episcopal-papal authority has laid down the law: Everything really happened historically the way the Bible describes it.

The "simple Bible readers," who obstinately keep asking whether everything actually did happen the way the Bible says, generally get nothing but unsatisfactory answers from the theologians. The reason for this is that a theologian who understands the Bible reader's doubts only too well, or who may even share them, can get into trouble and lose his or her license to teach as a Catholic. With the story of the Ascension, of course, the Catholic hierarchy is still fairly generous, because it views this miraculous tale as less necessary for maintaining its own position. But there are danger zones. To take one example, the virgin birth is indispensable for maintaining the dominion of clerical celibates. Above all, therefore, it must be interpreted historically, biologically, and literally. Under no circumstances may it be read as a thought model conditioned by the age it comes from.

Some have argued that the Christian faith is not belief in legends or fairy tales, that it has more essential material for its contents than the un-

conditional literal acceptance of a few top-of-the-charts New Testament
miracle stories. But this view is not shared by the Catholic hierarchy, and
so it's often totally unknown to the so-called simple believers. Often, in
fact, this insight is something these simple believers don't want to look at,
after having been disinformed, deformed, and infantilized by two thousand years of the Church's fairy-tale preaching.

CHAPTER ELEVEN

Pentecost

THE AUTHOR OF Acts of the Apostles has the richest imagination of all the New Testament tellers of fairy tales and legends. He is identical to the author of the Gospel of Luke, as we learn from the introduction to both works (Luke 1:1–3 and Acts 1:1–2). We owe him a debt of thanks for such lovely fairy tales as the story of Bethlehem with the child in the crib and of the twelve-year-old Jesus in the Temple, the earlier tale of Zechariah and Elizabeth, and all the others up to the Ascension after forty days. And now, shortly before the year 100, he brings us the story of the miracle of Pentecost, about which neither Paul nor the other Evangelists tell us anything.

Before the miracle occurs, Luke first has a special apostolic election take place, owing to the supposed betrayal and death of Judas. During his forty-day stay on earth after Easter, Jesus himself doesn't make any choice of his own; evidently he doesn't think it necessary. The apostles, on the other hand, feel that it's indispensable, for the sake of a verse in the Psalms ("His office let another take," Ps. 109:8). Of course the author of that verse never dreamed of the election of a new apostle centuries in the future. On this occasion Peter delivers a speech, in which he, speaking Aramaic to Aramaic-speaking Jews, strangely talks about "their language" (Acts 1:19). The fact that he treats his native tongue as a foreign language spoken by a foreign nation proves that the whole speech was fashioned from a later perspective and by a different author.

The disciple chosen is a young man named Matthias, who is here conjured out of oblivion only to sink right back into it. Nothing was ever heard of him before or after this—except for a few later legends and the "discovery" of empress mother Helena. She must have had a special flair for buried saints and sacred objects, because she found where the apostle Matthias was buried, dug him up, and had him brought to Rome. Now part of his body lies in Trier and another part in Rome.

The feast of Pentecost was a turbulent event. We are told that they were "all" together (Acts 2:1). This group, as we learned earlier in Acts 1:15–16, numbered about "120 persons," all men by the way, since Peter addresses them as "brothers" (Acts 1:16), and the text plainly puts him "among the brethren" (Acts 1:15). Then there comes a noise or roar from heaven, which thunders through the house and fills it from top to bottom. What was hitherto only audible now becomes visible: Suddenly tongues of fire are seen; one such tongue descends upon everyone participating in the assembly, and they begin to speak in many different tongues (i.e., languages). The apostles are not the only ones to receive the Holy Spirit; all those present (Acts 2:3), that is, the "brothers," do, too.

At Pentecost, the second of the three great pilgrimage festivals, great crowds of Jewish pilgrims streamed to Jerusalem. These Diaspora Jews, who are characterized as "devout men from every nation under heaven" (Acts 2:5) and who have gathered outside the house, hear the roughly 120 Christian men inside speaking in the languages of their homeland. "Are not all these who are speaking Galileans?" they ask, "And how is it that we hear, each of us in our own native language?"

The many languages being spoken by the 120 men are added up in a list that is long but neither correct nor up-to-date. The "Medes and Parthians," for example, had long since disappeared from world history. And "Judea" and its language are cited as a foreign country and a foreign language, even though the scene of Pentecost is being played out in Jerusalem, the capital of Judea. This shows that the whole event is a construct from a later, Gentile-Christian perspective. "In fact it is highly improbable that any Diaspora Jew would have understood such vernacular languages, to the extent that they survived in the more remote regions of the Middle East. . . . Actually the Jews in the areas listed spoke either Aramaic or Greek" (Ernst Haenchen, *Die Apostelgeschichte* [1971], p. 171).

Greek was the international language from around the time of Alexander the Great (323 B.C.) to about A.D. 200. In Jesus' day, Greek was spoken from the Tiber to the Tigris and beyond, especially by business-men, politicians, officers, and anyone intent on a career. Emperor Tiberius (A.D. 14-37), in whose reign Jesus was crucified, wrote Greek poems. Rome at the time was a bilingual city, speaking Greek as well as Latin. In the Middle East, Greek was increasingly supplanting Aramaic, which had been the language of that part of the world (since around 500 B.C.). In Jesus' time, Aramaic had sunk to the status of the language of the people—that is, of the illiterates. Many Jews, even simple folk, spoke Greek as well as Aramaic.

In the linguistic outburst described by Luke, some people outside the house mockingly suggest that the speakers are "filled with new wine" (Acts 2:13). But Peter stands up and explains that this isn't drunkenness, since it's only nine o'clock in the morning. He tells them that they, the "men of Israel" listening to him, murdered Jesus (Acts 2:22–23). Jesus, however, risen from the dead (he says nothing about the Ascension, al-though this is supposed to have happened only ten days before). Then Jesus received the Holy Spirit from the Father, and now, as they could hear and see, he had poured out the same Spirit.

Of course Peter also inserts an abundance of quotations from the Old Testament into his Pentecost speech. This was an important concern for the New Testament writers and their missionary work. They wanted to show that Jesus, his life and, above all, his death (which could have made him look to many people like a failure and a reject), had been prophesied in the Bible. This way they could prove that the Christians were the heirs of Jewish biblical tradition.

Many of the listeners convert and have themselves baptized, around three thousand souls (Acts 3:41), all of them men, since they are addressed in Acts 2:29 as "brothers." The whole Pentecost episode is a feast of male bonding and fraternization, since before their baptism the three thousand listening brothers ask the 120 polyglot brothers, "Brethren, what shall we do?" (Acts 2:37).

Pentecost is not the only time in Acts that the Spirit descends to earth. The Spirit comes down repeatedly, sometimes on individuals, sometimes on an entire group. The inhabitants of Samaria receive the Spirit (Acts 8:17), as does the audience of a sermon by Peter in Caesarea, who thereupon speak in tongues (Acts 10:44–48). Such glossolalia is incomprehensible speech uttered in a state of ecstasy. It is a religious phenomenon that creates the impression of mental derangement; and it was widespread in the early Church. Paul reports about it in chapter 14 of 1 Corinthians. Other recipients of the Spirit include the twelve or so men in Ephesus who also started speaking in tongues and even prophesied (Acts 19:6). Thus Pentecost differs from the other descents of the Spirit only in its date; essentially there are many Pentecosts in Acts.

One of these events deserves special attention, namely, the descent of the Spirit upon the Gentiles (Acts 10:44). For the universal expansion of the Church, this was more important than the fact that the apostles and the other Jewish men on hand were filled with the Holy Spirit. Despite the fact that they themselves have just received the Holy Spirit, the Jewish Christians are completely dispirited by this novelty: "While Peter was still saying this, the Holy Spirit fell on all who heard the word. And the believers from among the circumcised who came with Peter were amazed, because the gift of the Holy Spirit had been poured out even on the Gentiles. For they heard them speaking in tongues and extolling God" (Acts 10:44–46). The bewilderment of the Jewish Christians shows how crucial the event was. So, in the strict sense, we should speak of a Jewish Pentecost in Jerusalem and a hitherto unheard-of Gentile Pentecost in Caesarea. One interesting feature of the Pentecost in Caesarea is that a Roman centurion (literally the leader of a hundred men, perhaps the equivalent of our captain), is named at the head of those receiving the Holy Spirit. The officer's name is Cornelius. In Caesarea by the sea, the Roman procurator had his official headquarters, and a Roman garrison was lodged there as well. It's striking to see how the Holy Spirit has a certain weakness for top leaders, both ecclesiastical and military. This was not without consequences in church history. So the Church's head man in Jerusalem and the military's head man in Caesarea (higher-ups in the Roman army not being available at the moment) both received the Holy Spirit. Since then the two have worked together continually in the same spirit, though that spirit hasn't always been holy.

Thus there are both greater and lesser Pentecosts in Acts of the Apostles. This points to a tendency on the part of the author to describe the beginning of an era of the Church. Jesus had (mistakenly) expected the coming of God's Kingdom in the very near future: "Truly, I say to you, this generation will not pass away till all has taken place" (Luke 21:32). But when the Kingdom of God failed to arrive and the "last days" were extended indefinitely, the Christians knew how to handle it. After his account of the Ascension, with which he brings the Age of the Messiah to a close, the author of Acts turns once and for all to a new horizon. His subject is now the activity of the apostles and the Church as a whole, work that he sees as supported by the Holy Spirit and leading to participation in the same Spirit. Despite the tongues of fire, the events of Pentecost are rather obscure; but the official Church has made very good use of them. It views Pentecost as the day it was founded. Schott's Roman Missal typically says that "Pentecost is the birthday, the solemn consecration of the Church established by Christ." But the Church's leadership sees even more to be gained here. "From the first day on Pentecost onwards the Holy Spirit has been the soul of the holy Church, the mystical body of Christ. He animates, leads, teaches and protects it from all error." This is supposed to mean that since Pentecost the Church—which naturally means its leaders—is infallible.

Year in, year out, John Paul II keeps talking over Radio Vatican, in more and more languages—though not always intelligibly (the pope's English is particularly bad)—about Pentecost and the priesthood. This is not an accident: Thanks to this feast, he feels confirmed, elevated, glorified, and illuminated. By comparison, the Resurrection of Christ takes a backseat, because it affects everyone and lends the pope no special prominence.

At a theological symposium in the diocese of Essen shortly after the Second Vatican Council (1962–65), the first speaker was the Jesuit Karl

Rahner, followed by the then-bishop of Essen and later Cardinal Franz Hengsbach. On the subject of the council, Bishop Hengsbach said: "Well, the theologians [looking in Rahner's direction] will have quite a bit more work to process what the Holy Spirit inspired us bishops with at the Council." We have Acts' account of Pentecost (or what the Church has made of it) to thank for this sort of remark. There sat Karl Rahner, a great theologian, silent and modest and—in the bishop's eyes—spiritually subordinate to the bishop, because he had been given no inspiration from the Holy Spirit. And there stood Franz Hengsbach, a theological midget compared with Rahner, trumpeting his ownership of the Spirit.

Apart from such high and mighty papal-episcopal claims, the events of Pentecost produced little theology of any significance. Characteristically, for instance, Rahner and Vorgrimler's *Kleines theologisches Wörterbuch* (Little Theological Dictionary, 1961) has no entry at all for "Pentecost." It's still missing in the big four-volume *Sacramentum mundi* (The Sacrament of the World, 1967–69). What the twelve-volume *Kirchenlexikon* by Wetzer and Welte has to say about the subject is also insignificant: "Since the Holy Spirit was given to the Church . . . on the 50th day after Easter, the day on which the feast occurs is thus determined by the feast of Easter" ([1895] IX, 1974–75). This sort of self-evident statement may not be profound, but at least readers will never go wrong with it. (Incidentally, the word *Pentecost* comes from the Greek word *pentekoste,* "the fiftieth day.")

From the 2nd century B.C. onward, and hence in Jesus's day, the Jews celebrated Pentecost—the second of the three pilgrim feasts—not simply in thanksgiving for the harvest (as the earlier inhabitants of the land, the Canaanites, had done), but, more importantly, as *Simhat Torah,* "rejoicing of the law," in memory of the giving of the Law on Mount Sinai. As a day of remembrance of that event, Pentecost played for the Jews a role in salvation history. It was dedicated to the memory of God's alliance with his people. The Holy Spirit, by the way, had no special part in the Jewish feast of Pentecost. On the other hand, the Spirit no longer needed to be given to the Jews anymore, unlike the Church, which apparently didn't have the Spirit before this. Long before this, it had descended, as the "spirit of God," on the elders of the Jews (Num. 11:25). At that time the seventy elders of Israel likewise fell into ecstasy, so that the Christian feast of Pentecost was like a new edition of the ancient event.

In the opinion of the Christians, however, their Pentecost Holy Spirit was far superior to the Jews' "spirit of God," wherever or whenever or on whomever it may have been bestowed. The term "spirit of God" is used with many different meanings. But among Christians it was later mostly standardized and—even if not yet in the New Testament—personified and declared the third person of the Trinity, the latter definitively at the Council of Constantinople in 381.

With their "three persons" in one God, the Christians saddled themselves with intellectual problems vis-à-vis Jewish monotheism that could never be solved. But to Christians, an insoluble intellectual problem and an insoluble mindlessness were only proof of greater faith. Protestant and Catholic theologians alike have had their hands full explaining that the term *person* in the Trinity is not to be understood in the sense of "person" as otherwise understood by everyone. With a doctrine of the Trinity that almost all people misunderstand as really being about three "persons," one might suspect that something in it doesn't add up. But one will wait in vain for the theologians to admit that.

Since we're talking just now about the Trinity: The title "Son of God" in the Old and New Testaments is not, so to speak, copyrighted. There is no exact job description for it; and it is not understood in the sense that Christians later gave it, when they equated "Son of God" with "God." In the Old Testament, for example, angels or kings are called "sons of God." And in the Letter to the Romans, Paul calls "sons of God" all those "who are led by the Spirit of God" (8:14; cf. 8:19; 9:26). In Galatians Paul says: "You are all sons of God through faith" (3:26). In 2 Corinthians (6:18) "the Lord Almighty" says, "And you shall be my sons and daughters." (Note: The sons of God have since then been reduced to a single Son of God, and the daughters of God have all died out.) In Revelation God says: "He who conquers will have this heritage, and I will be his God and he shall be my son" (21:7). In the Sermon on the Mount it is said that the peacemakers "shall be called the sons of God" (Matt. 5:9). This is the exact same formulation that the angel Gabriel uses in speaking with Mary:

Jesus, he says, will "be called Son of God" (Luke 1:35). Now nobody ever thinks of seeing the peace movement as a movement of gods. And during the first three centuries, many people never thought of seeing Jesus, the "son of God," as God, simply equating him with God.

There were long struggles before that finally happened, in the year 325, at the Council of Nicea. Since then Christians no longer have the slightest problem with the idea that every Christmas God lies in the manger, wrapped in swaddling clothes. On the contrary, this fits in with their obliging and infantilizing theology, which really considers anything possible. Even the term "Mother of God" (Council of Ephesus, 431) no longer causes them any difficulties. Of course, nowadays we no longer use the term "God's grandmother" to refer to Saint Anne. Karl Rahner, alluding to the phrase in the "Hail, Mary," "blessed is the fruit of thy womb, Jesus," gives us pause by observing, "Naturally the divinity of her child is not the fruit of her womb" (*Schriften zur Theologie* [1984], XVI, 329). Thus the mother of the undivine Christ child, of Christ minus his divinity, should be called not the Mother of God, but simply and unmistakably, the mother of Jesus.

A similar suggestion was made more than a millennium and a half ago by Nestorius, the archbishop of Constantinople. He rejected the title Mother of God for Mary, arguing that Mother of Christ was the right one and that a God in swaddling clothes was too ridiculous a notion. For this reason in 431 at the Council of Ephesus, where the title Mother of God was officially conferred on Mary, Nestorius was condemned as a heretic and exiled to Upper Egypt. He died there around 451.

Back to the outpouring of the Holy Spirit in Acts. The Christian miracle of Pentecost has a strongly anti-Jewish accent. True, for the sake of the Christian propaganda miracles, the story employs images of fire and storm taken from Old Testament theophanies. For example, in Exod. 3:4 God speaks to Moses out of a burning thorn bush, while in 1 Kings 19:11 "the Lord passed by, and a great and strong wind rent the mountains." Above all, God had come down in fire to Sinai, the mountain where he gave the law and made a covenant with his people (Exod. 19:18; cf. Deut. 5:22ff.). But in opposition to, and competition with, the Jewish feast of

Pentecost, the Christians wanted to advertise themselves as the "true Israel." The Jews, from the Christian standpoint, had wasted, lost, and betrayed their own destiny, since they refused to believe in the Messiah and even murdered Jesus.

The New Testament's constant invoking of the Old Testament, the continual quotations and "prophecies" of Jesus, mean the opposite of a bond between Christians and Jews. They mean hostility. The Viennese historian Friedrich Heer illustrates this anti-Jewish motif with the example of the apostle Paul. Yet the point holds not just for Paul, but equally for the Peter of Acts and his Pentecost speech. Thus Heer writes in *Gottes erste Liebe: Die Juden im Spannungsfeld der Geschichte* ([1981] pp. 54–55):

> *Paul is the first founder and first organizer of the Church. He hails her as the new, the true Israel. This is one of the most revolutionary and fateful proclamations in world history. It tears Christianity out of the bosom of Judaism, and lays the triple foundation—in theology, in the history of theology, and in history—for the greatest predatory raid (from the Jewish standpoint) in world history. Compared with this, the plundering by the Romans of the Temple in Jerusalem, the plundering of the Library of Alexandria, all the great and terrible plunderings of treasuries, riches, and legal collections by the barbarians, Romans, Arabs, and Mongolians look petty indeed. This—as the Jews saw it—. . . greatest raid in world history carries off the Old Testament into the service of the New Testament: What for over 1,000 years Jewish prophets, priests, heralds, sons, and fathers of the Jewish faith had created by way of prayers, sacrifices, liturgy, poetry, or eloquence—amid unspeakable suffering and pain, long before and long after the Babylonian captivity—all this has now become the booty of the new Israel, the Church, is turned into the Church's inviolable legacy.*
>
> *Christendom thinks, meditates, prays, sacrifices, in its liturgy, in its psalter, in the breviary daily recited by priests, in*

the canonical hours of monks and nuns, with this property, with-
out which not a day, not an hour in the Church's year would be
imaginable—against the Jews, against the "perfidious nation of
the Jews."

It wasn't the Romans who crucified Jesus, it was the Jews: That is what Christians, with their friendliness toward the Romans and hostility toward the Jews, have been claiming from the very beginning. In his speech on Pentecost, Peter first says: "This Jesus, delivered up according to the definite plan and foreknowledge of God, you crucified and killed by the hands of lawless men" (Acts 2:23). Here the Roman presence at the crucifixion is admittedly still alluded to, but the Romans are mere agents and instruments of the Jews. A few sentences later we hear about "this Jesus whom you crucified" (Acts 2:36); the Romans aren't even mentioned. By "you" Peter means the people of Israel, and not just the pilgrims standing before him from all over the world. The historically false message of the God-murdering people of the Jews, which already runs through the Gospels, has now become an essential component of the anti-Jewish Christian message of Pentecost.

The whole description of the divine sending of the Spirit as an anti-miracle pitted against the Jewish Pentecost memory of the miracle on Sinai is theologically weak. Its anti-Jewish bias must be condemned; and this exploitation on the part of the Catholic hierarchy, so as to strengthen its own power, must be deplored.

But in this obscure story there is a line from the prophet Joel, which Peter places at the beginning of his sermon as a prophecy of the Christian feast of Pentecost: "This is what was spoken by the prophet Joel" (Acts 2:16). However, speaking as a man in an entirely male group, Peter doesn't pay any serious attention to it. Joel's programmatic line has not in fact been fulfilled at all. For this reason it deserves to be stressed and firmly held onto, because at a stroke its nonfulfillment convicts an arrogant male hierarchy of narrow-mindedness. What God says is: "I will pour my Spirit on all flesh, and your sons and daughters shall prophesy, . . . on my menservants and my maidservants in those days I will pour out my Spirit"

(Acts 2:17–18). This isn't the only passage in the Old Testament where Jewish tradition is friendlier to women than the Christian is.

If the Church's leaders claim in the Roman Missal that the Holy Spirit has come down on them ever since Pentecost, then this "and your daughters" is the norm of the Spirit against which they must be measured. Hence, no Holy Spirit ever came down on that all-male company then, because there is no Holy Spirit exclusively for men. Which is why, as things now stand, the Men's Church should for the time being keep silent about their Holy Spirit, keep silent at least until the Holy Spirit promised by the prophet Joel has really come down upon them.

CHAPTER TWELVE

The Fairy Tale
of Acts

WE HAVE ALREADY come to know two fairy-tale miracles from Acts of the Apostles: the Ascension and Pentecost. A third miracle concerns the course of the conversion of the apostle Paul. Note that the conversion itself was not a miracle, it actually happened. But the nature and circumstances of the conversion derive from the fantasy of whoever wrote Acts of the Apostles. In this context it should be mentioned that it's incorrect to speak, as people often do, of Saul's converting to Paul, as if after he became a Christian, Saul took on a new name that he hadn't had before, like a person entering a religious order. Rather, Paul had had two names from birth: a Jewish synagogue name, Saul (the name of a Jewish king from Paul's own tribe of Benjamin [see Rom. 11:1]), along with a Roman name, Paul, which came from his having been born a Roman citizen in Tarsus.

As a prelude to the story, Acts tells of Paul's "breathing threats and murder against the disciples" (9:1), as he persecuted the Christians. Paul had already been present at the stoning of Stephen. His conversion then took place on the road to Damascus, where he was headed to arrest Christians, "that he might bring them back bound to Jerusalem." The conversion is described in three parallel accounts that contradict one another on various details (Acts 9:1–19a; 22:3–16; 26:9–18). The first time the story is told by the author of Acts, the next two times it's ascribed to Paul himself.

The first account (9:1ff.) says:

Now as he journeyed he approached Damascus, and suddenly a light from heaven flashed about him. And he fell to the ground and heard a voice saying to him, "Saul, Saul, why do you persecute me?" And he said, "Who are you, Lord?" And he said, "I am Jesus, whom you are persecuting, but rise and enter the city, and you will be told what you are to do." (The men who were traveling with him stood speechless, hearing the voice, but seeing no one.)

By contrast we read in the second description (22:3ff.): "Now those who were with me saw the light but did not hear the voice of the one who was speaking to me." Thus in the first description the men heard but saw nothing, in the second they saw but heard nothing.

In the third description (26:9ff.) nothing is said about whether they heard or saw anything. But it doesn't matter, since none of the stories is true.

In the first and second stories the men come to a stop, while Saul crashes to the ground, but in the third they all fall down together. It's strange that the companions of the persecutor don't convert with him. In any case, Saul is now blinded, and his companions lead him to Damascus, where he is miraculously healed by a certain Ananias.

In contrast with the three legendary versions in Acts, we have an entirely different report in the letters of Paul. He says nothing about being blinded. In Galatians he writes about his conversion: "But when he who had set me apart before I was born, and had called me through his grace, was pleased to reveal his Son to me, in order that I might preach him among the Gentiles . . ." (Gal. 1:15–16). Such language is in sharp contrast to the three fantasies on a so-called moment of conversion. At such moments a person may see lights and hear voices and be dashed to the ground ten times in a row, but that sort of spectacle has nothing to do with conversion. Compared with Acts' version of the event, Paul's single sentence says more than could ever be expressed by some theatrical thunder en route to Damascus.

In 1 Corinthians (15:8) Paul once again speaks of his encounter with the risen Christ. This passage is usually translated as, "Last of all, as to one untimely born, he appeared also to me." It's a misunderstanding to take this "appeared" (Latin *visus*) to mean a vision, as if Paul "saw" something in a real, perceptible dimension. There is no seeing going on here. Our categories of sight are not appropriate to the event Paul has in mind. He means that something happened in which the presence of the Revealer was experienced existentially. This experience means more than an "appearance," more than a miraculous seeing and hearing. There is no way to define such perception and knowledge, which transcend every element of the senses, which embrace all of existence. But it's certain that such an encounter with Jesus, as Paul describes it, has nothing in common with the Damascus Show in Acts. In Galatians Paul describes the moment with the words "when he . . . was pleased to reveal his Son to me" (1:15–16). This terse "to me" strips the event of all external attention-getting features and leaves it in the discreet taciturnity of the unprovable.

In the third of the legendary accounts, we find a remark that Jesus is supposed to have made to Paul as he lay on the ground: "It hurts you to kick against the goad" (26:14). This is a quotation from *The Bacchae* by Euripides (d. 406 B.C.). It's no surprise to find a quotation from ancient literature; the only peculiar thing is that Jesus should quote a Greek proverb to Paul while speaking Aramaic ("in the Hebrew language"). But the really strange thing is that with both Jesus and Euripides we have the same "familiar quotation" and the same situation. In both cases we have a conversation between a persecuted god and his persecutor. In Euripides the persecuted god is Dionysus, and his persecutor is Pentheus, king of Thebes. Just like Jesus, Dionysus calls his persecutor to account: "You disregard my words of warning . . . and kick against necessity [literally 'against the goads'] a man defying god" (*Euripides V*, trans. William Arrowsmith [Chicago: Univ. of Chicago Press, 1959], p. 188).

Quite obviously the author of Acts has borrowed this Dionysus episode and relocated it near Damascus. Jesus even uses the same plural form of the noun (*kentra*) that Euripides needs for the meter of his line.

This fairy tale about Paul's conversion is harmless enough. But Acts also has evil and malicious fairy tales, such as the story of Ananias and

Sapphira: "A man named Ananias with his wife Sapphira sold a piece of property, and with his wife's knowledge he kept back some of the proceeds, and brought only a part and laid it at the apostles' feet" (5:1–2). The man, therefore, was acting in a completely legal and legitimate manner, since everyone has the right to sell some real estate, give a part to the Church, and hold onto the rest. But for the Church in Acts, this constituted embezzlement, since it didn't get the whole thing.

And so God's vengeance thus took its relentless course. Here at least God's mills grind quickly. First, Peter confronts the villain with his outrageous behavior: "Ananias, why has Satan filled your heart to lie to the Holy Spirit and to keep back part of the proceeds of the land?" Now, Ananias hadn't lied to the Holy Spirit at all, since he hadn't said a single word to the Holy Spirit—or at least nothing like that is mentioned here. And he hadn't embezzled anything, because the money was his; he simply wanted to keep part of it.

But Peter and, above all, the Holy Spirit evidently took a different view of things: They saw in his action a crime worthy of death. The poor man was punished with death on the spot: "When Ananias heard these word, he fell down and died [lit., gave up the ghost]" (5:5). The ghost or spirit that he gave up was not the great, divine Holy Spirit, but a totally godforsaken and small, poor human spirit, whose fate it was to come knocking on the wrong door—the Holy Spirit's. "The young men rose and wrapped him up and carried him out and buried him" (5:6).

Ananias's wife came three hours later to see her husband, knowing nothing about what had happened. It would have been asking too much of the apostles to have them, in addition to all their many other activities, inform Sapphira that her husband was now dead and buried. Besides, they were probably too busy counting the money. So Peter asks the widow, who doesn't even know that she is a widow, whether her husband's gift to the Church was the true purchase price of the property. This was absolutely none of his business, but she says yes, presumably out of fear. She also doesn't want to give a different answer from the one her husband might have given. So she says yes, but she shouldn't have, because by a divine miracle she, too, is instantaneously whisked from life to death. "When the young men came in they found her dead, and they carried her out and buried her beside her husband" (5:10).

This is the story of miraculous, divine, lethal punishment meted out to an only half-saintly couple. Nowadays we can comfort ourselves with the thought that this miracle is a fairy tale. But the shock remains. We shrink back from this method of promoting faith with horror stories, to exploit people and extort money from them with the description of such miracles.

In another passage of Acts we also meet God as a kind of lightning executioner. This time the victim is King Herod Agrippa I (10 B.C.– A.D 44), a grandson of Herod the Great. He dies not of a stroke or heart attack, but eaten by worms: "On an appointed day Herod put on his royal robes, took his seat upon the throne, and made an oration to them. The people shouted, 'The voice of a god, and not of man!' Immediately an angel of the Lord smote him, because he did not give God the glory; and he was eaten by worms and died. But the word of God grew and multiplied" (12:21–24).

We find a fairy tale, although a different one, about the death of Herod Agrippa I in Josephus. Here, too, the king dies suddenly, but not so quickly as in Christian tradition; this time after an interval of five days. He dies not eaten by worms and not blind to the folly of fame, but resigned to the will of God. But all this is connected to a mysterious owl that had once been shown to him by a Germanic seer. The seer had prophesied to Agrippa that he would have a happy death, but that the owl would be the messenger of his death: The next time he saw the owl, he would die five days later (*JA*, XVIII, vi, 7; LCL, pp. 123, 125, 127).

That is just what happens three years later. At festivities in honor of the emperor, Agrippa appears in a wonderful silver robe. At the sight of this, his flatterers cry out to him, "addressing him as a god. 'May you be propitious to us,' they added, 'and if we have hitherto feared you as a man, yet henceforth we agree that you are more than mortal in your being.' The king did not rebuke them nor did he reject their flattery as impious. But shortly thereafter he looked up and saw an owl perched on a rope over his hand. At once, recognizing this as a harbinger of woes just as it had once been of good tidings, he felt a stab of pain in his heart." He is seized by sharp pains, and says: "I, a god in your eyes, . . . am now under sentence of death. But I must accept my death as God wills it." And five days later he dies (*JA*, XIX, viii, 2; LCL, pp. 379, 381).

Incidentally, according to Josephus, this Agrippa, unlike his grandfather, was a good-natured soul. "Agrippa, on the contrary, had a gentle disposition and he was a benefactor to all alike. He was benevolent to those of other nations and exhibited his generosity to them also" (*JA*, XIX, vii, 3; LCL, p. 369). Evidently people hated foreigners even back then. All this, to be sure, is of no use to him when in Acts of Apostles God sentences him to be eaten by worms. While Jesus, for his part, spent his time tearing apart the superstitious link between sickness and guilt, the Christians—whenever it suited them—connected guilt, sickness, and death together again, beginning with King Herod Agrippa I all the way down to AIDS.

In chapter 14 of Acts, Paul and Barnabas show how a real Christian behaves upon getting, like Agrippa, exaggerated compliments. When Paul heals a cripple in the city of Lystra, the people who witness it cry out, "The gods have come down to us in the likeness of men!" They call Barnabas Zeus and Paul Hermes; and the priest of Zeus even wants to sacrifice oxen to them. "But when the apostles Barnabas and Paul heard of it, they tore their garments and rushed out among the multitude, crying, 'Men, why are you doing this? We also are men, of like nature with you'" (14:14–15). Thus the apostles escape the divine death penalty for pride.

Given the harshness of God's punishments, the Jewish magician in Cyprus, Bar-Jesus, was fortunate in his misfortune. After Paul arrives on the island, Bar-Jesus tries to turn the proconsul Sergius Paulus away from the faith.

> But Saul, who is also called Paul, filled with the Holy Spirit, looked intently at him and said, "You son of the devil, you enemy of all righteousness, full of all deceit and villainy, will you not stop making crooked the straight paths of the Lord? And now, behold, the hand of the Lord is upon you, and you shall be blind and unable to see the sun for a time." Immediately mist and darkness fell upon him, and he went about seeking people to lead him by the hand. (13:9–11)

For his sake, we hope that after God's hand turned against him, he found a human hand that was on his side.

Christians took action not just against magicians, but against books of magic as well. Christians have, alas, been burning books since the beginning of Christianity. But faith never overcomes superstition in this way, much as it may strive to. The stronger simply annihilates the weaker, and by this will to annihilate he proves nothing except his own superstition. This is quite apart from the fact that the "books of magic" burned by the newly converted Christians were certainly not weapons of the same caliber as the infamous *Hammer of Witches* (1487), a manual written by two Dominican friars that cost the lives of countless innocent women. The earlier texts were works with incomprehensible magic formulas and long series of mysterious words. They served, for example, to ward off demons and to protect people from harmful influences. "Many also of those who were now believers came, confessing and divulging their practices. And a number of those who practiced magic arts brought their books together and burned them in the sight of all; and they counted the value of them and found that it came to fifty thousand pieces of silver. So the word of the Lord grew and prevailed mightily" (19:18ff.).

With these and similar stories, Acts attempts to edify believers, to strengthen and discipline them in the faith. The whole book is a work of propaganda aimed at Gentile Christians and Gentiles who have not yet become Christians. The latter, it was hoped, would take a more positive attitude toward Christianity. Toward that end the title "Acts of the Apostles" doesn't mean ordinary actions, but grand, heroic, and miraculous deeds.

As a matter of fact, the apostles in Acts do perform many miracles, surely more than Jesus did. Generally these miracles are not described precisely but just mentioned en bloc. The apostles do "many signs and wonders" (2:43; 5:42). Stephen does "great wonders and signs" (6:8). The apostles also do "signs and great miracles" (8:13). In Malta Paul cures all the sick people on the island (28:9) and is otherwise, like Peter, active as a miraculous healer in multifarious ways. When Peter's shadow falls on the sick, they promptly get better, "so that they even carried out the sick into the streets, and laid them on beds and pallets, that as Peter came by at least his shadow might fall on some of them. The people also gathered from the towns around Jerusalem, bringing the sick and those afflicted with unclean spirits, and they were all healed" (5:15–16). If Paul's handkerchiefs or other pieces of laundry were laid upon the sick, they would recover: "And God did extraordinary things by the hands of Paul, so that handkerchiefs or aprons were carried away from his body to the sick; and diseases left them and the evil spirits came out of them" (19:11–12). There was actually nothing out of the ordinary in the fact that Peter also healed cripples (3:2ff.; 9:33), and Paul did the same (14:8).

As for resurrections from the dead, Peter and Paul managed only a total of two, each raising one person.

> Now there was at Joppa a disciple named Tabitha, which means Dorcas. She was full of good works and acts of charity. In those days she fell sick and died; and when they had washed her, they laid her in an upper room. Since Lydda was near Joppa, the disciples, hearing that Peter was there, sent two men to him entreating him, "Please come to us without delay." So Peter rose and went with them. And when he had come, they took him to the upper room. All the widows stood beside him weeping, and showing tunics and other garments which Dorcas had made while she was with them. But Peter put them all outside and knelt down and prayed; then turning to the body he said, "Tabitha, rise." And she opened her eyes, and when she saw Peter she sat up. (9:36–40)

Paul's raising of the dead was in no way inferior. It took place in Troas, the region where ancient Troy was located. Paul had been preaching for several hours, until midnight,

> and a young man named Eutychus was sitting in the window. He sank into a deep sleep as Paul talked still longer; and being overcome by sleep, he fell down from the third story and was taken up dead. But Paul went down and bent over him, and embracing him said, "Do not be alarmed, for his life is in him." And when Paul had gone up and had broken bread and eaten, he conversed

with them a long while, until daybreak, and so departed. And
they took the lad away alive, and were not a little comforted.
(20:7–12)

In brief, the "acts" of the apostles were mighty, and they themselves
were mighty men. Hence, it's no wonder that when they prayed, there was
an earthquake (4:31). When necessary, it could quake again, so as to free
them from their chains and open their prison doors: "But around midnight Paul and Silas were praying and singing hymns to God, and the prisoners were listening to them, and suddenly there was a great earthquake,
so that the foundations of the prison were shaken; and immediately all the
doors were opened and everyone's fetters were unfastened" (16:25–26).
The scene continues as in *The Bacchae* (which Jesus had already quoted on
the occasion of Paul's conversion). Euripides writes of the maenads who
were being kept in the city's prison: "The chains on their legs snapped
apart / by themselves. Untouched by any human hand, / the doors swung
wide, opening of their own accord" (Euripides, *The Bacchae,* in *Euripides*
V, ll. 447–48; p. 192; cf. ll. 497–98).

To maintain the balance between Peter and Paul, Peter has an experience in prison similar to Paul's. In lieu of an earthquake, he is helped by
an angel (12:6ff.). Thus the apostles preach a violent God who, as he leads
the Israelites through the wilderness into the promised land, "destroyed
seven nations in the land of Canaan [and] gave them their land as an in-
heritance" (13:19). This gives rise to hope that, if necessary, God will eradi-
cate more nations for the benefit of Christians. In the meantime, the Holy
Spirit keeps descending on them, or an angel appears to them. One time
even Jesus comes in person and passes on a brief exhortation: "The following night the Lord stood by him and said, 'Take courage, for as you
have testified about me at Jerusalem, so you must bear witness also at
Rome'" (23:11).

Along with the edification of believers, a second concern of Acts was
to harmonize theological tensions in the young Church. Acts idealizes the
infancy of Christianity. In reality, its early years were full of hard struggles
and bitter partisan conflict between Peter and Paul. On one side was the
grand old man of the apostles and an eyewitness to Jesus' life, and on the

other was the latecomer who had not known Jesus and instead invoked a vision, or whatever one wishes to call it, that he had after Jesus' death. The main point in dispute was, To what extent do Gentile Christians have to follow the law? Do they have to be circumcised and observe Jewish dietary rules?

In the Letter to the Galatians, written in the 50s, long before Acts, we can see still the glimmer of some of these conflicts in the early Church and of the clash between Peter and Paul. It's no longer clear to us who the particular groups involved were or how much power anyone had. In present-day discussions in the Catholic Church, the pope decides everything, and dissenters are immediately excluded. That makes the front lines a lot easier to make out. At any rate, Paul writes in Galatians: "But even Titus, who was with me, was not compelled to be circumcised, though he was a Greek. But because of false brethren secretly brought in, who slipped in to spy out our freedom which we have in Christ Jesus, that they might bring us into bondage—to them we did not yield submission even for a moment, that the truth of the gospel might be preserved for you" (Gal. 2:3–5).

In Antioch Paul even made a public charge (in the presence of all the members of the community) against Peter. Paul describes this dispute in Gal. 2:11–14:

> But when Cephas came to Antioch I opposed him to his face, be-
> cause he stood condemned. For before certain men came from
> James, he ate with the [Christian] Gentiles; but when they came
> he drew back and separated himself, fearing the circumcision
> party [Jewish Christians]. And with him the rest of the Jews
> acted insincerely, so that even Barnabas was carried away by
> their insincerity. But when I saw that they were not straightfor-
> ward about the truth of the gospel, I said to Cephas before them
> all, "If you, though a Jew, live like a Gentile and not like a Jew,
> how can you compel the Gentiles to live like Jews?"

Evidently, on the one side there was a group of Jewish Christians gathered around James (the brother of the Lord), and on the other, the increasingly strong Christian party gathered around Paul. Peter vacillated between the two fronts. When James and his representatives were away, he held the Eucharist with the Gentile Christians. When James or his people were in the neighborhood, he withdrew. When it came to the Gentile Christians, Peter the "rock" had no firm theological ground beneath his feet.

Acts contains not a single word about this dispute. The Protestant theologian Hans Joachim Schoeps writes that Acts has been "believed much too readily." In reality Acts is

> only a retrospective view of Christian origins written by one party (the winners). . . . Anyone used to evaluating texts critically has no choice but to rate it as a document of the second or even third Christian generation. Acts follows a clear didactic line and for this reason energetically cultivates the creation of legends, and reshapes persons and events according to its own standards. (Das Judenchristentum [1964], p. 10)

Thus Acts never mentions the conflict between Peter and Paul. It tries "to reduce the tension between these 'Hellenists' and the 'Hebrews' to a minimum" (Ernst Haenchen, Die Apostelgeschichte [1971], p. 113). The 'Hellenists' (Greek-speaking Diaspora Jews) who took a more liberal stand on the mission to the Gentiles than the "Hebrews" (Aramaic-speaking Jews in Palestine) felt slighted "because their widows were neglected in the daily distribution" (6:1ff.).

Thus the great rift that threatened to tear the young Christian world apart, the great conflict between Peter and Paul—of which the dispute in Antioch is only one example—never took place, as far as Acts is concerned. It is papered over with a declaration of harmony. Peter is even presented as the initiator of the mission to the Gentiles, converting, as mentioned, the first Gentile, the Roman centurion Cornelius (10:1ff.). During an ecstasy, Peter sees the heavens open, and a great sheet descends containing all the animals of the earth and air, both clean and unclean foods. A voice bids him slaughter and eat and recognize that no foods are really unclean. He must see that he is supposed to eat the foods of the Gentiles, which means going to the Gentiles and converting them. Accordingly, at the so-called Apostolic Council (chapter 15) Peter is the chief

spokesman of the mission to the Gentiles. It sounds as if Paul were ventril-
oquizing through Peter's mouth.

Even today the dispute between different groups in the early
Church, especially Paul's confrontation with Peter, is still being covered up
with banal conciliatory pronouncements and patchwork histories. At the
"Pauline centenary" in Rome in 1960, Cardinal Julius Döpfner delivered a
speech entitled "Paul and Peter: Saint Paul and the Primacy of Rome." In
it he makes Paul a witness to that primacy, although Paul never in his life
heard or said a word on the subject. Here is how he addresses the episode
at Antioch:

> At this point something should be said about the so-called fac-
> tum Antiochenum, *the confrontation between Paul and Peter in
> Antioch. It is true that after the Apostolic Council in Jerusalem
> that Peter had at first eaten with Gentile Christians. But when
> some people from James's circle arrived, he withdrew from them
> out of fear of this extremist group of Jewish Christians. Other
> Jewish Christians joined in this move, even Barnabas. Then
> Paul said, "I opposed him to his face, because he stood con-
> demned. . . ." The difference of opinion between Peter and Paul
> was not about any fundamental questions. At issue in Antioch
> was practical behavior, the possibility of Jews and Gentiles dining
> together. Out of pastoral prudence Peter felt obliged to make al-
> lowances for the feelings and difficulties of the hard-line visitors
> from Jerusalem. (Bibel und Kirche, 2/1961, p. 41)*

What Paul called "insincerity" (literally "hypocrisy") is nowadays
called "pastoral prudence."

The differences in the early Church as seen in Galatians were by no
means overcome by Paul's attack on Peter. In the course of time there were
more and more divisions among the Jewish Christians in Jerusalem. Many
clung to Jewish traditions and laws and continued to observe circumcision
and kashruth, kept the Sabbath, and took part in worship in the Temple. A
radical group demanded circumcision even from the Gentile converts to
Christianity, while others opposed this.

One group of radical Jewish Christians and vigorous opponents of Paul were the Ebionites (that is, the poor). Their first leader was James the brother of the Lord, and all the way into the second century they continued to choose their bishops from Jesus' family. Originally, Ebionite was a name of honor, since Jesus had declared that the poor were blessed. But they had enemies on all sides, and over the years the name fell into disfavor. They continued to think of themselves as Jews, but the Jews excommunicated them because they claimed Jesus was the Messiah and they rejected animal sacrifices (in time they became vegetarians). On the other hand, they were looked upon as heretics by the Gentile Christians because they were opponents of Paul. For example, unlike Paul, they did not view Jesus' death as a bloody act of atonement: They interpreted the Eucharist as a mere memorial of Jesus, substituting a chalice of water for the chalice of blood; and they deviated from orthodoxy in other ways. But the Romans lumped them together with the other Jews and Christians as potential insurgents. The Romans were indifferent to people's philosophy of life; they simply wanted to crush rebellions and unrest and, where possible, to nip them in the bud.

Over the following centuries, the main point of difference between the Ebionites and the mainstream Church turned out to be their rejection of the virgin birth. They believed that Jesus was the Messiah, but not that he had been born the Son of God. Rather, the Holy Spirit had united with Jesus at his baptism. In their eyes a Son of God born of a virgin was a notion derived from the pagan Greek world of myths and hence alien to Christian origins.

And because the Ebionites continued to reject this myth, they were treated as heretics by the Church at large, which was increasingly, and later on all but exclusively, made up of Gentile Christians. The Church Father Irenaeus of Lyon (d. ca. 202) writes in his *Against the Heresies:* "Their interpretation is false, who dare to explain the Scripture thus: Behold, a girl (instead of a virgin) shall conceive and bear a son. That is how the Ebionites say that he [Jesus] is Joseph's natural son. In saying this they destroy God's tremendous plan for salvation" (III, xxi, 1). In another passage Irenaeus observes: "The Ebionites are foolish. . . . For they refuse to realize that the Holy Spirit came over Mary, and the power of the Most High

PUTTING AWAY CHILDISH THINGS

overshadowed her.... Thus they deny the heavenly wine and wish to know nought but the water of this world" (V, i, 3).

Eusebius (d. 339) also writes about the Ebionites in his *Ecclesiastical History:* The Ebionites "had poor and mean opinions concerning Christ. They held him to be a plain and ordinary man who had achieved righteousness merely by the progress of his character and had been born naturally from Mary and her husband" (III, xxvii; LCL, p. 261). And: "Those who belong to the heresy of the Ebionites . . . affirm that Christ was born of Joseph and Mary, and suppose Him to be a mere man" (VI, xvii; LCL, II, 53). By damning the Ebionites as heretics, the Church Universal definitively cut itself off from its Jewish-Christian roots.

A third concern of Acts, along with edifying the community and downplaying conflicts, was to stress the malice of the Jews and, by contrast, to showcase the Romans' sense of justice. Next to the Gospel of John, Acts of the Apostles is the most anti-Judaic work of the New Testament. We have already seen this impulse in the story of Pentecost, which was an anti-Jewish propaganda feast. The charge that the Jews were the murderers of Christ was a constituent part of the message of Pentecost.

For example, the malice of the Jews is conspicuous in the speech of Stephen. Incidentally, much is unclear about Stephen's trial. Hans Joachim Schoeps doubts that there is anything to "the historicity of the supposed Hellenist deacon Stephen" (*Das Judenchristentum,* p. 40). At all events, in Acts' description of the scene we find an uneasy mixture of "a lynch mob and an orderly court session" (Haenchen, *Die Apostelgeschichte,* p. 265). Luke overlooks the fact "that the Sanhedrin . . . had no right whatsoever to issue such death sentences" (p. 286). In any case, the story of Stephen offered Luke "space for the great speech with which he could make clear his position vis-à-vis Judaism" (p. 266).

The speech that Luke inserts into Stephen's mouth is an abusive indictment in which the entire history of Israel is seen as the story of a long defection of a people from its God. Even the building of the Temple by Solomon takes place against God's will:

"Heaven is my throne, and earth my footstool. What house will you build for me, says the Lord, or what is my place of rest? Did

not my hand make all these things?" You stiff-necked people, un-circumcised in heart and ears, you always resisted the Holy Spirit. As your fathers did, so do you. Which of the prophets did not your fathers persecute? And they killed those who announced beforehand the coming of the Righteous One, whom you have now betrayed and murdered, you who received the law as deliv-ered by angels and did not keep it. (7:49–52)

This speech is the great final chord of a blast against an obdurate, depraved people; and it reveals a desire for the religious and moral annihilation of Israel.

The Romans, by contrast, appear as the benevolent force that protects Christianity. In the empire the rule of law prevails, and the Romans are continually kept busy trying to save Paul's life from the murderous Jews. In Paphos on Cyprus, the Roman governor is so impressed by the way Paul blinds the magician Bar-Jesus that he lets himself be converted to Christianity (13:12). When the Jews in Greece accuse Paul before Gallio, the governor of Achaia, "This man is persuading men to worship God contrary to law" (18:13), Gallio rejects the charge even before Paul has opened his mouth in self-defense. Gallio sees the whole thing as mere Jewish bickering (18:14–17).

The commandant of Jerusalem, Claudius Lysias (23:29), and later in Caesarea the two governors Felix (24:22) and Festus (24:4, 16, 25; cf. 26:32) reject the proposal to condemn Paul. To make sure that Paul arrives safely in Caesarea and doesn't fall victim to an attack by "more than forty Jews," half of the whole Roman garrison in Jerusalem is mustered out at night. This large band of Jewish assassins have sworn "neither to eat nor drink till they had killed Paul" (23:13f.). So Claudius Lysias assigns "two hundred soldiers with seventy horsemen and two hundred spearmen" to protect Paul from the Jewish conspirators and to bring him into the safe custody of the Roman governor, Felix, in Caesarea (23:23ff.). This is already the third time in only two days that the Romans have saved Paul from the hands of the Jews (cf. 21:32–33 and 23:10).

We have already met the Roman governor Felix (51/52–ca. 62) in connection with the uprising of the Zealots in the chapter on Good Friday.

He is the man whom Tacitus characterized as a "slavish soul" and who, according to Josephus, daily crucified a large number of rebels. Felix, of all people, is described in Acts as having a long conversation with Paul about Christianity:

> After some days Felix came with his wife Drusilla, who was a Jewess; and he sent for Paul and heard him speak upon faith in Christ Jesus. And as he argued about justice and self-control and future judgment, Felix was alarmed and said, "Go away for the present; when I have an opportunity I will summon you.". . . But when two years had elapsed, Felix was succeeded by Porcius Festus; and desiring to do the Jews a favor, Felix left Paul in prison. (24:24-27)

As for the "self-control" that in Paul's eyes the Roman governor was lacking, the situation was this: When her father, Agrippa, suddenly died, eaten up by worms, in 44, Drusilla (A.D. 38-79) was six years old. Her brother Agrippa later married her to King Azizus of Emesa. Josephus tells us how she came to marry the Gentile Felix:

> Not long afterwards Drusilla's marriage to Azizus was dissolved under the following circumstances. At the time when Felix was procurator of Judaea, he beheld her; and, inasmuch as she surpassed all other women in beauty, he conceived a passion for the lady. . . . Felix promised to make her supremely happy [n.b., Felix means "happy" in Latin] if she did not disdain him. She . . . was persuaded to transgress the ancestral laws and to marry Felix. By him she gave birth to a son whom she named Agrippa, and who died with his mother in the eruption of Vesuvius. (JA, XX, vii, 2; LCL, pp. 77, 79)

So it seems that Felix's lack of self-control consisted in his marrying a divorced woman, who had married her first husband at her brother's command. In any event, when Felix's successor, Festus, took office, he found Paul still a prisoner.

The scene with Paul and Festus is a parallel to the Jesus-Pilate scene, only this time Festus is sitting on the judgment seat (25:6) and Paul is the accused. Once again it is the Jews who are demanding the death of the accused, and once again it is the Roman governor who finds no guilt in the man charged with crime.

This all gives rise to the paradoxical circumstance that Paul is continually being found innocent by the Romans but never set free. Acts ends with Paul's living as a prisoner in Rome and preaching "openly and unhindered" (28:31). Like the Gospels before it, Acts does everything to document the good relations of the Christians with the Romans and to shift all the responsibility for Paul's Roman imprisonment (the reasons for which were ultimately no longer understood) onto the Jews. This is exactly what the Gospels had done with the crucifixion of Jesus. Thus the bloodcurdling ballad of Jewish injustice against God's saints, and the hymn praising Roman justice and the correctness of Roman officials, were repeatedly sung and spread throughout the Roman empire.

CHAPTER THIRTEEN

Peter in Rome?

THERE IS A church in Rome, as everyone knows, named after Saint Peter. And, as one may read in every theological lexicon, this church stands over the tomb of Saint Peter. Before St. Peter's was built, there was an earlier St. Peter's on the same spot, erected by the emperor Constantine in the year 320. Even back then it had grown into a mighty structure. Over the centuries there were additions and renovations, but the church nonetheless got so decrepit that in the course of rebuilding from 1506 to 1615 it was torn down. For about two hundred years, work continued on the new structure. Famous artists like Bramante, Raphael, Michelangelo, and Bernini took part in this process; and in the end they created, as Jacob Burckhard phrased it, the greatest "expression of unified power anywhere." The gigantic undertaking was financed by letters of indulgence that redeemed people from "temporal punishment" due to sin and that prompted the appearance of Martin Luther.

The idea that St. Peter's stands over Peter's tomb is important for the pope. It's one more confirmation of papal claims and papal power: Peter in the Vatican and the pope in the Vatican. This shows more than a mere personal closeness; it makes it especially clear that the pope is what he always has said he is: the successor of the apostle Peter. Of course, in some ways the pope is different from Peter. Among other things, Peter had a mother-in-law, and the pope has none. But although this theological distinction is by no means insignificant, the current pope studiously looks past it.

The urgent papal interest in owning or being enthroned over Peter's tomb gives rise, if not suspicion, to at least some questions. Does the pope have any right to invoke the name of the fisherman from the Sea of Galilee? Did Peter stay in Rome, did he die, and was he buried, there? Could it be that all such assertions are merely biased propaganda *ad majorem gloriam*, to the greater glory, of the papal throne? In any event, it's appropriate to investigate these claims.

First let's turn to what the New Testament has to say about Peter's career after the death of Jesus. According to Acts, he first stayed in Jerusalem, making only a brief side trip to Samaria (8:14). Another, likewise not very distant, journey takes him to Lydda (9:32ff.) and Caesarea by the seaside (10:1ff.). Then he returns once more to Jerusalem (11:1ff.). He is arrested by Agrippa I but set free by an "angel of the Lord" (15:1). He takes part in the Apostolic Council (15:1). There ends Acts' report on Peter.

While the events mentioned may all be legendary even in their details, nevertheless a clear general pattern emerges of Jerusalem as Peter's place of residence. It's surprising that Acts, which otherwise takes pains to strike a balance between Peter the supreme apostle and Paul the late apostle, says nothing about Peter's staying or dying in Rome. This despite the fact that the book was written after Peter's death, which, according to the Catholic Church, is supposed to have occurred about 64–67 under Nero, and that Acts is very well informed about Paul's stay in Rome.

We learn from Paul about a journey or a move by Peter to Antioch. "When Cephas came to Antioch . . ." (Gal. 2:11). Apart from this, the New Testament is silent about any places where Peter might have lived.

The advocates of Peter's having lived in Rome cite as proof the First Letter of Peter, which they think was actually written by Peter, and whose next to last verse is, "She [the church] who is at Babylon, who is likewise chosen, sends you greetings; and so does my son Mark" (1 Pet. 5:13). "Babylon" is taken by many theologians to indicate Rome: Jews of this period often used it as a code name for the capital of the empire.

Had Peter used the name Babylon for Rome, he would have thereby shown himself to be an enemy of the state and a conspirator against Rome and the Roman Empire. But the interest of Christians was exactly the opposite. They wanted to advertise their friendship with Rome and to dispel the odor of being a danger to the state. This reputation had clung stubbornly to them because of Jesus' execution by the Roman procurator Pontius Pilate. They were interested in good relations with the Romans and did everything possible to clear themselves of the suspicion of having taken part in the uprisings that led to the Jewish War and to the destruction of Jerusalem in the year 70.

Only for the Jews, but not for the Christians, was Rome the capital city of the enemy. Jews used the code name of Babylon to express both their hostility to the Roman forces occupying their homeland and their hope that God would destroy this center of godlessness as soon as possible.

After the Jewish War, which ended with the conquest and leveling of Jerusalem, and after the mass suicide of almost one thousand Zealots when the Romans stormed the fortress of Masada in the year 73, there were isolated Jewish uprisings against the Romans in the early 2nd century. The very last revolt took place, as already mentioned, from 132 to 135 under Bar Kochba (son of the star), whom some Jews venerated as the Messiah.

On the occasion of this uprising, there were sharp conflicts between Jews and Jewish Christians. Since the Jewish Christians believed the Messiah had already come, they looked upon Bar Kochba as a competitor of Jesus; and they did not join in the struggle against the Romans. "In the persecution of 135 by their own compatriots the last Jewish Christians of whom we know died as martyrs" (Hans Joachim Schoeps, *Das Judenchristen* [1964], p. 33). Around 150 the Christian Justin Martyr wrote: "In the recent Jewish War, Bar Kochba, the leader of the Jewish uprising, ordered that only the Christians should be subject to terrible torments unless they renounced and blasphemed Christ" (1 *Apology*, 31).

The young Church was in the process of spreading through the Roman Empire; and the thought of making Rome the real Christian metropolis made more sense to Christians than the destruction of the city. The First Letter of Peter is not only not stamped with hostility to the Roman state, it even makes propaganda for it: "Be subject for the Lord's sake to every human institution, whether it be to the emperor as supreme, or to governors as sent by him to punish those who do wrong and to praise those who do right. . . . Fear God. Honor the emperor" (1 Pet. 2:13–14). It is unthinkable, therefore, that Peter would label Rome with the hostile name of Babylon. Hence Babylon may not be equated with Rome, and this letter was not written from Rome.

Where was the letter written then? The simplest answer would be, in Babylon. At this time, Babylon in Mesopotamia was a rather large city and had a Jewish colony. One cannot swap the difficult question of how Peter came to be in Babylon for the no less difficult one of how he came to be in Rome—and then explain that it's more likely he went to Rome, even though it's not less likely he came to Babylon.

On the Christian thesis that Peter was in Rome, Voltaire observes: "How bad must things be if to prove that this Peter was in Rome, one must claim that a letter ascribed to him, dated from Babylon, was actually written in Rome. . . . Following this interpretation a letter dated from St. Petersburg must have been written in Constantinople" (Voltaire, "The Luncheon of Count Boulainvilliers" 2).

But there is something else: The so-called First Letter of Peter was not written by Peter at all, but, as Voltaire says, merely ascribed to him. The letter does begin: "Peter, an apostle of Jesus Christ, to the exiles of the Dispersion in Pontus, Galatia, Cappadocia, Asia, and Bithynia . . ." (1 Pet. 1:1). But despite this introduction, many theologians argue that, like the rest of the letter, it was never written by Peter.

We may get a hint as to the fate of Peter from chapter 21 of John's Gospel: "Truly, truly I say to you, when you were young, you girded yourself and walked where you would; but when you are old, you will stretch out your hands, and another will gird you and carry you where you do not wish to go. (This he said to show by what death he was to glorify God)" (John 21:18–19). This chapter is a later addition to the Gospel. One might infer from the passage that Peter died a martyr's death, but not that he died in Rome or that he died in some particular fashion, such as by crucifixion.

As for evidence outside the New Testament, the most important source cited by the proponents of Peter's being in Rome is the First Letter of Clement. Clement was bishop of Rome, thus in present-day Catholic terminology he was the pope. He wrote the letter to the Church in Corinth around 96. But it by no means follows from Clement's letter that Peter was ever in Rome. On the other hand, the *Lexikon für Theologie und Kirche* is absolutely certain that "Clement I (1 Clem. V–VI) [attests to] Peter's death as a martyr in Rome during the persecution by Nero" (VIII, 340).

This is a completely unjustified assertion, because the passage in question says:

> *Through jealousy and envy the greatest and most righteous pillars of the Church were persecuted and contended unto death. Let us set before our eyes the good apostles: Peter, who because of unrighteous jealousy suffered not one or two but many trials, and having thus given his testimony went to the glorious place which was his due. Through jealousy and strife Paul showed the way to the prize of endurance; seven times he was in bonds, he was exiled, he was stoned, he was a herald both in the East and in the West, he gained the noble fame of his faith, he taught righteousness to all the world, and when he had reached the limits of the West he gave testimony before the rulers, and thus passed from the world and was taken up into the Holy Place—the greatest example of endurance.* (The Apostolic Fathers, *trans.* Kirsopp Lake [Cambridge, MA: Harvard Univ. Press (LCL), 1985], I, p. 17)

This text has two striking features: First, Clement characterizes both apostles as victims of "jealousy and envy," evidently meaning intrigues. Here we catch a glimpse of the great partisan conflicts in the early Church. Even back then envy played a large part in human relations. Second, Clement says of Paul merely that he evangelized "in the East and the West," pressing forward to "the limits of the West." This could be understood to mean Rome or (more likely) Spain. But in any event, it's Paul and not Peter to whom the reference concerning "the West" applies. And it is overstraining the text to read into the sentences about Peter anything about a stay in Rome. Instead the fact remains that nowhere, and certainly not in this passage, is there any early evidence that Peter was ever in Rome.

Nor can we infer from Clement's letter that Peter died a martyr. The Greek verb *martyrein* means "to be a witness," "to give testimony." Only from the middle of the 2nd century on was the word used in the sense of "to suffer a martyr's death." In this passage—and in the two other passages of the letter where it occurs (XXXVIII, 2; LCL, p. 75, and LXIII, 1; LCL, p. 81) it means "to bear witness," in the usual sense. With the "many trials" that he had to endure on account of "jealousy and envy," Peter bore witness to Christ. This point is confirmed by the Catholic theologian Peter Stockmeier in *Bibel und Leben,* a journal published by the Catholic Bible Society of Stuttgart. He stresses that "the text does not say that Peter bore witness (*martyrein*) by dying but by suffering trials" ("Die Römische Petrustradition—das Petrusgrab," in *Bibel und Leben,* 2/1978, p. 51).

Anyone wishing to be convinced that *martyrein* is not simply a synonym for "martyrdom" can readily do so by consulting Acts 7:58. Here at the stoning of Stephen, the first Christian martyr, it is not Stephen himself who is designated a "martyr," but the witnesses who put down their clothes before they stone him: "And the witnesses (martyrs) laid down their garments at the feet of a young man named Saul."

The first unmistakable claim that Peter was in Rome does not appear until late, namely, in the letter from Dionysius of Corinth (ca. 170) to the Romans. Eusebius of Caesarea (d. 339) quotes this letter in his *Ecclesiastical History:*

> *And that they were both martyred at the same time Dionysius, bishop of Corinth, affirms in this passage of his correspondence with the Romans: "By so great an admonition you bound together the foundations of the Romans and Corinthians by Peter and Paul, for both of them taught together in our Corinth and were our founders, and together also taught in Italy in the same place and were martyred at the same time." (EH, II, xxv, 2; LCL, I, 183)*

But this passage proves only that around 170 Dionysius of Corinth was convinced that Peter had spent time in Rome and that he died a martyr's death. The letter dates from an age when such a conviction had long been *de rigueur* for reasons of church politics. The bishops of Rome in particular had an interest in styling themselves the successors of Rome's first bishop—Peter.

When we examine the details of Dionysius's account, it turns out to be without historical foundation. In no way were Peter and Paul "our founders" in Rome. In his letter to the Romans, Paul writes that he has "longed for many years to come to you," but has always been hindered from doing so (Rom. 15:22–24). He emphasizes that the faith of the Roman Church has already been "proclaimed in all the world" (Rom. 1:8). In other words, the Christian community in Rome had already been founded before Paul came to visit.

Paul wrote Romans in 54 or 57. But there were Christians in Rome as far back as 49. This is clear from an edict of Emperor Claudius in that year: "Because the Jews at Rome caused continuous disturbances at the instigation of Chrestus [i.e., Christ], he expelled them from the City." This is the account given by Suetonius (born ca. A.D. 70, date of death unknown) in his "Life of Claudius" (25, 4; *The Twelve Caesars*, trans. Robert Graves [Baltimore: Penguin, 1957], p. 197).

At that time—that is, long before Paul was in Rome—there must have been sharp conflicts between Jews and Christians, between old believers and new believers, leading to Claudius's edict of expulsion. In Acts 18:2 we learn about one such Jewish Christian, "a Jew named Aquila, a native of Pontus, lately come from Italy with his wife Priscilla, because Claudius had commanded all the Jews to leave Rome." Paul stayed with them in Corinth.

Dionysius's claim that Peter had founded the Roman Church together with Paul is just as false as his assertion that Paul was its founder. His further claim that Peter had founded the Church in Corinth is likewise untrue, since it had been founded by Paul alone (Acts 18:1–17).

The wishful thinking about Peter's having been in Rome and having founded the Christian community there solidified after 170. Around 190 the Church Father Irenaeus (d. ca. 202) writes: "After the blessed apostles (Peter and Paul) had founded and established the church in Rome, they conferred the episcopacy upon Linus for the administration of the church. . . . He was followed by Anacletus. After him Clement was the third to hold the episcopacy" (*Against the Heresies* III, iii). Thus, according to Irenaeus, the first bishop of Rome was Linus.

Eusebius agrees (*EH*, III, ii; LCL, I, 91; and III, xxi; LCL, II, 241). According to ancient catalogs of the popes, Linus is supposed to have taken office while Peter was still alive, serving as bishop of Rome from 55 to 67 (Heinrich Joseph Wetzer and Benedikt Welte, *Kirchenlexikon*, VIII, 2077). Other ancient church writers also affirm that Linus and not Peter was Rome's first bishop (cf. *Bibliothek der Kirchenväter* [1932], "Eusebius" II, 101).

On the other hand, the learned elder and later antipope Hippolytus (d. 235) claims that Peter was the first bishop of Rome. He says that Pope Victor (ca. 189–98) was "the thirteenth bishop after Peter" (Eusebius, *EH*, V, xxviii; LCL, I, 517). Over the course of time, this tradition has prevailed over the other, which made Linus the first bishop of Rome.

One more legend needs to be mentioned: the story that Peter was crucified in Rome upside down (the latter at his own request). Here we see fantasy playing an even larger role than it does in the traditions about Peter as a whole (where it was already very busy). The legend is to be found in the apocryphal Acts of Peter (composed around 180–90). There Peter says: "I request you, executioners, crucify me head-downwards—in this way and no other. And the reason, I will tell it to those who hear." But once he is hanging upside down on the cross, all that he pronounces is some confused symbolism: "Men whose duty it is to hear, pay attention to what I shall tell you at this very moment that I am hanged up. You must know the mystery of all nature, and the beginning of all things, how it came about . . ." and so forth (37–38; *NTA*, II, 319).

In the Roman Missal (Peter's feast day is 29 June) this strange crucifixion is treated as a historical fact. According to the Acts of Peter, the dead saint was taken down from the cross by a certain Marcellus, bathed in milk and wine, anointed, and buried in Marcellus's own tomb along with a "very costly stone vat with Attic honey." (For these services Marcellus, too, found a place in the Missal, with his feast day on 7 October.) When Nero heard of Peter's death, he flew into a rage because he would have liked to have punished him more severely. But then he saw a vision at night and thereafter left the Christians in peace, for the time being at least (*Acts of Peter* 38–41; *NTA*, II, 318–20).

Thus John Paul II is certain that Peter was in Rome, that he founded the Christian community there, was the first bishop of Rome, and suffered martyrdom in Rome; and as bishop of Rome, John Paul II is Peter's successor. Thus a legend has come to its logical conclusion.

Alongside the Peter-Rome tradition there was also a completely different Petrine tradition that had nothing to do with Rome. We learn this, too, from Eusebius's *Ecclesiastical History,* where the author calls Ignatius of Antioch (d. ca. 110) the "second after Peter to succeed to the bishopric of Antioch" (III, xxxvi; LCL, I, 281). The first successor was named Evodius. According to Origen, too (*Hom. VI in Lucam*), and Jerome (*De vir. ill.* 16), Peter was the first bishop of Antioch. Nowhere is there any report that at some point he gave up this bishopric. No one would ever have maintained that Peter went to Rome and died there except for the bias in favor of Rome's claims of power and the Roman papal succession. Hence, the alternative story, that Peter had a bishopric, and a permanent one at that, in Antioch has at least as much credibility as the first.

As for the archaeological findings, Peter Stockmeier has it right when he says: "We can say a priori that even the [archaeologist's] spade was unable to close the gap of uncertainty that, as far as written tradition goes, had always existed about Peter's death. (As is well known, the Acts of the Apostles is silent on the subject.) Owing to the state of the sources the Roman Petrine tradition still lies in a dubious light. However much interpreters may have made up their minds on the subject, the obscurity has yet to be cleared up" (Stockmeier, "Die Römische Petrustradition," p. 51).

Not until relatively late do we find any statements about Peter having a tomb in Rome; and shortly after that, we hear of his tomb being elsewhere in the city. So the tradition was split almost from the outset. The first witness to a tomb of Peter comes from a certain Gaius, who was active in the Roman Christian community around the year 200. At the time, not only Rome, but various other cities in the empire as well, engaged in disputes over the possession of tombs of the apostles. Each side wanted the graves in order to prove the correctness of its religious views and the importance of its own community.

Thus Gaius got into an argument with Proklos, the leader of a prophetic Christian sect known as the Montanists. To prove that the Montanist teaching was right, Proklos cited the existence in Hierapolis (evidently a center of Montanism) of the tombs of the apostle Philip and his daughters. Gaius fought back with the heavy artillery of the tombs of Peter and Paul in Rome: "But I can point out the trophies of the Apostles, for if you will go to the Vatican or to the Ostian Way you will find the trophies of those who founded the Church" (Eusebius, *EH*, II, xxv; LCL, I, 183).

By invoking the tombs, Gaius thought he had checkmated his opponent, because the question of who's right is decided by whose tomb you are sitting on. Actually, this mode of argument doesn't convince everyone, but it was popular back then. Like Gaius and Proklos citing the tombs of the apostles, Bishop Polycrates of Ephesus backed up his position on the proper date for Easter by pointing out that the grave of the apostle Philip was in Hierapolis: "Therefore we keep the day undeviatingly, neither adding nor taking away, for in Asia great luminaries sleep. . . . Such were Philip of the twelve apostles, and two of his daughters who grew old as virgins, who sleep in Hierapolis, and another daughter of his, who lived in the Holy Spirit, [and who] rests at Ephesus" (Eusebius, *EH*, V, xxiv; LCL, I, 505). The dispute over the date of Easter revolved around the question of whether Easter should always be celebrated on a Sunday or on the 14th day of the month of Passover (Nisan), regardless of what day of the week it fell on.

Thus around 200 Gaius knew about a tomb of Peter on the highway to Ostia on the Vatican. But it's clear from a Roman festive calendar from 354 that back around the year 260 people were convinced that the tombs of Peter and Paul lay on the Via Appia underneath the later Sepulchre-Basilica of San Sebastiano. Confronting these two tombs of Saint Peter, Catholic church historian Hubert Jedin notes in resignation:

> *Ultimately there are no reliable data about the way Peter was executed and buried. So the possibilities that we have (burning of the body after execution, mutilation of the corpse, interment in a mass grave, refusal to surrender the body to the Christians) continue to remain so many open questions. These difficulties taken together have thus far not been satisfactorily resolved. Hence they make it impossible, for the present, to accept the idea that the*

excavations have positively brought to light Peter's tomb or its
original site. . . . Despite all the hypotheses the site of the cult of
the apostles on the Via Appia remains the great unsolved puzzle.
(History of the Church *[1963]*, I, *140*)

Peter Stockmeier speaks of the "cult of Peter in Rome, which is split between San Sebastiano and the Vatican. . . . The uncertainty gets even worse when we reflect that there is no information whatsoever about how Peter was buried (individual tomb, mass grave, or cremation)" (Stockmeier, "Die Römische Petrustradition," pp. 54–55).

Relics of Saint Peter, however, are widely available. Saint Ambrose (d. 397), a Father of the Church, is supposed to have been a busy collector of such relics. Peter's head is kept, along with Paul's, in the papal altar of St. John Lateran. Numerous other smaller body parts are scattered all over Italy (cf. *LThK*, VIII, 342). A few of Peter's possessions have, amazingly, been preserved as well. First there are the two chains that are stored in a Roman church named Ad Vincula Petri (at Peter's chains). The first chain comes from the imprisonment (mentioned in Acts 12:1–17) under Herod Agrippa I, from which Peter was freed by an angel. There is no word on who made off with the chain, the angel or Peter. At first it dropped out of sight, but Eudoxia, the wife of Emperor Theodosius the Great, miraculously tracked it down and brought it to Rome around 437. The second chain comes from Peter's imprisonment under Nero in Rome, where it was preserved and venerated from the very beginning. In honor of these chains, people built churches in Rome and Constantinople, and every year on 1 August the Church still celebrates the feast of Saint Peter in Chains. Beyond that, there is a table of Saint Peter, at which he said mass when he came to Rome. The owner of the table and the house it was located in belonged to a senator named Pudens. This individual had received Peter into his house and had gotten himself and his family baptized by Peter. On the site where Pudens's house once stood there now stands the church of St. Pudenziana, named after him. The table, or at least a part of it, is in the church. The other part is enclosed in the high altar of St. John Lateran (Wetzer and Welte, *Kirchenlexicon* [1895], IX, 1854–55, 1865).

We also have the chair of the apostle, kept, as is only proper, in St. Peter's itself. A church in Venice, San Pietro a Castello, has a second chair of Saint Peter, which comes from the time when Peter was still bishop of Antioch. Then there is a staff of Saint Peter, about which there are various stories in circulation. According to one of them, Peter gave this walking stick to Eucharius, who then used it to bring the dead Saint Maternus back to life. Maternus later took the staff to Trier, whence it came to the local cathedral upon the founding of the diocese of Limburg. But a piece of it and the head are in the treasury of the Cathedral of Cologne (*LThK*, VIII, 342).

CHAPTER FOURTEEN

The Apocrypha

THE NEW TESTAMENT didn't fall from heaven as a finished book. For centuries, battles were fought over which texts should be part of it and which not. There were many Gospels, stories about the apostles and letters by them, and apocalypses in circulation. The ones chosen to be "Scripture" were selected because in the eyes of the Church back then, they had a binding character. These writings make up the contents, the so-called canon ("guideline" or "norm"), of the New Testament.

This canon was slow to develop. Around the year 200 it took on fairly firm shape, but it did not yet contain the twenty-seven "books" in today's New Testament. On the other hand, it did contain a series of texts that were later eliminated as "apocryphal." In the year 367 all twenty-seven books of the New Testament were officially listed in the Thirty-ninth Easter Letter of Bishop Athanasius of Alexandria, "Since . . . some guileless persons may be led astray from their purity and holiness by the craftiness of certain men and begin thereafter to pay attention to other books, the so-called apocryphal writings, being deceived by their possession of the same names as the genuine books . . ." (NTA, I, p. 59).

Some books of the New Testament, however, did not win general recognition until the 5th or 6th century. These were the seven "Catholic" (meant for the general public) Epistles (the Letter of James, the two

Letters of Peter, the three Letters of John, and the Letter of Jude), along with the Letter to the Hebrews. As late as the 10th century, the Revelation of John was still not accepted everywhere.

The opposite of the canonical Scriptures are the so-called Apocrypha. The latter were not accepted into the canon, although some of them had stood side by side enjoying equal status with the texts that were later canonized. The word *apocryphal* means "kept hidden," but it soon came to sound like inauthentic and false. Despite this opposition between genuine and false Scriptures, the Church has drawn many a stimulus for its faith and teachings from the Apocrypha; and it has used passages from the Apocrypha when they seemed useful for bolstering its doctrinal position.

The Apocrypha are divided, according to their content, into Gospels, Apostolic Letters, and Apocalypses. There are three different types of Gospels, but they cannot be sharply distinguished. First, there are Gospels related to our four Gospels, especially to the Synoptics. Some of these were composed independently of the canonical Gospels; some were modeled after them. Second, there is the group of Gnostic Gospels, from Gnosticism (*gnosis* meaning "knowledge"), a pessimistic, world-denying, and often antisexual religious movement. Shortly before the beginning of the Christian era, Gnosticism made its way into the West from the East (probably from Persia) and proved to be the most dangerous competitor that Christianity had to face. Third, there are so-called legend Gospels, in which events from Jesus' life are simply spun out with free-ranging fantasy. These are often not mere legends: They reveal a clear Gnostic bias. They are hostile to the body and they glorify virginity, and so the line separating them from the second group is hazy. These legendary Gospels have played a crucial role in the formation of Catholic piety.

Also part of this third group are the so-called infancy Gospels, presenting details from Jesus' childhood years. The best known of these is the already mentioned *Protevangelium of James,* composed around 150. The author calls himself James and wants to create the impression that he is the Lord's brother. This apocryphal Gospel has played a major role in the Church's teaching, in Christian piety, and, above all, in art. What Protestant theologian Oscar Cullmann says about the infancy Gospels in general is particularly true of this one: "In Antiquity, in the Middle Ages, and in the Renaissance these texts had a greater influence on literature and art than the Bible did" (Wilhelm Schneemelcher, *Neutestamentliche Apokryphen* [1990], I, 333).

"James" recounts the miraculous birth of Mary, and in the process we learn the hitherto unknown names of Mary's parents, Joachim and Anne. Again, one of the characteristics of legend formation is that unknown persons are supplied with names. We then read about Mary's life as a Temple virgin, which includes the historically false but poetically fine touch: "And he [the priest] placed her on the third step of the altar, and the Lord God put grace upon the child, and she danced for joy with her feet, *and the whole house of Israel loved her*" (7:3; *NTA*, I, 378).

"And Mary was in the temple nurtured like a dove and received food from the hand of an angel" (8:1; *NTA*, I). There isn't a single theologian in the world who believes that this notion of Mary as a Temple virgin has any historical basis. Nevertheless, to this day, we have the feast of the "Presentation of the Blessed Virgin Mary" (21 November), which Pope Sixtus V ordered the whole Church to celebrate in 1585. The *Protevangelium* goes on to describe Mary's marriage with Joseph. Special attention is given to her biological virginity, undamaged by the birth of Jesus.

The discovery of Mary's intact hymen at this point is not exactly distinguished by discretion. One might note instead traces of a theological pornography, as sexual fantasies unfold under the mantle of piety. The text is as follows:

> *And the midwife came out of the cave, and Salome met her. And she said to her: "Salome, Salome, I have a new sight to tell you; a virgin has brought forth, a thing which her nature does not allow." And Salome said: "As the Lord my God lives, unless I put (forward) my finger and test her condition, I will not believe that a virgin has brought forth." And Salome went in and made ready to test her condition. And she cried out saying: "I have tempted the living God; and behold, my hand falls away, consumed by fire!" And she prayed to the Lord. And behold, an angel of the Lord stood before Salome and said to her: "The Lord God has heard your prayer. Come near, touch the child, and you will*

be healed." And she did so. And Salome was healed as she had re-
quested, and she went out of the cave. (19:3-20:4; NTA, I, 384-85)

We have the *Protevangelium of James* to thank for more than just the cave or grotto where Jesus was born (Luke speaks only of a manger, presumably in a stable). James has also given us the midwife's guarantee that Mary's hymen remained intact during the birth of Jesus. This *virginitas in partu* (virginity during birth) is the middle section of Mary's tripartite and total virginity prescribed by the Catholic Church as an article of faith.

But we are most indebted to the *Protevangelium of James* for its answer to the question, What to do with Jesus' brothers? The image of a virginal conception, so widespread in the ancient world, is also found in Matthew and Luke and is no more to be taken literally than the creation of Adam, related in Genesis, from a clod of earth. It originally had nothing to do with the later Catholic virginity-mania and hostility to sex. It was instead an image of God's creative activity in making Jesus—the second man, as Paul calls him (1 Corinthians 15)—just as God's forming man from the dust was an image of his creative activity in making Adam, the first man.

Thus the New Testament image of virginal conception is not a symbol of Mary's sexual intactness. It does not emphasize or glorify her virginity, but harmonizes perfectly well with the brothers and sisters of Jesus (mentioned in Matthew 13 and Mark 6) that Mary and Joseph had after Jesus. There are four brothers cited by name: Jacob, Joses, Simon, and Judas. Jesus also had "sisters" (hence, at least two), whose names aren't given and, therefore, a total of at least six younger siblings.

The narratives of the virgin birth in pagan antiquity and the two in Matthew and Luke are not about the chastity of the mother but the splendor of the son. They aim to glorify the son, not the virginity of his mother.

For example, Speusippus, a nephew of Plato (d. 348/347 B.C.), reports that there was a widely believed story in Athens that Plato was a son of Apollo. Up until Plato's birth, his father, Ariston, had abstained from sexual relations with his wife, Perictione (Diogenes Laertius III, i, 2). Just as with Ariston, we learn that Joseph "knew her [Mary] not until she had borne a son" (Matt. 1:25). Just as Plato later got siblings (e.g., Glaucon,

Adeimantus, and the mother of Speusippus), so did Jesus, according to the same Gospel of Matthew that reports his virgin birth (13:35).

But under the influence that Gnostic hatred of sex had on early Christianity, the so-called "virginity before birth" (*virginitas ante partum*) was misunderstood as the inauguration of a lifetime as a virgin. Everything that has to do with normal children and the normal way of getting them was now kept far from Mary. Her whole personal world was cleansed of human progeny, because children always point to sexuality. Among the pagans, by contrast, a later real and normal childbearing career, as we see with Plato's siblings, was never impaired by the image of the virgin birth. But because of Christianity's neurotic hostility to sex, this image of the supernatural was taken as grounds for outlawing the real and the natural. Jesus' brothers and sisters were felt to be disturbing and quite literally problem children. As stains on their mother's virginity, they had no right to live. They had to be theologically aborted.

The *Protevangelium of James* tries to answer this question of Mary's postpartum virginity, the third and last part of her total virginity. That is, it grapples with the question of Jesus' brothers and sisters so as to satisfy the antisexual and provirginity believers. The solution is to make Joseph a widower who brought the children from his first marriage along with him:

> When she [Mary] was twelve years old, there took place a council of the priests, saying: "Behold, Mary has become twelve years old in the temple of the Lord. What then shall we do with her, that she may not pollute the temple of the Lord?" [through menstruation]. And they said to the high priest: "You stand at the altar of the Lord; enter (the sanctuary) and pray concerning her, and what the Lord shall reveal to you we will do." And the high priest took the vestment with the twelve bells and went into the Holy of Holies and prayed concerning her. And behold, an angel of the Lord (suddenly) stood before him and said to him: "Zacharias, Zacharias, go out and assemble the widowers of the people ... and to whomsoever the Lord shall give a (miraculous) sign, his wife shall she be." And the heralds went forth and spread out through all the country round about Judaea; the trumpet of the

*Lord had sounded, and all ran to it. . . . And the priest said to
Joseph: "Joseph, to you has fallen the good fortune to receive the
virgin of the Lord; take her under your care." (But) Joseph answered him: "I (already) have sons and am old, but she is a girl. I
fear lest I should become a laughing-stock to the children of Israel." And the priest said to Joseph: "Fear the Lord thy God, and
remember all that God did to Dathan, Abiram and Korah, how
the earth was rent open and they were all swallowed up because
of their rebellion. And now fear, Joseph, lest this happen (also) in
your house." And Joseph was afraid and took her under his care.
(8:2-9:5; NTA, I, 378-79)*

Cowed by the threat of this curse, therefore, Joseph was ready for
marriage with Mary. The painters who depict Joseph as an old man in
contrast to the youthful Mary are relying on this legend. A gray-haired
Joseph is a narrative device to avoid having Mary's virginity endangered
by the impetuosity of Joseph's youth.

In the period that followed, however, the *Protevangelium*'s pious
attempt to interpret Jesus' siblings as stepbrothers and stepsisters proved
to be insufficiently pious. Ultimately, the stepsiblings were destined to be
banished both from Mary's house and from the doctrinal edifice of
Catholicism. The man who took charge of driving out Mary's—or only
Joseph's—children was a Father of the Church, Saint Jerome (d. 419/20).
Jerome objected to the *Protevangelium*. As he explains, it is a "godless
and apocryphal daydream" to believe that Joseph had children from an
earlier marriage: Joseph had to be a virgin to match the virgin Mary (*Ad
Matth.* 12).

Jerome dispatches not only the stepsiblings but, above all, the root
cause of the annoyance they caused: the brothers and sisters mentioned in
the New Testament. He does this by inventing the cousins of Jesus, who to
this day still flit about in Catholic commentaries. Jerome, it develops, was
having a violent altercation with a layman named Helvidius, because the
latter, following Mark 6 and Matthew 13, maintained that Jesus had had
brothers and sisters. Thus Helvidius was challenging Mary's postpartum
virginity.

196 PUTTING AWAY CHILDISH THINGS

In 383 Jerome wrote a piece entitled "Against Helvidius, or the Perpetual Virginity of Mary." The reasons adduced against Helvidius are more or less the same that Catholic theologians advance even today when anyone raises the issue of Jesus' brothers and sisters. The person of Mary clearly demonstrates the moral superiority of virginity.

As a matter of fact, the situation wasn't as Jerome and his fellow bachelor theologians, up to and including John Paul II, had imagined: Virginity wasn't prized because Mary was a virgin; Mary was made a perpetual virgin because virginity was idolized.

The legend of the virgin birth, which began in the New Testament for the purpose of glorifying Jesus, after the manner of a Hellenistic legend about a son of god, logically culminates in a pair of phantom Christian celibates: Joseph loses all his children, and Mary holds onto only one of hers. "You assert that Mary did not remain a virgin, but I go still further and assert that Joseph lived as a virgin" (*Against Helvidius,* 19).

In order to send the brothers and sisters of Jesus to the devil once and for all, the *Protevangelium of James* was cited (thanks to Jerome's strictures) by a famous papal document, the *Decretum Gelasianum.* Part of this decree goes all the way back to Damasus (366–88), who was pope in the time of Jerome. The *Protevangelium* now appears in the catalog of books that must be rejected. At the end of its list of heretical books, the decree says: "This and that which is similar to it . . . we declare not only to be repudiated but to be excluded by the whole Roman Catholic Church, and with its authors and supporters of its authors to be condemned to the unbreakable fetters of anathema for all eternity."

In the meantime, the center of the legend of the virgin birth is no longer the son but the virgin. Siblings wouldn't have done Jesus any damage. They wouldn't have detracted from his divinity. Instead, with the beautiful image of Jesus as a brother with brothers and sisters, they would have underscored the humanity he shared with them, illustrating rather than obscuring the truth that Jesus was everyone's brother. But because of the supposed perpetual virginity of his mother, Jesus was not allowed to have siblings. On this point he had to bow to the dictates of Mariology.

Thus ever since Jerome's day, Catholic commentators have taken care of the problem of Jesus' "condemned" brothers and sisters by degrading them to more distant relatives. This is done, for instance, with the argument that "in Semitically influenced texts [sic] the word [brother] is readily used to mean more distant relatives" (J. Blinzler, LThK, II, 715). It's remarkable, though, that the New Testament otherwise can distinguish quite well between brothers and relatives: When Jesus' parents can't find their missing twelve-year-old, who has remained behind in Jerusalem, they look for him among "kinsfolk" and not "brothers" (Luke 2:44). Jesus makes the same distinction: "When you give a dinner or a banquet, do not invite your friends or your brothers or your kinsmen" (Luke 14:12). Likewise, in Luke 21:16, Jesus distinguishes between "brothers and kinsmen."

But Jesus' brothers and sisters are caught up in a hopeless struggle to survive. Catholic theologians will always claim that brothers can also be kinsmen; they will never concede that brothers just might be brothers and sisters, sisters.

Jerome was scandalized by another detail of the *Protevangelium:* the two midwives. In his piece against Helvidius he writes: "There were no midwives there, nor was there any business for any other women. She [Mary] herself wrapped the child in swaddling clothes. She herself was both mother and midwife. 'And she laid him,' it says, 'in a manger, because there was no room for him in the inn' [Luke 2:7]. This passage refutes the fantasies of the Aprocrypha, since Mary personally wrapped the child in swaddling clothes" (*Against Helvidius,* 8).

The reason why the midwives were superfluous at Jesus' birth is that Mary had no labor pains and so managed perfectly well without a midwife. For the pain of giving birth and everything connected with it—his is the opinion of many Catholic theologians to this day—are God's curse and punishment for the Fall. "I will greatly multiply your pain in childbearing," he tells Eve, "in pain you shall bring forth children" (Gen. 3:16).

Jerome thought exactly like his contemporary Augustine on this point: Mary conceived Jesus virginally, without having to be ashamed of any sexual pleasure, and so she gave birth without pain (*Enchiridion* 34). Augustine throws in a snappy little rhyme here (a sort of ad for painless do-it-yourself birthing): "With no shame [*sine pudore*] in her conceiving, / Mary's childbirth brought no grieving [*(cum) dolore*]" (*In serm. De nativit.*). Unfortunately, other women can't take advantage of this method because Mary is the only exception to the rule that conception means shame.

Thomas Aquinas, who is even now the chief custodian of Catholic antisexuality, repeats this Augustinian couplet, and then for his part takes exception to the "misrepresentation" of the apocryphal *Protevangelium*, which Jerome has already and quite rightly attacked. Like Jerome, Aquinas points to Luke's Christmas narrative, where Mary herself wraps her child in swaddling clothes (*S.Th.* III q. 35 a. 6).

According to this bachelors' theology—the one thing here that really has no shame—it's only the other mothers who are stuck with God's curse and the need for help from midwives. Incidentally, the pagans already had the absurd (male) notion that a painless delivery proved the great merits of the newborn (boy). Plutarch reports that when Cicero was born, "his mother was delivered without pain or labor" (*Lives*, p. 1041).

Along with the *Protevangelium of James* there is another important infancy Gospel—the Gospel of Thomas ("The Account of Thomas the Israelite Philosopher Concerning the Childhood of the Lord"). This was presumably composed about the second half of the 2nd century. It was popular in the early Church and found a broad audience. This Gospel aims to present the child Jesus as a sort of Superboy. But the miracles he does often leave the reader uneasy: "After this again he went through the village, and a lad ran and knocked against his shoulder. Jesus was exasperated and said to him: 'You shall not go further on your way,' and the child immediately fell down and died' (4:1; *NTA*, I, 393).

After a few more such tales of homicide in this Gospel, Joseph finds himself at his wit's end and begs Mary, "Do not let him go outside the door, for all those who provoke him die" (14:3; *NTA*, I, 397). Alongside these we also find stories about Jesus' raising the dead. But they hardly weaken the impression of Jesus as a dangerous little monster.

In the period that followed, the natural law of legend proliferation took effect, and the two older infancy Gospels (of James and Thomas) were expanded. At the same time they were stripped of any offensive material (*NTA*, I, 404). The most significant of these later compositions is the Arabic infancy narrative with miracles performed by the child Jesus.

Thanks to this Gospel, legends of Jesus' infancy became known to Muslims. Muhammad even incorporated a few of them into the Qur'an.

The influence of this apocryphal Arabic infancy Gospel on Islam can be seen, for instance, in the greeting from the embassy of the Islamic Republic of Iran in Bonn on 4 January 1980:

> *Response of the Imam Khomeini, December 12, 1979. . . . In the name of the compassionate and merciful God, I congratulate all oppressed nations of the world, the Christian nations and my Christian fellow-citizens on the birthday of Christ. Everything that has to do with Jesus was a miracle. It was a miracle that he was born of a virgin. It was a miracle that he could speak in the cradle. It was a miracle that he brought . . . peace to humanity.*

Here Khomeini is referring to Sura 3:41, where the angel of the annunciation says to Mary: "And he will speak with men in the cradle," and to Sura 19:31, where the child Jesus delivers a brief address, beginning with the words "Behold, I am Allah's servant."

Most Catholics are unaware of the fact that as a result of the influence the Christian Apocrypha had on the Qur'an, the Virgin Mary plays a not insignificant role in it, and that, according to the Qur'an, Maria conceived virginally. Luke's annunciation scene appears in full detail in the Qur'an. This is Sura 3:42: "She [Mary] spoke [to the angel]: 'My lord, how should I have a son, when no man has touched me?' He said: 'Thus Allah does what he wills; if he has resolved on a thing, he merely says to it: "BE!" and it is.'" In Sura 3:52, the angel further tells Mary: "Behold, before Allah Jesus is equal to Adam. He created him out of the earth, and when he said to him, 'Be!' he was" (cf. also Sura 19:16ff.).

The Qur'an, by the way, clearly and correctly expresses what Luke meant—namely, that this is a creative action by God and not a sexual relationship between God and a woman. These parallels to the annunciation in the Qur'an are also one more clue that divine sonship and virgin birth are not inseparably linked, since despite his birth from a virgin, Jesus is not considered by Muslims to be the Son of God.

And so the vision of Mary's virginity in the Apocrypha has traveled a long distance, all the way to the Qur'an and to Pope John Paul's fixation on virginity. Apart from that, we are indebted to the fantasy of the Apocrypha for many details of the modern-day Christmas idyll. Anyone who approaches the life-size crèches one sees inside or outside churches, or who puts up a smaller crèche beneath the family Christmas tree, is entering an apocryphal fairyland.

In the Armenian infancy Gospel, the Magi have become three kings, two of whom are brothers (although this latter notion has dropped out of the Catholic book of fairy-tale images). Gaspar (Caspar) rules over Arabia, Melqon (Melchior) over Persia, and Balthasar over India (*NTA*, I, 405).

From the Gospel of Pseudo-Matthew, another infancy Gospel, which was written in the West around the 8th or 9th century, the ox and ass at the manger have trotted all the way to the modern world. Pseudo-Matthew combines the birth cave of the *Protevangelium of James* and the stable with the manger from Luke: "On the third day after the birth of our Lord Jesus Christ holy Mary went out from the cave, and went into a stable and put her child in a manger, and an ox and an ass worshipped him" (14:1; *NTA*, I, 410).

This work, however, contains an unchaste touch: Despite the previously mentioned papal condemnation of his first marriage, Joseph is still presented as a widower, and he still has the children from his first marriage, Jesus' stepsiblings, whom Jerome fought against so vigorously. The text therefore had to be purified; then it was renamed the "Story of the Birth of Mary." Finally, in 1298, it was incorporated by Archbishop Jacobus de Varagine into his *Golden Legend*, which became a world-famous book of edification and likewise made the "Birth of Mary" famous.

The core of the imaginative embellishments in the apocryphal Gospels is not merely Jesus' birth but his Passion as well. The latter is described by the Acts of Pilate, which was composed in the 5th century, but with some parts going back to the 2nd century. Ever since that time, it has also been called the Gospel of Nicodemus. As the name suggests, Pilate plays a special role in the story. In keeping with Christian bias, he is further relieved of any responsibility in Jesus' death. Conversely, the same bias continues to lay the burden of guilt on the Jews. So close an understanding has developed between Pilate and Jesus here that Pilate asks advice from Jesus on the matter of his sentence.

Jesus wants to be executed on account of the Old Testament prophecies. The text says literally: "Then the governor commanded the Jews to go out from the praetorium, and he called Jesus to him and said to him: 'What shall I do with you?' Jesus answered Pilate: 'As it was given to you.' Pilate said: 'How was it given?' Jesus said: 'Moses and the prophets foretold my death and resurrection'" (4:3; *NTA*, I, 455). In the Acts of Pilate, we also learn the names of the robbers who were crucified with Jesus: Dysmas and Gestas. Dysmas is the one who converted (9:4–5; *NTA*, I, 458).

Included in the Acts of Pilate is the Paradosis Pilati (Tradition of Pilate). In it Pilate is accused by Emperor Tiberius on account of the execution of Jesus (who in the meantime has come to be seen as a just man even in the eyes of the emperor). Pilate explains that he let Jesus be crucified "because of the unlawful insubordination of the lawless and godless Jews." "Filled with anger," Tiberius thereupon orders Licianus, "chief governor of the East," to make the Jews slaves and prisoners of war, to hound them out of Judea and scatter them among all nations. This is because they "committed a lawless crime in forcing Pilate to crucify Jesus who was acknowledged as God. . . . Licianus carried out [the] terrible instructions and destroyed the whole Jewish nation, and those who were left in Judea he scattered as slaves among the nations." (Note: Here we find the catastrophe of the Jewish War and the downfall of the Jewish state in A.D. 70 in their Christian interpretation as God's punishment of the deicide.)

The emperor condemns Pilate to death by the sword. Before the execution, Pilate prays a Christian—that is, anti-Jewish—prayer: "Lord, do not destroy me with the wicked Hebrews, for it was through the lawless nation of the Jews that I raised my hand against you." After the prefect has cut off Pilate's head, "an angel of the Lord received it. And when Procla his wife saw the angel coming and receiving his head, she was filled with joy, and immediately gave up the ghost, and was buried with her husband" (*NTA*, I, 483–84).

In the Acts of Pilate (Gospel of Nicodemus) we also learn something about Joseph, the rich man from Arimathea (a town in the hill country of Ephraim), who the Gospels say took the body of Jesus down from the cross and buried it. The Jews, it seems, had requited his good deed by locking him in prison, a "house with no windows." But Jesus entered the prison in person, kissed him, and set him free:

> And at midnight as I stood up and prayed, the house where you shut me in was raised up by the four corners, and I saw as it were a lightning flash in my eyes. Full of fear I fell to the ground. And someone took me by the hand and raised me up from the place where I had fallen, and something moist like water flowed from my head to my feet, and the smell of fragrant oil reached my nostrils. And he wiped my face and kissed me and said to me: Do not fear, Joseph. . . . I looked up and saw Jesus. (15:6; NTA, I, 466)

Joseph of Arimathea is venerated as a martyr; his feast is on 17 March (along with Saint Patrick).

According to later legends, Joseph of Arimathea stood under the cross and gathered in a cup drops of blood from Jesus' wounds. He took this cup (which later became the Holy Grail) with him to England, where he was sent by the apostle Philip in the year 63. In England Joseph founded a city named Glastonbury. Later, the Grail got lost in England, and the Knights of the Round Table searched for it in vain. In the 19th century, Joseph's relics were taken to Italy; one of his arms is to be found today in St. Peter's (Heinrich Joseph Wetzer and Benedikt Welte, *Kirchenlexikon* VI, 1865).

Mary Magdalen plays a special role in the Apocrypha. Of course, she has some importance in the New Testament as well, since she is one of the women who accompany Jesus and support Jesus and his group "out of their means" (Luke 8:2). Anyone who has money and supports other people with it always has a say in things. Mary is also important in the New Testament as a witness to the Resurrection (Mark 10; Matthew 28; Luke 24; John 20). But the total domination by men that soon swept over the Church quickly put an end to the initially equal rights of Christian women.

Thus early on in the Catholic Church, women were no longer permitted to teach (as they originally did) and were absolutely barred from any position with power over a man. Instead they had to concentrate their energies on childbearing, as the forged Letter to Timothy says (1 Tim.

2:12ff.). (On the subject of forgeries, see the next chapter.) By contrast, several Gnostic Gospels speak a different language on this subject.

In the Gospel of Mary (Magdalen), composed in the 2nd century, Mary Magdalen comforts the disciples after Jesus' departure and shares with them revelations that she has gotten from Jesus. But she runs into unbelief and mistrust. Peter says: "Did he then [the Savior] speak privily with a woman rather than with us, and not openly? . . . Has he preferred her over against us?" Another disciple named Levi intervenes on behalf of Mary Magdalen: "If the Savior hath made her worthy, who then art thou, that thou reject her? Certainly the Savior knows her surely enough. Therefore did he love her more than us" (*NTA*, I, 343).

In 1945 (two years before the discovery of the Dead Sea Scrolls at Qumran) the number of the Apocrypha was increased by a sensational find at Nag Hammadi in Egypt. It was a Gnostic library that included Gospels in which Mary Magdalen frequently appears, for example, in the 2nd-century Gospel of Philip: "Reference is made to the 'three holy women' who walked continually with the Lord: his mother Mary and her sister . . . and Magdalene, whom men called his companion" (32b; *NTA*, I, 277). According to this text, Jesus is evidently not a Lord completely surrounded by "brothers," as it sometimes seems in the New Testament. Further on it says, "The Redeemer loved Mary Magdalen more than all the disciples, and he often kissed her on her mouth" (55b; Schneemelcher, *Neutestamentliche Apokryphen*, p. 161).

These kisses are not to be understood in the erotic sense; rather, they are analogous to the "holy kiss" often mentioned by Paul (Rom. 16:16, etc.). In any case, all sorts of conflicts arise with the brothers. The text of the Gospel of Philip goes on to say: "The other disciples came to her and reproached her. They said to him: 'Why do you love her more than us all?' The Savior answered and said to them: 'Why do I not love you as much as her?'" In the Coptic Gospel of Thomas, also found in Nag Hammadi, from the middle of the 2nd century (and some parts as early as the 1st century), Peter voices his displeasure: "Let Mary go out from among us, because women are not worthy of the Life" (114; *NTA*, I, 343).

The answer, though, that Jesus gives Peter is not satisfying and testifies to another kind of misogyny: "Behold, I shall lead her, that I may make her male, in order that she also may become a living spirit like you males" (logion 114, *NTA*, I, 522). While Christianity quickly turned hostile to both women and sexuality, these Gnostic circles were evidently only antisexual. They did not share the views of the male-dominated Christian Church on leadership positions for women.

The notion that women in a ideal state must become men was not unusual. Jerome, for example, says: "As long as a woman lives for birth and children, there exists the same difference between her and a man as between body and soul. But if she wishes to serve Christ more than the world, she will cease to be a woman and will be called 'man,' because we wish her to be elevated to the perfect man" (*Commentary on Ephesians*, 5). In a similar vein, Saint Ambrose (d. 397) writes about Mary Magdalen: "Jesus says to her: 'Woman.' She who does not believe is a woman, and she is still addressed with the term that refers to her bodily gender. For the woman who believes becomes the perfect man" (*Corpus Scriptorum Ecclesiasticorum Latinorum* 23, 3, 514). And Thomas Aquinas, that pillar of the Church and of antisexuality (d. 1274), concurs with this therapy of masculinization for women. "By taking the vow of virginity or of widowhood and becoming betrothed to Christ, they are elevated to the dignity of a man [*promoventur in dignitatem virilem*]" (1 Cor. cap. 11, lectio 2).

Contemporary feminist theologians were initially satisfied with the stronger position of women in the Gnostic Gospels, but lately their enthusiasm has cooled off. More recent discussion has taken on a "more sober" tone, as Protestant theologian Luise Schottroff says, because "in the same texts alongside features of Gnostic tradition that do justice to women we find an even stronger set of statements full of contempt for women." This raises the question "whether the dualistic overall framework of Gnostic thinking . . . , with its hatred of the body, might not be assigning to women a role that alienates them from themselves, despite the strong role of women as bearers of revelation" (in *Wörterbuch der feministischen Theologie* [1991], pp. 157–58).

Among the apocryphal Acts of the Twelve Apostles we have already mentioned the Acts of Peter (composed ca. A.D. 180–90) with their description of Peter's crucifixion. The apocryphal Acts of Paul (ca. A.D. 185–95) report Paul's legendary death by decapitation. This takes place on orders from Nero, to whom Paul had already prophesied, "And if thou behead me, this will I do: I will arise and appear to thee (in proof) that I am not dead, but alive to my Lord Christ Jesus." And that's just what happens. When he is beheaded, milk and not blood "spurted upon the soldier's clothing." And after his death Paul makes good on this threat. He comes before Nero and tells him, " 'Caesar, here I am—Paul, God's soldier. I am not dead, but alive in my God. But for thee, unhappy man, there shall be many evils and great punishment, because thou did unjustly shed the blood of the righteous, and that not many days hence!' And when he had said this Paul departed from him" (*NTA*, II, 385–86). Furthermore, by the next morning Paul has also arisen from the dead. He stands with two other men, a certain Longus and the centurion Cestus, at his own tomb, praying together with them.

This fantastic tale is the Church's grounds for claiming (in the Roman Missal, for instance) that Paul's beheading was a historical fact. The decapitation of Paul in Rome is just as true or just as false as the observation that milk rather than blood spurted from his corpse.

We know nothing about how Paul really died. On the other hand, the *Lexikon für Theologie und Kirche* (VIII, 340) finds "testimony" in the First Letter of Clement (ca. A.D. 96, mentioned in the last chapter) not only for Peter's death as a martyr but for Paul's as well. Such claims can be made only in the hope that readers will simply copy the text, instead of checking the sources. What the passage in question actually says is:

> Through jealousy and strife Paul showed the way to the prize of endurance; seven times he was in bonds, he was exiled, he was stoned, he was a herald (of the Gospel) both in the East and the West, he gained the noble fame of his faith, he taught righteousness to all the world, and when he had reached the limits of the West he gave his testimony before the rulers, and thus passed from the world and was taken up into the Holy Place—the greatest example of endurance. (V:5-7)

Church historiographers understand the text in the way that best suits their needs. The Greek verb *martyrein* (in "he gave his testimony") cannot be read in its later sense of "undergo martyrdom," as the previous chapter pointed out with regard to parallel remarks about Peter.

The effort to turn both Paul and Peter into martyrs, although early sources know nothing about this, can be explained by the rage for martyrdom in the early Church. The most important herald of this enthusiasm was Ignatius, bishop of Antioch. He wrote seven letters around A.D. 110 while he was being transported to Rome to be thrown to wild beasts in the Colosseum. One of the privileges of the Romans was watching condemned prisoners who had been sent from the provinces being put to death in circus spectacles. Ignatius's letters are ranked among the highest of Catholic texts because they are considered the most significant evidence of the time immediately after the New Testament. Ignatius is the most important of the "Apostolic Fathers," that is, not the fathers of the apostles, but the fathers of the Church who were the closest, at least in time, to the apostles. Another member of this group is the author of the First Letter of Clement.

Because of Ignatius's great importance and his martyr's death, hardly anyone ever dared to criticize him. But in reality he was a reckless self-destroyer, a neurotic seeker of martyrdom, and a religious masochist. And he has stood sponsor to the morbid addiction to martyrdom of many Catholic saints. On the way to Rome he wrote, among other things, a letter to the Romans whose main point is that under no circumstances should steps be taken to save him.

Such religious fanatics are not found exclusively in Christianity, but they do abound there, because Christian theology approves Jesus' death on the cross as the will of God.

These devout maniacs are utterly indifferent to the fact that they are making other human beings into executioners and hangmen. In other words, they are contributing not to the spread of love among their fellows, but to the spread of cruelty.

Ignatius writes to the Romans and begs them to let him die his martyr's death without any interference: "I am afraid of your love" (Kirsopp Lake, trans., *The Apostolic Fathers* [Cambridge, MA: Harvard Univ. Press (LCL), 1985], I, 227). "For neither shall I ever have such an opportunity of attaining to God, nor can you, if you be but silent, have any better deed ascribed to you. . . . Grant me nothing more than that I may be poured out to God, while an altar is still ready" (II, 227, 229). Christianity's greatest commandment is no longer love, as it was for Jesus. For Ignatius the greatest good deed is to let him die the grim death he has been condemned to—without interfering, without even contradicting him. He wants to be a sacrificial offering to God, who obviously approves of human sacrifice.

> I am writing to all the churches, and I give injunctions to all men, that I am dying willingly for God's sake, if you do not hinder it. I beseech you, be not an unseasonable kindness to me. Suffer me to be eaten by the beasts, through whom I can attain to God. I am God's wheat, and I am ground by the teeth of wild beasts that I may be found pure bread of Christ. Rather entice the wild beasts that they may become my tomb, and leave no trace of my body. . . . Beseech Christ on my behalf, that I may be found a sacrifice through these instruments. (IV, 231)
>
> I long for the beasts that are prepared for me; and I pray that they may be found prompt for me; I will even entice them to devour me promptly; not as has happened to some whom they have not touched from fear; even if they be unwilling of themselves, I will force them to it. . . . Let there come on me fire, and cross, and struggles with wild beasts, cutting and tearing asunder, rackings of bones, mangling of limbs, crushing my whole body, cruel tortures of the devil, may I but attain to Jesus Christ! (V, 233)

Thus for this unfortunate saint, shortly before he was thrown to the wild beasts. Terrible things hanging over one's head can derange a person. To that extent, we have no right to judge the question of whether anyone who doesn't want compassion for himself can represent the compassion of God for others.

In any event, the Christian ideal of martyrdom was a contributing factor to Peter and Paul's not being allowed to die a normal death. Never mind the fact that the word *martyrein* in the text of the First Letter of Clement didn't have the later sense of "suffer martyrdom." Kittel's *Theologisches Wörterbuch zum Neuen Testament,* a standard Protestant reference work, notes in its analysis of *martyrein* in Clement:

> *Equally remarkable is the total absence in Ignatius of the use of this whole group of words in the sense of martyrdom. Ignatius is filled with the idea of martyrdom. The whole conceptual content connected with this idea is richly developed in his letters. He is an imitator or bearer of Christ. As someone going to martyrdom he is in the process of truly becoming Jesus' disciple. But he never speaks of* martyrein. . . . *That is, Ignatius has no notion of the later use of this term.* ([1942] IV, 511)

But that is of no consequence. Wherever possible, the early Christians are portrayed as persecuted, ideally as martyrs. Should the ancient texts tell a different tale, the translator at least tries to supply some martyred corpses. Whenever they can, Catholic theologians translate *martyrein* and *memartyremenos* (meaning "someone of approved character") as "suffering a martyr's death"—unless the next line shows the person in question alive and well.

Thus, for example, in Ignatius's Letter to the Ephesians (12), where the author speaks of the Apostle Paul, the classic German *Library of the Fathers of the Church* translated *memartyremenos* as "martyred." But in Ignatius's letter to the Philadelphians the same word is rendered as "of good repute." The reason is that in the latter case, the passage concerning the deacon Philo of Cilicia goes on to say, "who even now is serving me. . . ." So Philo was lucky to have gone on serving Bishop Ignatius. Otherwise the *Library of the Fathers of the Church* would surely have sent him to a martyr's grave (*Apostolische Väter* [1918], pp. 122, 146).

Upon closer inspection, the passage in 1 Clement can actually be read the other way around, as an indication that Paul was *not* executed in Rome. Clement says that Paul "reached the limits of the West." This means Spain, and such a trip can only have taken place after Paul's stay in prison and his trial. In fact, alongside the later, unreliable tales of his beheading in Rome, we also meet (for example, in the apocryphal Acts of Peter) other tales, similarly unreliable, about his acquittal in Rome and a subsequent journey to Spain. According to these sources, after his acquittal Paul had a "vision, the Lord saying to him, 'Paul, arise and be a physician to those who are in Spain'" (1; *NTA*, II, 279).

And even the so-called Muratori canon (composed at the end of the 2nd century and named after its discoverer, Ludovico Antonio Muratori, d. 1750) speaks of a journey by Paul to Spain. It makes the following comment on Luke's Acts of the Apostles: "For 'the most excellent Theophilus' Luke summarizes the several things that in his own presence have come to pass, as also by the omission of the passion of Peter he makes quite clear, and equally by (the omission) of the journey of Paul, who from the city (of Rome) proceeded to Spain" (35ff.; *NTA*, I, 44).

Paul did, in fact, plan a trip to Spain; he speaks about it in Romans: "I hope to see you in passing as I go to Spain" (15:24). It's possible that he got to Spain, but it's also possible that this note in Romans led people to conclude that at some point he carried out his intention and hence must have gone there. In any case, we know nothing about his death.

The Acts of Paul extolled not only the deeds of men, and Paul in particular; they also helped to make one woman famous, at least in antiquity and the Middle Ages. They not only called this fairy-tale figure into life, they also provided her with enormous sanctity, gave her worldwide importance and even cultic honors (her feast is 23 September). The lady is Saint Thecla. The Acts of Paul have largely been lost, but the Story of the Deeds of Paul and Thecla, which originally formed part of it, have been preserved.

Here is the story: Thecla heard Paul preach in Iconium and converted to Christianity. Part of her conversion involved breaking with her fiancé, Thamyris, for the sake of chastity. The unhappy Thamyris is told: "He [Paul] deprives young men of wives and maidens of husbands, saying: 'Otherwise there is no resurrection for you, except ye remain chaste and do not defile the chaste'" (12; *NTA*, II, 365). The furious bridegroom has Paul arrested. Paul is then banished, and poor Thecla is condemned to be burned to death. But a miraculous downpour of rain and hail saves her. She meets Paul again and goes with him to Antioch. Here a certain Alexander falls in love with her, but she pays him no heed. Then she is condemned to fight wild animals. During the parade that precedes the contests, she is tied to a wild lioness; but she sits down on the beast, and the lioness licks her feet. Later another fierce lioness defends her against a bear and a lion. Then she springs into some water that happens to be nearby, baptizing herself. The seals in the water can't eat her because suddenly they all die. More beasts are set on her, but they all fall asleep. "And they bound her by the feet between the bulls, and set red-hot irons beneath their bellies that being the more enraged they might kill her" (35; *NTA*, II, 362).

This pious ecstasy, by the way, is not quite PG-13, because all through her many trials Thecla remains naked. But in the end she is saved and meets Paul again. On commission from him, she preaches the word of God. She is supposed to have died peacefully around the year 100, aged ninety, in Seleucia, and a whole series of Church Fathers called her an "apostoless."

Over the tomb of this fairy-tale woman a basilica was later built that developed into a busy pilgrimage center. According to a contemporary report, Thecla worked thirty-one miracles. Emperor Zeno (471–91) then had a second church built in her honor. In Constantinople there were as many as four churches dedicated to Saint Thecla. There was a shrine to Thecla in Jerusalem, and in Cyprus five villages were named after her. In many cities of Europe one can find relics of Thecla: Her head is in Milan, an arm that King James II of Aragon had acquired in Armenia went first to Barcelona, then to Tarragona. There she became the city's patroness. Her relics were also carried to Cologne (St. Gereon), as well as to Bologna and Chartres (Wetzer and Welte, *Kirchenlexikon*, XI, 1481).

The summit of pious fantasy in the Apocrypha is the Letter of Jesus to King Abgar V Ukkama ("the Black") of Edessa in Mesopotamia, composed at the end of the 3rd century. It should come as no surprise that someone would produce a work by Jesus, because fantasy always tends to up the ante. Eusebius (d. 339) assures us that he saw the letter of Jesus with his own eyes. This King Abgar had heard of Jesus' miracles, as Eusebius reports, and, since he was sick, he wished to be cured by him. To this end he sent the runner Ananias with a letter to Jesus, who immediately replied in writing. Eusebius writes: "There is nothing equal to hearing the letters themselves, which we have extracted from the archives, and when translated from the Syriac they are verbally as follows . . ." (*EH*, I, xiii; LCL, pp. 89, 91).

To make a long story short, Jesus writes that at the moment he is short of time. First he has to go (after his death) to heaven, but then he'll send a disciple to cure the king, which is what happens. The famous nun Egeria (or Aetheria or Eucheria), who probably came from southern France and visited Edessa in 384, tells us about her adventures there in her *Peregrinatio Egeriae* (Egeria's Pilgrimage). She spoke with the bishop of Edessa and learned that "Abgar and many others after him, when a siege threatened, brought Jesus' letter to the gate, read it there, and immediately the enemy dispersed" (*NTA*, I, 389).

CHAPTER FIFTEEN

Forgeries and
False Authors

JESUS AND THE Church are two different things. Jesus had long been dead and gone home to heaven when the Church came into being. It had, as it were, engendered and given birth to itself. It does claim to be the child of the Holy Spirit, who came down from heaven with fire and storm on Pentecost fifty-two days after Jesus' death. On Pentecost the Spirit founded the hierarchy and the papacy, and ever since then the Church has possessed the Holy Spirit. But this Holy Spirit is no Spirit to be possessed, because it blows where it wills and not where the Church or anyone else wants it to. We can assume, therefore, that the Church is merely a product of its own spirit.

One very special lightning bolt from the Spirit was the so-called Donation of Constantine. In it Emperor Constantine (d. 337) showed great generosity toward the Church: "We have transferred our [Lateran] palace and all the provinces, places, and towns belonging to the city of Rome, to Italy, and to the West to the most blessed supreme pontiff, our father Silvester, the universal pope, and to his—or his successors'—power and sway." The date, official seal, and signature of the emperor authenticated this donation. Constantine, the absolute monarch, thus gave to the pope all of the western Roman Empire; and the popes became the successors of the Roman emperors in the West. Constantine himself was content with the East, "because the earthly emperor should not have authority where the head of the Christian religion [the pope] has been appointed by the heavenly emperor [Jesus]."

Yet it was all a swindle, a handmade-homemade inside job, an ecclesiastical forgery. From it, of course, the Church got inestimable advantages in power and possessions, and that for centuries. The forgery had been cooked up in the papal chanceries around the middle of the 8th century; it was not exposed until the 15th century. The detective was a humanist, critic of the papacy, and high official of the Roman Curia, Lorenzo Valla (d. 1457). But his work exposing the fraud wasn't published until 1517 by Ulrich von Hutten at the beginning of the Reformation. The Catholic side did not admit the whole deception until much later. The *Lexikon für Theologie und Kirche* writes, "Since the middle of the 19th century . . . the contents of the Donation of Constantine have been considered a forgery from the Catholic standpoint" ([1961] VI, 484). The Church is like the Italian postal service in that the system seems to take its own sweet time.

Along with this donation to the Church by Constantine one might speak of a donation to the Church by Jesus. It might be said that Jesus donated the whole world to the Church, so that it could play games of domination with it. And in fact the Church did to a large extent turn the earth into its playground, to play out its adventures, with such fatal games as "Persecuting the Jews," "Crusades," "Inquisition," and "Extirpating the Indians," and many others in the same vein. But the copyright on these games belongs to the Church, and not to Jesus.

Throughout the New Testament, we meet traces of this donation of the world to the Church by Jesus. The world becomes a task and, for that very reason, a gift. The very last words of Jesus before his Ascension concern this task: "You shall be my witnesses in Jerusalem and in all Judea and Samaria and to the end of the earth" (Acts 1:8). It all depends on what Jesus meant by the "end of the earth." Did that mean Galilee, which many Jews looked down upon and actually saw as a kind of "end of the earth"? Or did Jesus mean that the apostles should leap over Galilee and immediately press forward to the real ends of the world as his "witnesses"? Regardless of what Jesus meant, the Church has planted the ends of the world far off, taking him to mean the whole region between Cape Deshnev in

Siberia up on the right to Cape Horn below on the left—in other words, all the way to the "round world's imagined corners." The Church has always gone for the whole, for the total package, one might say. And this total Church developed into a totalitarian Church, which is why its leaders failed to be real "witnesses" of Jesus.

Jesus has been turned from the preacher of salvation to Israel that he wanted to be ("I was sent only to the lost sheep of the house of Israel," Matt. 15:24) into an unforeseen rescuer of the Gentiles all over the world, whether they wanted to be rescued or not. Jesus has been transmogrified from a Jewish preacher and prophet into a cosmopolitan-universal ruler, into a Roman Catholic lord of the world. In the process, Jesus, who loved his enemies, has been turned into an enemy of many people. His "witnesses" have largely proved to be false witnesses.

To the mind of the Church's representatives, various means were justified for spreading Christianity, for winning and maintaining power. These included forgery, of which the Donation of Constantine wasn't the first. Karlheinz Deschner, a critic of the Church, has dealt with such forgeries. Upon hearing the term "Christian West," citizens of the First World are liable to feel a frisson of profound satisfaction. That is because "Christian West" seems so redolent of piety and righteousness. But if they read Deschner, such people will find their soup full of hairs. His work is painfully disturbing to Christian ignorance and arrogance. For example, the third volume of his *Kriminalgeschichte des Christentums: Die alte Kirche* (1990) addresses the subject of forgeries in, among other places, the New Testament.

When it comes to New Testament forgeries that can't be dodged, Christian textbooks usually cite mitigating circumstances. The argument runs along the lines of, "The modern notion of intellectual property was unknown in the ancient world." Deschner shows that this is by no means true. In this context he also attends to the question of what right, if any, the Bible has to be termed the Word of God. This is an issue that should be interesting, above all, to Protestants, because the Catholic dictatorship of the pope is matched by the Protestant dictatorship of Scripture.

Forgeries of many sorts can be found in the New Testament. For example, words are put into Jesus' mouth that make him a propagandist for the Church and its powers. One such forgery occurs in Matt. 28:19, when Jesus bids the disciples, "Go therefore and make disciples of all nations, baptizing them in the name of the Father and of the Son and of the Holy Spirit." Jesus had no intention of founding a "church" and certainly not a "church universal." For an authentic example of Jesus' view, consider Matt. 10:5–6, which expresses the exact opposite of a universal commission: "These twelve Jesus sent out, charging them, 'Go nowhere among the Gentiles, and enter no town of the Samaritans, but go rather to the lost sheep of the house of Israel.' " Two further authentic passages are Matt. 15:24, "I was sent only to the lost sheep of the house of Israel," and Matt. 10:23, "You will not have gone through all the towns of Israel, before the Son of Man comes."

Jesus had no idea of a mission to the Gentiles, an idea that first occurred to Paul. "Thus the historian will have to judge that Jesus' saying in Matthew 28:19a was not composed until the mission to the Gentiles, thanks to Paul's life work, had become an unassailable operation of the Church, and the mission to the Jews had moved into the background" (Johannes Weiss and Wilhelm Bousset in *Die Schriften des Neuen Testament* [1917], I, 389). Jesus himself—and all theologians have by now acknowledged this—believed that the Kingdom of God would be coming soon. But that is the opposite of a world mission in the grand style.

Hans Küng is right when he says:

> The historical Jesus . . . counted on the world's coming to an end
> in his own lifetime. And for this coming of God's kingdom he
> doubtless did not want to found a special community distinct
> from Israel, with its own creed, its own cult, its own constitution,
> its own offices. . . . All this means that in his own lifetime Jesus
> never founded any church. He had no idea of founding and or-
> ganizing a large-scale religious operation that would have to
> be created. . . . Neither for himself nor for his disciples did he
> think of a mission among the pagan nations. (Christ Sein [1976],
> pp. 338-39)

In connection with the charge to evangelize and baptize the world (Matt. 28:19), Schalom Ben-Chorin makes an important point: "It is not insignificant for our case that this passage, as Professor Pines of Hebrew University in Jerusalem has proved, is missing in the oldest manuscripts before the Council of Nicea (325)" (*Paulus* [1986], p. 23).

According to Matthew, in Jesus' charge, "Go therefore and make disciples of all nations," the speaker is the risen Christ, whose death is behind him. Contemporary theologians, too, like to put it this way: "Here we have the post-Easter Jesus speaking." They use this phrase not only at points in the Gospels, as here in Matthew, where Jesus is saying something *after* his Resurrection. No, theologians cite the post-Easter Jesus even when the Evangelists have put words into the *pre*-Easter Jesus' mouth that he could not possibly have said during his lifetime. The theologians consider this fully legitimate, since they feel the Evangelist is interpreting Jesus correctly by putting into his earthly mouth the words that he definitely said or would have said, though only after his Resurrection.

Thus here in Matthew 28 the speaker is, according to the Evangelist, the risen Jesus. But, the skeptic will ask, how can a risen man be speaking, since the resurrection stories featuring a dead man returned to life must be understood as legendary images? No tape recorder could have captured the voice of the risen Christ. That, by the way, is a point that Protestant theologians, almost without exception, will concede, though not all their Catholic colleagues, more inclined to believe in miracles, would agree. But even the Protestants who admit that no tape recorder could pick up the voice of the risen Christ still have no problem believing everything that, according to Matthew, he is supposed to have said. For them, Matthew has Jesus say only what he really did say (even if it could never have been taped).

"The post-Easter Jesus," in other words, is completely in the palm of the Church's hand. Furthermore, each Christian denomination assumes the right to interpret the words of the post-Easter Jesus in a manner that suits its particular point of view. For Catholics this means the papal, standardized reading; for Protestants, the professorial, pluralistic one. First the Church (in this case the Evangelist) lends Jesus its voice, then it interprets what he says. Thus the Church is sure to avoid any surprises, and Jesus never says anything false. His lines have been precensored and improved upon by the Church.

The Church has turned Jesus into its propagandist. For this reason we take everything that presupposes or discusses or promotes the existence of a Church as interpolations by the authors of the Gospels into Jesus' original sayings. That includes Jesus' hailing Peter as the rock on which he will build his church (Matt. 16:18), since Jesus never meant to found a church. It makes no difference at all whether this passage is a later addition, as some theologians think, or was present in Matthew from the very beginning. In either case, it's not Jesus who's speaking here; it's the early church, which was interested in having such a leadership position and authority figure because of its growing hierarchical structure.

In the inauthentic chapter 21 of John—that is, in a later addition to the actual Gospel—the idea of a deputy is already clearly developed. Peter becomes the shepherd of the flock of Christ. He takes over the functions of Jesus, the former and actual shepherd, as his representative. Shortly afterward, the Church began to think that the important thing was not the person of Peter. The Church decided that the office Peter held was the bedrock foundation of the Church, and that Jesus established it permanently. With this concept we have the popes as Peter's successors and Christ's deputies, and the papacy as the foundation of the Church.

The Evangelists put words in Jesus' mouth that he never said and impute to him actions—for example, miracles—that he never did. But that's not all: The Evangelists themselves are not the persons the Church maintains they are. In the German translation of the New Testament by Josef Kürzinger (1970), we find in the Introduction to the Gospel of Matthew the traditional claim: "According to the most ancient tradition, which can be demonstrated as far back as the beginning of the 2nd century, the first Gospel comes from the apostle Matthew, also called Levi, the son of Alphaeus." All that sounds good: "most ancient tradition" sounds good; "demonstrated" sounds good. "Apostle" guarantees an eyewitness, and such a precise citation of his name and his father's name wins our trust.

The "most ancient tradition" that Kürzinger speaks of derives from Bishop Papias around the year 140. All the later sources copy this one. Papias's work (*Explanations of the Lord's Words*) has been lost, but fragments of it have come down to us in the form of quotations in other authors. In them we find this statement about Matthew: "Matthew collected the oracles [of Jesus] in the Hebrew language, and each interpreted them as best he could" (Eusebius, *Ecclesiastical History,* III, xxxix, 16; LCL, p. 297).

But Matthew's Gospel was originally written in Greek and is not a translation. For this reason theologians today are all but unanimous in concluding that what Papias says does not apply to Matthew's Gospel as we have it. And when, for example, the Protestant-Catholic "Unity Translation" of 1980 continues to speak about the "old church tradition" of an original Aramaic version, it is refusing to acknowledge the findings of serious scholarship. Contrary to Papias, the Apostle Matthew is by no means the author of the Gospel according to Matthew, as shown by the fact that it was written in Greek. Furthermore, Matthew is dependent on Mark, which even the Church has always considered not to be the work of a disciple. Matthew takes over almost all Mark's material, Mark's sequence of events, and, for the most part, Mark's wording. It is incomprehensible that an eyewitness (the Apostle Matthew) would choose to depend so radically on a non-eyewitness (the author of Mark).

The real author of Matthew is unknown. Its language shows the Gospel's author to have been a cultivated speaker of Greek, who relied on various traditions and sources (in particular the Gospel of Mark). The experts disagree on whether he was a Gentile or a Jewish Christian. He is more likely to have been a Gentile, since a Jewish Christian would have had a hard time adopting the legend of the virgin birth, which is alien to the religious and imaginative world of Judaism. Such a legend, by contrast, might readily flow from the pen of a Gentile Christian. There were numerous Hellenistic tales of divine sons being begotten through alliances of gods with human women, and the author would have known of them. The time of composition is generally accepted as from A.D. 80 to 90.

We know nothing about the author of Mark, which is generally reckoned to be the oldest of the Gospels. Once again, Kürzinger cites tradition: "According to a uniform, very early tradition the second Gospel comes from John Mark, the co-worker of St. Peter." This "very early tradition" is our old friend Papias. Eusebius quotes Papias:

"Mark became Peter's interpreter and wrote accurately all that he remembered, not, indeed, in order, of the things said or done by

the Lord. For he had not heard the Lord, nor had he followed him, but later on, as I said, he followed Peter, who used to give teaching as necessity demanded but not making, as it were, an arrangement of the Lord's oracles, so that Mark did nothing wrong in thus writing down single points as he remembered them. For to one thing he gave attention, to leave out nothing of what he had heard and to make no false statements in them." (EH, III, xxxix, 15; LCL, p. 297)

If so, then the Gospel of Mark would be a rendering of Peter's disorganized reports about Jesus. And in fact, the events in Jesus' life would have followed a different sequence from the one in Mark. Papias claims that Mark was a disciple of Peter, but most scholars characterize that as inaccurate. In the New Testament, John Mark always appears only as Paul's companion on his missionary journeys. Mark must have been composed around the year 70, but we don't know where.

Just as church tradition ascribed the Gospel of Mark to a companion of Peter, it assigned the Gospel of Luke to a companion of Paul. Such a balancing out of origins suggests itself to the untrained imagination from a desire to give equal rank to the two apostles. Just as Mark is supposed to have gotten his information from Peter, so Luke presumably got his from Paul. Irenaeus writes around A.D. 190 that Luke "wrote down in a book the gospel preached by Paul" (*Against the Heresies* III, i, 1), and that Luke and Paul were inseparable (III, xiv, 1).

In the Muratori canon, also known as the Muratori fragment, composed around A.D. 200 by an unknown author, which contains an account of the canonical (recognized by the Church) Scriptures, we are told: "The third Gospel book, that according to Luke. This physician Luke after Christ's ascension, since Paul had taken him with him as an expert in the way (of the teaching), composed it in his own name according to (his) thinking. Yet neither did he himself see the Lord in the flesh" (3–7; NTA, I, 43).

Protestant theologians in particular challenge these two reports. They stress that Pauline theology is completely alien to Luke and especially to Acts (both have the same author). For this reason "Luke the beloved physician" (Col. 4:14) and "co-worker" of Paul (Philem. 24) cannot be the author of the Gospel according to Luke. In Luke "the real Paul, the man known by both his disciples and his adversaries, is replaced by a Paul as a later age thought of him. The earliest days of the Church are not described here [in Acts] by someone who had personally experienced most of it," writes Ernst Haenchen in his commentary (*Die Apostelgeschichte* [1977], p. 124). The only thing we can definitely say about the author of Luke is that he was a Gentile Christian who wrote cultivated Greek. The time of composition would have been from around A.D. 80 to 90.

On the subject of the Gospel of John, Kürzinger writes:

> According to a reliable tradition, which can also be supplemented by the Gospel's testimony to itself (cf. 21:24), its author is John the son of Zebedee. As one of the first disciples he belonged to the leading group of disciples. A well-founded tradition maintains that as a very old man in Ephesus (Asia Minor), between A.D. 90 and 100 he composed the notes for the Gospel that was published by his disciples.

The first person to say anything about the author of the fourth Gospel is again Bishop Irenaeus of Lyon around 190. He writes: "Last of all John, the disciple of the Lord, who rested on his bosom, published his Gospel during his stay in Ephesus in Asia" (*Against the Heresies* III, i). The Muratori fragment offers a strange story of how the Gospel was composed: "The fourth Gospel, that of John, [one] of the disciples. When his fellow disciples and the bishops urged him, he said: Fast with me from today for three days, and what will be revealed to each one let us relate to one another. In the same night it was revealed to Andrew, one of the apostles, that, whilst all were to go over [it], John in his own name should write everything down" (9–16; *NTA*, I, 43).

This time Kürzinger and conservative Bible scholars have to dispense with Bishop Papias, whom they otherwise like to bring in as an expert on who wrote what. That is because, according to Papias, by the time the fourth Gospel was being composed John was already dead. In a work by Philippus of Side from the 5th century, we find a quotation from the second book of Papias's work: "John, the theologian and his brother James were murdered by the Jews." And in a Syrian martyrology from the year 411, which relies on older sources, we read under 27 December: "John and James, the apostles in Jerusalem." As a matter of fact, the Gospels of Mark and Matthew suggest that John had died before the composition of these two Gospels, which were themselves written before the Gospel of John. John and James, the hot-tempered brothers and sons of Zebedee, wanted to blast an inhospitable Samaritan village with fire from heaven (Luke 9:54). They had ambitious plans, to which their mother, according to Matthew, lent enthusiastic support: They wanted to take the seats immediately to the right and left of Jesus in the kingdom of heaven. So at least in their spirited careerism today's church officeholders are following the path of the apostles.

Jesus asks them: "You do not know what you are asking. Are you able to drink the cup that I drink, or to be baptized with the baptism with which I am baptized?" And when they answer yes, Jesus says: "The cup that I drink you will drink; and with the baptism with which I am baptized, you will be baptized; but to sit at my right hand or left is not mine to grant, but it is for those for whom it has been prepared" (Mark 10:35–40; cf. Matt. 20:20ff.). Incidentally, the other ten grumble about the pair's pursuing the best positions, probably because they were pursuing them themselves.

There can hardly be any doubt that in his answer to the brothers Jesus is speaking about their death as martyrs. This prophecy would probably not have gotten into the text if it hadn't already come true. Most likely the prophecy was put into Jesus' mouth after the death of James and John. This is known as a *vaticinium ex eventu,* a prophecy made after it has been fulfilled. At the time when Mark (which Matthew is based on) was being composed, that is, around A.D. 70, people were evidently convinced that both James and John had died violent deaths. Acts 12:1ff. reports the execution of James by Herod Agrippa I around the year 44. We have no account of the death of John. Nor can we explain why the knowledge of his violent death, which was still a vivid memory when Mark and Matthew were written and could even be found in Papias, was later lost.

Kürzinger refers to both the "reliable tradition" (we have seen how that tradition contradicts itself) and to the "supplementary" testimony that the Gospel gives on its own behalf. Concerning the latter we learn from 21:24 about "the disciple whom Jesus loved, who had lain close to his breast at the supper" (John 21:20). "This is the disciple who is bearing witness to these things, and who has written these things; and we know that his testimony is true." The 21st chapter of John is a later appendix and comes from a different hand than the Gospel itself. In this appendix the "beloved disciple" is characterized as the author of the Gospel. But that still leaves us completely in the dark as to who the author is.

This figure of the "beloved disciple," who is mentioned both in the body of the Gospel and in chapter 21, thoroughly clouds up the picture. The beloved disciple is part of the "Johannine Question" (the problem of why the Fourth Gospel is so different from the Synoptics). It has exercised theologians since the 18th century, and even more so since the early 19th century, after more and more doubts were raised about whether the Fourth Gospel had been written by an apostle.

The point is that the beloved disciple, that "enigmatic figure" (Rudolf Bultmann), is *not* identical to any of the apostles, not even to John the son of Zebedee, as many falsely believe. It seems as if the author of John, whoever he was, worked into the Gospel a figure with whom he himself identified. Through this character he used his pious fantasy to transform himself into an eyewitness of the time and a favorite disciple of Jesus. He painted himself, so to speak, into his own picture.

It's interesting that this beloved disciple is regularly contrasted with Peter. At the Last Supper Peter doesn't ask Jesus directly who the traitor is but bids the beloved disciple ask for him (John 13:24). He is presumably that "other disciple" who followed Jesus into the court of the high priest, while Peter stayed outside and was only led in by this "other disciple" (John 18:15–16). And so in 19:26 the beloved disciple stands loyally under the cross, even as Peter has meanwhile repeatedly denied his Lord and, like the other apostles, is too cowardly to remain with Jesus in the hour of death. After the Resurrection, Peter and the beloved disciple run to the tomb. The latter is naturally the faster, even though he doesn't enter the grave first (John 20:4–5). The beloved disciple believes immediately in the Resurrection, while nothing is said about whether Peter believed, too. Still later in the appended chapter 21 we can sense this contrast between Peter and the beloved disciple: Peter does not recognize the risen Lord, but the beloved disciple does so quite readily (John 21:7).

If the beloved disciple is presumably the product of authorial fantasy, then so is the whole scene beneath the cross. In it this disciple, as the Wetzer and Welte *Kirchenlexikon* puts it (VI, 1537), received "as a reward, Jesus' most precious legacy," namely, his mother. It's also scarcely conceivable that the other three Evangelists would not have mentioned the presence of Jesus' mother and a disciple under the cross, if they really had stood there.

In the following centuries a rich cycle of legends grew up around the real Apostle John, the son of Zebedee, who is falsely believed to be the author of the Fourth Gospel. In accordance with the law of legend formation, over time more detailed information came to light. During the persecution of the Christians under Emperor Domitian (81–96), John was brought to Rome, "where, after he had been plunged into boiling oil and had suffered no harm, was then banished to an island," as Tertullian (d. after 220) reports (*De praescriptione haereticorum* 36). And finally, according to Irenaeus, after the death of Domitian, he was back in Asia Minor until the time of Trajan (98–117) (*Against the Heresies* II, xxii, 5). So he would have lived to a very old age. Some people believed, as Augustine (d. 430) tells us, that he never died: "But as they say, he did not die, but lies there like a dead man, and so he was buried in his sleep; and until the second coming of Christ he will remain so and meanwhile he gives notice that he is alive by stirring up the dust. It is believed that this dust is set in motion by the breath of one resting there, so that it rises up from the depths to the surface of the grave mound" (*Comm. in Joh.* CXXIV, ii).

Epiphanius, bishop of Salamis (d. 431), presents John with the most splendid of Christian testimonies: He says that John remained a virgin. Actually, Epiphanius wasn't the first one to do this. Long before him the apocryphal Acts of John, the Pistis Sophia, and the Gospel of Bartholomew, all from the 3rd century, had awarded John the same honor. This was the reason why Jesus had entrusted Mary to him beneath the cross: "As the Redeemer hung on the cross, he turned, as it says in the

Gospel of John, and saw the disciple whom the Lord loved, and said to him, speaking of Mary: Behold, your mother; and to her he said: Behold, your son. . . . Why did he not rather give her to Peter? Why not to Andrew, Matthew, or Bartholomew? Evidently he gave her to John because of his virginity. . . . He wanted to show that she is the mother and protectress of virginity" (*Medicine Chest against the Antidicomarianites*, X. The Antidicomarianites were heretical opponents of Mary's perpetual virginity who maintained that after Jesus' birth Mary and Joseph had sexual relations).

As with the legendary King Midas, who turned everything he touched into gold (which left him with nothing he could eat), so everyone who came into contact with Mary turned into a virgin. The first one affected by this was her husband, Joseph. Now John (according to Epiphanius, Joseph had already died). A perpetual virgin couldn't be saddled with a married man or a widower. A contemporary of Epiphanius, Jerome, nailed down the truth concerning the widower Joseph from the *Protevangelium of James:* For a female virgin the only fitting companion was a male virgin. And so Joseph and John must be virgins.

In his youth, however, John had tried to get married three times, but Jesus had always prevented him. The first time he appeared to him and said: John, I need you. The second time he stopped John by means of sickness. The third time he made John blind for two years so that he couldn't see women anymore. By the time he regained his sight, Jesus had also enlightened his understanding, so that John no longer wanted to get married (Acts of John 113, from the 3rd century).

Still later we learn from the virginal John's last words that ever since his youth he had rejected the thought of marriage. Those last words were as follows: "O Lord, thou who from my infancy until this age has preserved me untouched by woman, thou who hast kept my body from them so that the mere sight of a woman excites abhorrence in me. O gift [of God], to remain untouched by the influence of women!" (Pseudo-Titus Epistle from the 5th century, *NTA*, II, p. 159).

Conservative theologians also attribute to the Apostle John the Book of Revelation, the last book in the Bible. For that reason it is often called the Secret Revelation of Saint John. Speaking of its author, Kürzinger writes: "John explicitly calls himself the author (cf. 1:1, 4, 9, 22:8). The most ancient tradition, with few exceptions, sees in this the apostle John, the author of the Fourth Gospel and the three Letters of John. Language and style as well as content, to be sure, show striking peculiarities vis-à-vis the other writings of John." Kürzinger doesn't point out that the "peculiarities" are so peculiar that it's impossible to accept the same author for the Fourth Gospel and Revelation.

The differences between Revelation and the Gospel of John had caught the attention of readers even back in antiquity. In his *Ecclesiastical History*, Eusebius quotes Bishop Dionysius the Great of Alexandria (d. 264/265):

> *Some indeed of those before our time rejected and altogether impugned the book, examining it chapter by chapter and declaring it to be unintelligible and illogical, and its title false. For they say that it is not John's, no, nor yet an apocalypse [unveiling], since it is veiled by its heavy, thick curtain of unintelligibility; and that the author of this book was not only not one of the apostles, nor even one of the saints or those belonging to the Church, but Cerinthus, the same who created the sect called "Cerinthian" after him, since he desired to affix to his own forgery a name worthy of credit.... But for my part I should not dare to reject the book, since many brethren hold that the interpretation of each several passage is in some way hidden and more wonderful. (EH, VII, xxv; LCL, p. 197)*

Today most Protestant and many Catholic theologians recognize that the Gospel of John and Revelation must have had different authors. But we still don't know who wrote Revelation.

Thus when it comes to the Gospels, Acts, and Revelation, we are dealing with writings that were later assigned false authors by some editor. But in the Apostolic Letters we meet "original" forgeries, that is, works in which the author pretends to be someone other than himself. The First Letter of Peter, only one in a whole series of such forgeries, has already been mentioned.

The Second Letter of Peter is likewise a forgery. "Simeon Peter," it begins, "a servant and apostle of Jesus Christ, to those who have obtained a faith of equal standing with ours in the righteousness of our God and savior Jesus Christ" (2 Pet. 1:1). While Kürzinger defends the authenticity of this letter, the Unity Translation at least explains that "in the second chapter [the author] relies on statements from the Letter of Jude. Thus it is often assumed that this book was not composed until after the death of the apostle."

When in Catholic theology such forged claims of authorship are conceded, they are nevertheless played down or justified. This, we are told, is a "legitimate, widespread custom," by the *Lexikon für Theologie und Kirche* (VIII, 867). There's no denying that such forgeries were widespread in the early Church, but that doesn't make them legitimate. It was and is religious counterfeiting.

The following Pauline letters are probably not authentic: Ephesians (which begins, "Paul, an apostle of Jesus Christ by the will of God" [1:1]); Colossians ("Paul, an apostle of Jesus Christ by the will of God" [1:1]); and 2 Thessalonians. Most certainly inauthentic are the three so-called pastoral Epistles: 1 Timothy ("Paul, an apostle of Christ Jesus by command of God" [1:1]); 2 Timothy ("Paul, an apostle of Christ Jesus by the will of God"[1:1]); and Titus ("Paul, a servant of God and an apostle of Jesus Christ" [1:1]).

Catholic theologians now generally acknowledge that the three Pastoral Letters are not by Paul. Many of them also admit the inauthenticity of Ephesians and Colossians. The director of the Catholic Bible Society in Stuttgart, Paul-Gerd Müller, offers pointers for getting people to understand this "in religion classes, Bible discussion groups, and adult education." He advises "careful and constructive [discussion] of the pseudonymous nature of Ephesians and Colossians" (*Bibel und Kirche*, 3/1981, 265).

Here, on the one hand, the fact of forged authorship is admitted, but on the other, it's minimized. The word *pseudonym* is no longer understood colloquially in its etymological meaning of "lying name," but as a nom de plume or stage name invented by the author. Using a nom de plume is legitimate and something altogether different from claiming to be the Apostle Paul.

Thanks to this diluting of the force of "pseudonym" the reader or listener is once again being deceived. Writers using noms de plume are not doing what the New Testament forgers are trying to do: to cover themselves with the mantle of apostolic authority supplied by "the will of God."

The Church reacts very gingerly to the question, How do I tell this to my child? It has a hard time breaking with this sort of divinely sanctioned swindle. The Church sets great store by the apostolic authority of New Testament authors, because such authority can always be converted into ecclesiastical greatness.

Women in particular are given all sorts of pious directives in both the presumably false and the certainly false letters of Paul. And down through history the Church has toiled tirelessly to get women to take such exhortations to heart: "Wives, be subject to your husbands, as to the Lord. For the husband is the head of the wife, as Christ is head of the church. . . . As the church is subject to Christ, so let wives also be subject in everything to their husbands" (Eph. 5:22–24). "Wives, be subject to your husbands, as it is fitting in the Lord" (Col. 3:18). "Women should adorn themselves modestly and sensibly in seemly apparel, not with braided hair or gold or pearls or costly attire but by good deeds, as befits women who profess religion. Let a woman learn in silence with all submissiveness. I permit no woman to teach or to have authority over men; she is to keep silent. For Adam was formed first, then Eve; and Adam was not deceived, but the woman was deceived and became a transgressor. Yet woman will be saved in bearing children" (1 Tim. 2:9–15).

And 1 Peter sings the same tune: "Likewise you wives, be submissive to your husbands. . . . Let not yours be the outward adorning with braiding of the hair, decoration of gold, and wearing of fine clothing" (3:1, 3).

There used to be an official notice on bank notes in Germany: "Anyone who counterfeits or forges bank notes or acquires such counterfeit or forged notes will . . . be punished." It's too bad that this kind of warning, with "Letters of the Apostles" replacing "bank notes," isn't printed on the New Testament Letters. Perhaps the Church would be a little more restrained in its constant dissemination of those Letters. Perhaps it would cut down on the use of the expression "Word of God," not just for the false Letters but also for the genuine ones. For all their genuineness, not one of them has ever been anything more than the word of man.

CHAPTER SIXTEEN

Hell

HEAVEN IS THE realm of God; Hell is the realm of a goddess, at least in the Germanic languages, including English. The name says it: Hell is the realm of Hel, the goddess of death. But that's no reason for being terrified, because she wasn't an evil goddess, and Hell wasn't an evil kingdom until it was transformed into a grim place of horror.

The name of the goddess Hel has faded or disappeared in our Christian-masculine world of ideas, but her kingdom has been preserved, if only in name. It has been given a Christian renovation and, most important, furnished with infernal fire. As the Church's threat against all sinners and all its enemies, Hell serves the holy purpose of cradle-to-grave intimidation.

Yet the kingdom of the goddess Hel was at first not bad at all. Hel and Hell are ultimately connected to words signifying protection and covering, such as *hall* (a covered place), *hole,* and *helmet.* Thus the goddess was the hider, the one who enveloped and protected the dead. Hell is the house where the dead reside and take their last rest, as in their mother's womb. No merciless God awakes them in the name of justice to enter a hellish existence full of meaningless suffering.

The negative rededication of Hel's silent realm began in Germanic times, no one knows at exactly what point, when fallen heroes were selected by the god Odin and transferred to Valhalla, the (male) warrior's paradise. A garden of paradise would have been out of place among the Germanic tribes because of the cold winters; hence, heaven was a hall for feasting. Nonheroes and noncombatants remained in the kingdom of Hel.

The Germanic religion is not the only one that first and foremost gave dead warriors hope of heavenly consolation: "The idea that the soldiers fallen in war share a privileged lot in the Beyond is extremely widespread. Thus among the Aztecs the ordinary dead go down into the underworld, but warriors fallen in war go to the sun; the slain at Thermopylae became heroes" ("Krieg," in *RGG* [2nd ed., March 1929], 1304).

A similar pattern developed in Judaism, from which Christianity adopted its hope of resurrection. Here, too, there was at first a silent kingdom of the dead, though without a goddess, which took in the dead indiscriminately for eternal time or timeless eternity. This was Sheol (Hades in Greek), the underworld. (For the Greeks, too, Hades was initially not a place of punishment for some people; it harbored all the dead without exception.) According to the Book of Job, Sheol lies deeper than the ocean (Job 26:5). The region of the dead is the "land of forgetfulness" (Ps. 88:13), the place of complete darkness, which has no relation to the upper world. Thence there is no return to the world of light, as Proverbs (2:19) says, "None who go to her come back, nor do they regain the paths of life. Those who dwell there remain dead and can no longer praise the Eternal" (Ps. 6:6).

Ecclesiastes (Qoheleth or the Preacher), composed around 250 B.C., is the most melancholy book in the Old Testament—"Vanity of vanities, says the Preacher! All is vanity!" (Eccles. 1:2). Ecclesiastes goes so far as to claim that "the fate of the sons of men and the fate of beasts is the same; as one dies, so does the other. They all have the same breath, and man has no advantage over the beasts. . . . All go to one place; all are from the dust, and all turn to the dust again" (Eccles. 3:19–20). In the ninth chapter the author urges his audience to enjoy life, "for there is no work or thought or knowledge or wisdom in Sheol, to which you are going" (Eccles. 9:10). Everyone there is equal—equally sad, that is.

Scarcely a hundred years later, in the very latest book of the Old Testament, the Book of Daniel (composed ca. 165 B.C.), there is some movement in the underworld. For the first time in the Hebrew Bible, we find clear evidence of faith in the resurrection. "And many of those who sleep in the dust of earth shall awake, some to everlasting life, and some to shame and everlasting contempt" (Dan. 12:2). It's not yet clear whether everyone or only "many" will be raised.

But some Jews said that neither many nor all but none will be raised. The Sadducees were still saying that in Jesus' day. They rejected belief in the resurrection because it was not attested to in Holy Scripture. That is, the Sadducees didn't consider Daniel part of the Bible. The canon was not definitively fixed by Jewish scholars until A.D. 90 after centuries of controversy. By that time the Temple had been destroyed (in A.D. 70), and as the party of the priestly aristocracy, the Sadducees had lost their influence.

Incidentally, Daniel is the last book in the Bible (or Old Testament) only for Jews and Protestants. For Catholics that would be the Wisdom of Solomon, which was composed sometime between 80 and 30 B.C. The Catholic canon of the Old Testament adds seven more books, some of which were written after the Book of Daniel: Judith, Tobit, Ecclesiasticus, the Wisdom of Solomon, Baruch, and the first two Books of the Maccabees. They are known as the deuterocanonical (or second canon) Scriptures. Unlike Jews and Protestants, Catholics follow not the first or Hebrew canon, but the second, the Greek or Alexandrian canon.

At any rate, Daniel contains the first evidence of faith in the resurrection. The so-called apocalypse of Isaiah (24-27): "Thy dead shall live; their bodies shall rise" (Isa. 26:19) likewise comes from this late period. In the deuterocanonical Scriptures, for example, in the Wisdom of Solomon, that faith comes forward even more boldly and sounds like a protest against the pessimistic teaching of Ecclesiastes: "Ungodly men . . . reasoned unsoundly, saying to themselves, 'Short and sorrowful is our life, and there is no remedy when a man comes to his end, and no one has been known to return from Hades. Because we were born by mere chance, and hereafter we shall be as if we had never been'" (Wisd. of Sol. 1:16–2:2). "But the souls of the righteous are in the hands of God. . . . In the eyes of the foolish they seem to have died, but . . . their hope is full of immortality. . . . But the ungodly will be punished as their reasoning deserves"

(Wisd. of Sol. 3:1–10). The formulations about life after death are strongly colored here by the Greek doctrine of the immortality of the soul.

The fact that in the 2nd century B.C. there was movement in Sheol, where the dead had slept forever, is connected with the Maccabean wars. Like Valhalla among the Germanic peoples, heaven among the Jews first came into view for the warriors (read "martyrs"). With that, the realm of the dead was degraded to the abode of nonheroes and civilians. In the Book of Enoch, a widespread and beloved Jewish collection, the so-called vision of the shepherds (ca. 135–15 B.C.) seems to speak of a resurrection only for the martyrs (the Maccabean warriors) (Enoch 90:33; see Hermann Strack and Paul Billerbeck, *Kommentar zum Neuen Testament aus Talmud und Midrash*, IV, 1167–68).

But almost immediately this twofold military division turned into a moral division between good and evil. The transition from military to ethical categories is not as surprising as it may seem at first glance, because war and religion have always been a harmonious couple. Thus it's no accident that the Romans had only one word for (a) military prowess and (b) ethical virtue, namely *virtus*. (The term comes from *vir*, "man.") That is because the first noble class to arise in human history was based on the muscular strength with which the stronger not only obtained material advantages over the weaker, but at the same time treated themselves to glory and honor. Virtue and morality are always the first thing the victors claim for themselves and deny to the vanquished.

The occasion for the Maccabean wars was this: Ever since the time of Alexander the Great (d. 323 B.C.), Palestine had been getting hellenized. That is, the Greek mode of life began to pervade native Jewish ways. With the Seleucid (Greek-Syrian) forces of King Antiochus Epiphanes IV (175–64 B.C.) occupying the country, this led to continually escalating conflicts. In the year 169 Antiochus actually forced his way into the Temple — an enormous sacrilege in the eyes of the Jews, who had forbidden Gentiles to enter it under pain of death. Antiochus finally forbade all sacrifices, keeping the Sabbath, circumcision (which the Greeks had always mocked anyway), and he set up an altar to Zeus Olympios in the Temple. In response to this, a resistance group of freedom fighters arose around the priest Mattathias and his three sons: Judas, called the Hammer (Maccabee), Jonathan, and Simon. In the course of their campaign, the Temple was liberated.

The question of life after death is as old as the human race, because death always raises the question of a future existence. At times of heightened demand for soldiers motivated to fight and ready to die, this question becomes urgent. Under certain circumstances it opens itself to answers that others have given before. For example, Pericles, the great Greek general and famous orator (d. 429 B.C.), had long before the Maccabees found meaningful answers from what might be called the chaplain's point of view. In his solemn address honoring the Athenians who had fallen on Samos he said, according to Plutarch: "They were become immortal like the gods. For . . . we do not see them (the gods) themselves, but only by the honors we pay them, and by the benefits they do us, attribute to them immortality; and the like attributes belong also to those that die in the service of their country" (*Lives,* trans. John Dryden [New York: Modern Library, 1932], p. 188).

Again, long before the age of Maccabees, belief in life after death had penetrated the consciousness of the Greeks—in Plato, in Stoicism, in the mystery religions, and in popular beliefs. But for the Jews, a still more important influence than Greek ideas of immortality seems to have been Persian belief in the resurrection. The Jews had been in extremely close contact with the Persians, because from 539 to 333 B.C. they found themselves under Persian sovereignty.

The founder of Persian religion was Zoroaster (probably 7th–6th century B.C.). He was, by the way, a passionate opponent of all bloody sacrifices and thus fell afoul of the priests of Mithra because they sacrificed bulls. The Persian notions of the fate of humans after death are written down in the Gatha, sacred Scriptures that go back to Zoroaster: For three days the human soul remains with its dead body. At the dawn of the fourth day, the soul betakes itself to the Cinvat bridge, which spans the abyss of Hell. There the good and evil deeds of the individual are weighed. The scale determines the judgment. If the good deeds prevail, the soul is led to Paradise.

The wicked, on the other hand, plunge from the bridge into Hell, which lies below. There they are tortured until the resurrection. At the general judgment, all souls recover their bodies and are definitively judged by the wise creator God Ahuramazda (Ormuzd). The wicked return to Hell, but only for three days. Then one and all, the good and the wicked, and the entire earth, are drenched in purifying fire, in a flood of molten metal. For the good this is like a bath in warm milk, for the wicked it's like hellfire. But they, too, are cleansed by it. Indeed the whole earth is cleansed by fire, and thanks to this cleansing it is turned into Paradise, where everyone will dwell in perfect bodies. (Christians today have not gone much beyond this; the only progress is that their Hell is eternal.)

Modern-day visitors to Bombay are shown the "towers of silence" on Malabar Hill. On top of the towers, shielded from the curiosity of photographers, Parsee corpses are laid out for the vultures to feed on. As the name indicates, the Parsees come from Persia. They are the guardians of ancient Persian religion, having migrated to India in response to the Islamization of Persia. The Parsees are an influential and respected Indian ethnic group that has spread all over India and has set the pace for industrialization in India. Their center is Bombay. Cremation is customary in India, but the Parsees have a cult of fire, and corpses would pollute the flames. Even today this cult, now thousands of years old, is stronger than the shudder of fear that may strike some Parsees at the sight of the "towers of silence."

Fire has since become familiar to Christians as the central feature of Purgatory and Hell. This derives from both Persian and Greek, particularly Stoic, notions of the end of the world.

Thus it was relatively late by comparison with other religions when at the time of the Maccabean wars in the 2nd century B.C. the thought of life after death became a certainty among the Jews. Tacitus stresses the connection between waging war and belief in an afterlife as characteristic of the Jews. We have already mentioned Tacitus (d. A.D. 120), the most important and embittered opponent of Judaism and Christianity in pagan antiquity. Under the influence of the Jewish War and the downfall of Jerusalem and the Jewish state, he came to view the Christians as a dangerous group of Jewish insurgents, as one more terrorist organization among a people already so aggravating to the Romans.

Jews or Christians, it was all the same to Tacitus. And with the same bitterness that he speaks about the Christians in connection with Nero's conflagration of Rome (see Chapter Seven), Tacitus turns against the Jews here. They strike him as people who, motivated by their faith in the resurrection of their fallen or executed rebels, love to wage war and seek death. In the long series of reproaches that he levels at the Jews, who "regard as profane all that we hold sacred; . . . [but] permit all that we abhor," Tacitus writes: "They believe that the souls of those who are killed in battle or by the executioner are immortal; hence comes their passion for begetting children and their scorn of death" (*Histories*, trans. Clifford Moore [Cambridge, MA: Harvard Univ. Press, 1979], iv–v; LCL, p. 183).

Incidentally, Tacitus considered King Antiochus IV the bringer of Greek cultural development, which the Jews were badly in need of: "King Antiochus endeavored to abolish Jewish superstition and to introduce Greek civilization; the war with the Parthians, however, prevented his improving this basest of peoples" (*Histories*, V, viii; LCL, p. 189).

Thus the Maccabean martyrs are the first to reshape the eternal monotony of Sheol, the Jewish kingdom of death. For these warriors (then for other pious souls as well) belief in an eternal life means that residence in the underworld, first, has a time limit and, second, is totally transformed. Sheol now gets different sections: For the just, a pleasant sort of waiting room for the resurrection is set up; for the godless, there is an area of interim punishment until the final judgment, after which the punishment will become eternal.

In Jesus' day only the Sadducees continued to view Sheol as the eternal and unchanging kingdom of the dead. They believed in neither punishment nor reward in the Beyond, and they denied the resurrection. But the majority of the Jewish people followed the Pharisees and their faith in the resurrection, and Jesus shared the Pharisaic standpoint. In his parable of the rich man and poor Lazarus (Luke 16), Hades is divided into two sections by a "great chasm." In one section the rich man suffers "great pain" in a fire, in the other Lazarus the poor man sits in "Abraham's bosom," where conditions are pleasant and there is plenty of water.

The Greek doctrine of immortality changed the thinking of some Jews. Now they believed that the souls of the just no longer went, even temporarily, like Abraham and Lazarus, into the kingdom of the dead. Instead they went off immediately to the heights of heaven. That was the view of the Essenes, who are nowadays more or less identified with the community at Qumran. Josephus writes about their belief in immortality:

> For it is a fixed belief of theirs that the body is corruptible and its constituent matter impermanent, but that the soul is immortal and imperishable. Emanating from the finest ether, these souls become entangled, as it were, in the prison house of the body . . . but when they are released from the bonds of the flesh, then, as though liberated from a long servitude, they rejoice and are borne aloft. Sharing the belief of the sons of Greece, they maintain that for virtuous souls there is reserved an abode beyond the ocean, a place which is not oppressed by rain or snow or heat, but is refreshed by the ever gentle breath of the west wind coming in from the ocean; while they relegate base souls to a murky and tempestuous dungeon, big with never-ending punishments. The Greeks, I imagine, had the same conception when they set apart the isles of the blessed for their brave men, whom they call heroes and demigods, and the region of the impious for the souls of the wicked down in Hades. (JW, II, viii, 11; LCL, pp. 381, 383)

Josephus also describes his personal belief: "Their souls [i.e., of people who die naturally] remaining spotless and obedient, are allotted the most holy place in heaven, whence in the revolution of the ages, they return to find in chaste bodies a new habitation. But as for those who have laid mad hands upon themselves, the darker regions of the nether world receive their souls" (JW, III, viii, 5; LCL, p. 681).

Thus in the image conjured up by the parable of the rich man and Lazarus, the good dead people dwell in a special section of Sheol. But, as the Essenes and Josephus see it, Sheol, the world of the dead, has lost all contact with the pious. And this trend continued. According to Rabbi Jochanan ben Zakkai (d. ca. A.D. 80), the souls of all the good people arrive immediately after their death in the Garden of Eden. This Eden is a halfway house to the resurrection. Thus the good no longer make any temporary stop in Sheol, which is turned into the place for punishing the godless. The erstwhile kingdom of all the dead, good and evil, has become a place of damnation.

But Sheol was increasingly losing its importance not just for the good, but ultimately for the wicked, too. In Jewish writing from around 130 B.C., a second place suddenly popped up alongside Sheol: the valley of Gehinnom, a place of terror that had never been, like Sheol, the destination of good people. As time went on, this Gehinnom increasingly superseded Sheol as the place of punishment.

In the New Testament, both places, Sheol and Gehenna, still remain side by side: The actual Hell and ultimate place of punishment for the wicked is *Gehinnom* ("Gehenna" in Greek): Matt. 5:22, 5:29–30, 10:28, 18:9, 23:15, 23:33; Mark 9:44, 45, 47; Luke 12:5; James 3:6. *Sheol* (or *Hades*) is now just the place for the transitional state experienced by all the dead, a waiting room for the good and a temporary place of punishment for the wicked until the resurrection and the subsequent last judgment. Here in Hades both the rich man and Lazarus wait for the final decision (Matt. 11:23, 16:18; Luke 10:15, 16:23; Acts 2:27, 31; Rev. 1:18, 6:8, 20:13–14). By the end of the first century of the Christian era, however, Jewish scholars believed that Gehinnom was the only place of punishment, both temporary and eternal, for the wicked. Sheol no longer had any importance; it had been, so to speak, swallowed up in Gehinnom. Thus with the emergence of belief in the resurrection in the 2nd century B.C., Sheol, the world of the dead, increasingly lost its significance for warriors and for the good, and by the end of the 1st century A.D. it no longer meant anything even to the wicked.

Gehinnom, the eternal Hell of the New Testament, was originally a notorious valley of terror south of Jerusalem. It was also called the Valley of Fire, and it owed its ill repute to the child sacrifices that are supposed to have been offered up in the fire there. Such human sacrifices are reported, for example, of King Ahaz (8th century B.C.; 2 Kings 16:3) and King Manasseh (7th century B.C.; 2 Kings 21:6). By about 130 B.C. this valley of horrors had become the scene of the last judgment in Jewish literature; and in the New Testament, which was written in Greek, it gave Hell its Greek name: Gehenna.

The two main instruments of punishment in Gehenna are, first, fire, and second, darkness, two things that don't go together. They were associated because the darkness from the realm of the dead (Hades or Sheol) was added on to the fire that had been bound up with Gehenna from the first. Thus, as Gehenna slowly took the place of Sheol, Hell became the dark and fiery kingdom of the dead.

The Dead Sea Scrolls speak of the "night of eternal fire" (1QS II, 8; TEWFQ, p. 75, composed 2nd/1st century B.C.). Hell becomes a "black fire" or a "dark fire" (Strack and Billerbeck, Kommentar, IV, 1079, 1084). Thus in the New Testament we read about the "darkness" of Hell, where "men will weep and gnash their teeth" (Matt. 8:12; 22:13; 25:30). The weeping from pain was originally predicated of the people suffering in the fires of Hell. The darkness, as mentioned, was added to the fire later on.

But it's not just that Hell borrows darkness from the realm of the dead; the realm of the dead borrows fire from Hell. In Jesus' parable the rich man in the realm of the dead, in Hades (Sheol), is waiting amid the flames for the Last Judgment.

From the outset, Jewish scholars assigned a purifying, reconciling power to hellfire. Thus Hell was simultaneously, as it were, a purifying Purgatory. In the first half of the 1st century A.D., there was a controversy between the school of Rabbi Shammai and the school of Rabbi Hillel: Rabbi Shammai's supporters said that the mediocre souls would be cleansed of their sins by the fire of the Last Judgment and would then come to the place of bliss. Hillel's partisans said that the mediocre wouldn't go to the fire of Gehinnom at all, that is, at the Last Judgment they would enter Paradise.

By the end of the 1st century A.D., when Gehinnom had also turned into the temporary place of punishment, its fire too was regarded as a purifying one. Rabbi Akiba (d. A.D. 135) thought that this would be an advantage for certain "godless individuals." After twelve months in the fire, their guilt would be wiped away. Moreover, a dead person's survivors could shorten the time served in Gehinnom through intercessory prayer and almsgiving (Strack and Billerbeck, *Kommentar*, IV, 1045). But unlike the Persian hellfire, which eventually purifies all humans and brings them into Paradise, here some people remained excluded from bliss. According to Rabbi Akiba and his followers, the following persons would not be admitted: freethinkers, people who read the noncanonical books, and heretics.

But there is one group of people who will definitely not go to Gehinnom: "Three [sorts] will not see the face of judgment in Gehinnom: Those who suffer from grinding poverty, abdominal diseases, and creditors. Some add to this: anyone married to a nasty wife" (Strack and Billerbeck, *Kommentar*, IV, 1071). Such persons have all had their Hell on earth beforehand.

This theological mixture of humanity and inhumanity in constructing Hell led in the end to a state of tangled confusion. Thus there are people who, some rabbis thought, would go to the provisional Hell in Gehinnom but who would not rise at the Last Judgment, because they would have been annihilated by the fire and have ceased to exist. Others again "will sleep an eternal sleep and not wake up," and so they, too, will not rise up at the Last Judgment—for example, the generation from the time of the Flood, the generation of the Tower of Babel, the Egyptians drowned in the Sea of Reeds, the troops of Nebuchadnezzar, and the underage children of the Gentiles. Then around A.D. 300, Rabbi Abbahu drew the logical conclusion and said that only the just would rise up. But the schools of Hillel and Shammai had taught that all human beings would be raised (Strack and Billerbeck, *Kommentar*, IV, 1178–89).

The first ones to manage to put order into the chaotic Hell of Jewish theologians were their Christian counterparts. But before this centuries-long task, the first step was taken by turning Jesus into a preacher of Hell—although he had never been any such thing. It's also noteworthy that Paul, the earliest writer in the New Testament, while he uses terms such as death, rejection, and downfall to describe missing one's definitive human vocation, does not speak of any Hell.

Even John, the latest of the four Evangelists, refrains from any Hell fantasies. Catholic theologian Georg Baudler stresses the fact that in the Gospel according to John, "which concentrates on God's self-revelation as love, . . . we see a clear tendency to separate from God any active . . . judging, sentencing, and casting out" ("Jesus und die Hölle," in *Theologie der Gegenwart*, 3/1991, 166).

Jesus talks a lot less about Hell than one might assume from the Church's threatening gestures. And the little he does say has been put into his mouth after the fact. Matthew is the main Evangelist who makes Jesus use Hell as a threat. But Bultmann has shown that the phrase "weeping and gnashing of teeth," which Jesus repeats six times (Matt. 8:12; 13:42, 50; 22:13; 24:51; 25:30), is an editorial insertion. It is used to explain and reinforce the original discourse material and does not come from Jesus (*Die Geschichte der synoptischen Tradition* [1961], p. 352). The one passage in Luke where "weeping and gnashing of teeth" occur is characterized by Bultmann as "a threatening saying that has nothing to do with Jesus" (p. 122). Georg Baudler comes to a similar conclusion:

> Hence it is of the highest theological importance that the images of Gehenna do not belong to Jesus' poetic vocabulary. Scholars who have researched the parables are agreed that those images were subsequently inserted into the body of Jesus' parables (mostly by the Matthew-community). All the divine tribunals and images of Hell that appear in Jesus' parables are later interpolations, and in some cases they actually wreck the structure of the original parable. (*Theologie der Gegenwart*, 3/1991, 167)

Of Jesus' discourse about the Last Judgment, where the good are separated from the wicked, the good saved and the wicked condemned and consigned to the flames ("Then he will say to those at his left hand, 'Depart from me, you cursed, into the eternal fire prepared for the devil and his angels'" [Matt. 25:31–46]), Bultmann writes: "[Here] Christian tradition has borrowed Jewish material and put it into Jesus' mouth" (Bultmann, *Die Geschichte*, pp. 132–33).

Jesus was no preacher of hellfire. His appearance in the synagogue of Nazareth left a deep impression on those who were present ("And all spoke well of him and wondered at the gracious words which proceeded out of his mouth" [Luke 4:22]). This scene shows that he omitted the talk of threats and punishment so common in the biblical prophets.

In Jesus' day the Jewish synagogue service, which remains to this day the model of both Catholic and Protestant services, took place on Saturday morning, on Saturday afternoon, and again on Monday and Thursday. Mondays and Thursdays courts were in session and markets open. Many country folk came into the towns then and had an opportunity to attend a service, something they could not do in their villages.

The services included readings from Scripture (standing) and a subsequent sermon (sitting). The readings came first from the Torah, then from the prophets. Reading the Scriptures was not the privilege of a special class: "Even an underage boy, even a woman" could do the reading (Strack and Billerbeck, *Kommentar,* IV, 157). The readers were called up by the overseer of the synagogue. If possible, a priest would be summoned first, then a Levite, then the others. They were informed the day before so that they could prepare themselves. Since by the time of Jesus, Hebrew was no longer the mother tongue of Jews, after every verse (in readings from the prophets after every three verses) a translator would render into Aramaic what had just been read.

In Jesus' day the reading from the prophets, unlike the reading from the Pentateuch, was not prescribed, so the reader could choose the text himself. Luke writes (4:16–19):

> *And he came to Nazareth, where he had been brought up; and he went to the synagogue, as his custom was, on the sabbath day. And he stood up to read; and there was given to him the book of the prophet Isaiah. He opened the book and found the place where it is written: "The Spirit of the Lord is upon me, because he has anointed me to preach good news to the poor. He has sent me to proclaim release to the captives and recovering of sight to the blind, to set at liberty those who are oppressed, to proclaim the acceptable year of the Lord."*

Thus Jesus closes his reading of Scripture (Isa. 61:1–2) with the words "the acceptable year of the Lord" (Isa. 61:2a). He breaks off in the middle of Isaiah's sentence, which goes on "and the day of vengeance of our God" (Isa. 61:2b). This vengeance will be taken at the end of time on the "enemy."

Then Jesus delivers a brief sermon, as was customary after the reading from the prophets. Luke continues: "And he closed the book, and gave it back to the attendant, and sat down; and the eyes of all in the synagogue were fixed on him. And he began to say to them, 'Today this scripture has been fulfilled in your hearing'" (Luke 4:20–21). Thus at the beginning of his career as a teacher, in a sort of preview of coming attractions, Jesus makes it clear that the vision of eschatological revenge belongs neither to his mission nor to his message.

There is yet another scene in the New Testament, reported by both Matthew and Luke, where Jesus pointedly neglects to speak of revenge and retribution at the end of time:

> Now when John heard in prison about the deeds of the Christ, he sent word by his disciples and said to him, "Are you he who is to come, or shall we look for another?" And Jesus answered them, "Go and tell John what you hear and see: the blind receive their sight and the lame walk, lepers are cleansed and the deaf hear, and the dead are raised up, and the poor have the good news preached to them. And blessed is he who takes no offense at me." (Matt. 11:2–6; cf. Luke 7:22–23)

The answer that Jesus sends to John the Baptist is a combination of quotations from Isaiah, namely, 29:18–19, 35:3–4, and again, as in the synagogue in Nazareth, 61:1. In all three quotations Jesus drops the words of revenge and retribution. Thus he skips Isa. 29:20: "And all who do evil shall be cut off"; Isa. 35:4b: "Behold your God will come with vengeance, with the recompense of God"; and again, as in Nazareth, Isa. 61:2: "and the day of vengeance of our God."

So although Jesus was the exact opposite of a hellfire preacher, only with the coming of Christianity did Hell come into its own, and begin its triumphal march. The Church has fashioned itself less into a preacher of a heaven than into a tireless preacher of Hell. It has found its divinely backed threats of Hell the most convenient way to compel religious obedience from the terrified minds of the faithful. The Church's pastors have cultivated a horror of God in their sheep, transforming him into a kind of watchdog and hellhound to guard them. To make it easier to lead a willing flock, they claimed that God barks and bites and broils. To the extent that they have succeeded in this, they have caused love for God to atrophy. If life in the next world resembles the Church's teaching, some of the dead might greatly prefer not rising and landing in the Hell of the Christian God, but continuing their eternal sleep in the original Hell of the goddess Hel beneath the World Tree, Iggdrasill.

The Church's knowledge about Hell constantly grew in scope. Around three hundred years after his death in 253, Origen, the greatest scholar of Christian antiquity, was damned by the Synod of Constantinople (543) because he had denied the eternity of infernal punishment. "Whoever says or believes that the punishment of evil spirits and godless men is only temporary and will end after a certain time, and that then there will be a complete restoration [*apokatastasis*] of the evil spirits and godless men, let him be anathema."

The ancient Church boasted a long series of other theologians who were supporters of Origen and rejected the idea of endless punishment in Hell. But they were all given the same sentence passed against Origen. Even after the condemnation in 543, the controversies over Origen, which had been going on for centuries, did not let up. In the course of church history, theologians have continually arisen to deny the eternity of Hell. But the preachers of eternal Hell prevailed and even took care, for example, that this eternity of woe should start up as soon as possible.

In the year 1336 Pope Benedict XII in his constitution *Benedictus Deus* determined that the pains of Hell begin immediately after death: "We further declare that, as God has universally ordained, the souls of those who die in mortal sin descend into Hell at once, where they are tormented by infernal agonies."

In 1442 the Council of Florence announced that all people who do not convert to Catholicism will go to Hell. The Holy Roman Catholic Church "firmly believes, confesses, and proclaims that neither the heathens nor the Jews nor the heretics and schismatics will have a share in eternal life, but will enter the eternal fire that has been prepared for the devil and his angels, if they do not join the Church before their death."

This old tradition explains why even Dante (d. 1321) in his *Divine Comedy* didn't dare to let any unbaptized persons into Heaven—neither

Plato nor Aristotle nor, above all, his guide, Virgil, whom he so venerated. He had to assign them a place in Limbo at the entrance to Hell. Not until five hundred years after the Council of Florence (1438–45) did the Second Vatican Council (1962–65) issue a more ecumenical communiqué about the fate of non-Catholics in the afterlife (even though this immediately stirred up unrest among the missionaries).

This soothing message for the pagans and disturbing message for the Christians went as follows: Article 16 of the "Constitution on the Church" (*Lumen Gentium*) states that "whoever through no fault of his own does not know the Gospel of Christ and his Church . . . can obtain eternal salvation." And article 2 of the "Declaration on the Relations of the Church with the Non-Christian Religions" (*Nostra Aetate*) of 28 November 1965 goes further, maintaining that "the other religions spread throughout the world are also striving in one fashion or another to counter the restlessness of the human heart, by pointing the ways: with teachings and rules of life as well as holy rites. The Catholic Church rejects none of all that is true and holy in these religions."

As mentioned, these conciliar texts aroused great concern among people working in the missions, because their jobs seemed to be in danger. This led to the Second Vatican Council's issuing a "Decree on the Missionary Activity of the Church" (*Ad Gentes*), dated 7 December 1965, which says in article 7: "Thus it is necessary that all be converted to him [Jesus], who becomes known through the preaching of the Church, and that they be incorporated both into him and into his body, the Church, through baptism. . . . Even though God can lead to faith, by ways that he knows, people who through no fault of their own are ignorant of the Gospel, . . . it is still necessary for the Church to proclaim the Gospel."

Such phenomena, suggesting that Hell was being phased out, left some missionaries frustrated. One Suso Brechter, the Benedictine arch-abbot of St. Ottilien in Munich, did what he could to comfort them. In his official commentary on that article 7, he wrote:

A large number of active missionaries were worried about the all too positive assessment of alien religions and of the possibility of salvation for non-Christians that had supposedly been expressed

by the Council in the Constitution on the Church (article 16) and
in the Declaration on the Relations of the Church with the Non-
Christian Religions (article 2). They demanded that a clear posi-
tion be taken on these problems and that an official statement be
issued on the necessity of the missions even after the Council, in
order to have a solid theological foundation for their work, which
is so difficult and burdened with responsibility.

The reverend commentator then continues in a comforting vein (comforting for the missionaries, not for the heathens): The council has not "reached a decision on the salvific value of the non-Christian religions," and "at least up till now the traditional solution has by no means been fundamentally shaken" (*LThK*, "Das Zweite Vatikanische Konzil" [1968], III, 40). So the missionaries can heave a sigh of relief and continue as before. The worst has been averted, for the time being. The worst would have been that without the Church and the missionaries everybody would get to heaven and nobody would go to Hell anymore. One wonders, though. Since Vatican II, God has been able to save those who are unbelievers "through no fault of their own," "by ways that he knows"—in other words, besides the straight paths of the Christians, God is also familiar with the crooked paths of the pagans. But one wonders whether the missionaries haven't recently been wreaking havoc, because for the most part all they manage to do is destroy pagan innocence. As soon as the missionaries show up, their innocence—and guiltlessness—is lost. The saving clause about those who ignore the Gospel "through no fault of their own" no longer applies to people once the missionaries have descended on them.

The fire in Hell must not be understood as a mere image or manner of speaking. "All of Church tradition," the well-known Catholic theologian Michael Schmaus tells us, "agrees that it is actual fire." He goes on: "Anyone who abandons this view is distancing himself from the general consensus of the Church. To do so, therefore, involves a dangerous risk." Schmaus makes the following point:

Also important is a statement by the Penitentiary (in Rome)
dated April 30, 1890. A confessor from the diocese of Mantua
asked how he should deal with a penitent who told him that he

did not believe in the fire of Hell, but looked upon it as a
metaphor for the pains of Hell. The answer given was that such
penitents were to be carefully instructed, and if they stubbornly
persisted in their thinking, they could not receive absolution.
(Katholische Dogmatik [1959], IV/2, 492-93).

In other words, the unfortunate fellow is in danger of being plunged into hellfire for lack of sufficient faith in it.

What proportion of humanity is damned, and what proportion is saved? Augustine (d. 430) can inform us that "the majority of humans will not be among the blessed" (*Enchiridion*, XCVII). The fact that Christianity turned into a religion of divine damnation is essentially due to this greatest of the Church Fathers. For Augustine the entire human race is a *massa damnata*. Only a smallish part will be saved, and this minority must constantly be aware of "what the whole human race actually deserved," namely, eternal damnation (*Enchiridion*, XXV).

Especially painful—for mothers at any rate—is Augustine's teaching that unbaptized children must taste the fire of Hell, "even though in a less painful fashion than those who have heaped personal sins on themselves" (*Letter to Paulinus*, XXIX). Augustine's most intelligent opponent was Bishop Julian of Eclanum, and because of that opposition he found his way into church history as a great heretic. Julian calls the God of Augustine a "persecutor of the newborn, who throws tiny babies into the eternal flames" (Augustine, *Opus imperfectum contra Julianum*, I, xlviii).

The Church's doctrine of unbaptized infants' suffering the pains of Hell shows that, for all its protests, the Church is certainly no advocate for the unborn. Of course, the consequences are even worse when the Church, after its own fashion, *does* play advocate for the unborn. Alphonsus Liguori (d. 1787), who until the middle of this century set the standard for Catholic moral theology, once tackled the question of what to do when an unborn child is in danger of dying before birth and hence before baptism. In this context he discusses at length "whether the mother is obliged to let her body be cut open so that the child can be baptized." He comes to the following decision: The mother must endure the possibility of her death through being cut open if in exchange there is a probability that the child can be baptized and thus attain eternal life. But if her death is certain and the possibility of the child's baptism is not certain, then the mother is not obliged to accept certain death (*Theologis Moralis*, VI, n. 106).

Bernhard Häring, the best-selling moral theologian of the mid-20th century, wrote in 1967: "If there is no hope of insuring the child's life and above all its baptism in any other way, then the mother is obliged to undergo this sort of operation" (*Das Gesetz Christi* [1967], III, 225). Note that the important thing is "above all its baptism." By "this sort of operation" Häring understands Caesarean section, or cutting through the pelvis or the interpubic disk, which is to be undertaken "under certain dangers for the mother." The idea is to pluck the unborn child from God's hellish hands and give it over to God's heavenly hands. To do that, a mother has to make a few sacrifices, and in past centuries, owing to inferior medical skill, not a few mothers lost their lives protecting their children from Hell (Uta Ranke-Heinemann, *Eunuchs for the Kingdom of Heaven* [New York: Doubleday, 1990], pp. 305-10).

However, since about the 12th century, many theologians have built a special Hell for unbaptized children. They believe that God does not plunge these children into the lower regions of hellfire, but settles them on a sort of margin or fringe (*limbus* in Latin) of Hell, generally known as Limbo. As late as the 19th century, theologians argued over whether the infants suffered pains there. But in 1886 the Wetzer and Welte *Kirchenlexikon* ventured to say that this "wasn't even probable" (IV, 768).

In our century it is now certain that they "suffer no physical pain. This opinion is today morally certain, although it was challenged by Augustine and many others" (*Dictionnaire de la Théologie Catholique* [1932] II, 366). As people become more humane, God does, too. A few theologians of our day have therefore simply abolished the whole business of Limbo for unbaptized children.

But one still runs into opinions like that of one Father Wasser in the parish of St. Hubert in Essen. Around 1970 this good priest used to tell the children preparing for their first communion, "Before baptism you were the devil's children. Through baptism you are God's children." Some of the pupils were deeply disturbed by all this.

When something's on fire, something must get burned. What the devil uses for fuel, whether wood or coal or gas or oil, is a point the Church has not yet defined. The Wetzer and Welte *Kirchenlexikon* suggests the possibility of sulfur ([1889] VI, 116). Maybe he uses something altogether different. In any case, he could get an enormous supply of fuel if he simply heated Hell with the mountains of paper bescribbled by theologians and church officials drafting their doctrines of eternal punishment.

With its teaching on Hell, the Church has stood Christ's teaching on its head. It has turned his good news into bad news, turned a God of love into a God of cruelty. Christ demands of human beings that they be ready to forgive and be reconciled, and backs up these demands by pointing to an irreconcilable God. It doesn't help things when the theologians, as they have ever done, try to give Hell a lofty meaning: "The meaning of hell," writes Michael Schmaus, "is not the improvement or education of a person, but the glorification of God, of the holy, the compassionate, the truthful, and just God" (*Katholische Dogmatik* [1959], IV/2, 507).

Lately, many theologians, particularly Catholics, who feel obliged to keep Hell even though they don't want to, try appeasing their conscience with a compromise: "Hell exists as a possibility, but we're not obliged to believe that there's anyone in it." This is one of the many halfhearted dodges that only make Christianity even less credible. In the message of God's love, the doctrine of the possibility of Hell makes no sense. What Jesus preaches overcomes all the sermons on Hell.

CHAPTER SEVENTEEN

Jesus and the Dead Sea Scrolls

IN RECENT YEARS there has been much discussion of the relationship between Jesus and the people of Qumran. (They were presumably members of the group of Jews whom we have come to know as Essenes, primarily thanks to Josephus.) In *The Dead Sea Scrolls Deception* (Summit, 1992), British journalists Michael Baigent and Richard Leigh claim that a considerable portion of the Dead Sea Scrolls, which were discovered between 1947 and 1956, have been withheld from the public and kept under lock and key. This, we are told, is the fault of the Vatican and, above all, Cardinal Ratzinger.

Such claims only show how deep the mistrust toward the Vatican runs, and how thoroughly convinced people are that the Vatican is opposed to every kind of enlightenment and scientific progress. Galileo has not yet been forgotten. In this case, however, justice demands the acknowledgment that the Vatican and Cardinal Ratzinger are not guilty, even if only because in an age of mass media the obscurantists are no longer capable of locking up scholarly/scientific findings or simply making them disappear. But the real reason is that questions concerning the historical Jesus leave the Catholic hierarchy more or less indifferent. It's enough for them that Jesus lived and, above all, that he was crucified. As far as his words and deeds go, the crucial thing is interpretation, and the pope is in charge of interpretation anyway. Not all the Qumran texts have been published, and that can rightly be considered a scandal, but it's not a plot by Ratzinger. The real culprit is jurisdictional disputes and a lead-footed bureaucracy.

A lost goat, the story goes, got the stone rolling. And a shepherd boy, Muhammad adh-Dhib ("Muhammad the wolf") was supposedly the one who did the rest. One day in 1947, on the northwest shore of the Dead Sea, while searching for that goat, he stumbled onto a cave with clay jars. They contained, not the golden treasures the boy hoped for, but ancient scrolls from the so-called Qumran sect. This community is so named because the valley (wadi) of Qumran and its ruins (khirbet) lie near the site of the finds. Further explorations were undertaken, and between 1951 and 1956 they uncovered the remains of a large, monasterylike settlement with residences, workplaces, warehouses, baths, cisterns, fortifications, and so on, even one large and two smaller cemeteries. In the large cemetery, laid out in careful order, around eleven hundred men were buried, while in the two smaller ones, in not so careful order, lay about a hundred graves, including those of seven women (buried with meager bits of jewelry) and four children.

The community probably settled in Qumran sometime after the middle of the 2nd century B.C., building on the ruins of a much older Israelite fortress. In 31 B.C. the settlement was abandoned after an earthquake and fires, but it was rebuilt and resettled in the years 4–1 B.C. In A.D. 68, during the Jewish War, the whole site was destroyed by the Romans. Roman soldiers maintained an outpost in Qumran all the way till the end of the century. In the course of the Bar Kochba rebellion (132–35), the last uprising against the Romans, Jewish guerrillas had a base there. But after the rebellion was crushed, Qumran remained deserted.

The dig uncovered forty previously inhabited caves. In eleven of these caves, known as 1–11 Q, manuscripts were found that had presumably been stashed away at the outbreak of the Jewish War. The scrolls and fragments are of leather, with the exception of a few papyrus Scriptures. Excavators also found two copper scrolls (actually plates) with a list of hidden treasures.

The writings can be divided into three groups:

The first (making up about a fourth of the total find) consists of copies of Old Testament books. These are extremely important because they are one thousand to twelve hundred years older than the hitherto oldest known complete Hebrew manuscript of the Bible (from A.D. 1008). With the Bible manuscripts from Qumran, the textual fidelity of previously available manuscripts could be checked and confirmed. Strangely enough, the only book of the Bible missing is Esther.

The second group consists of the Apocrypha and Pseudepigrapha. These Apocrypha are the writings that were accepted in the Catholic Old Testament, but not in the Hebrew Bible or the Protestant Old Testament. The Pseudepigrapha are similar ancient Jewish writings that were rejected by all sides. Since the canon of the Hebrew Bible wasn't fixed until A.D. 90, it was still fluid at the time of the Dead Sea Scrolls.

The third group contains original writings by the Qumran community itself, for example, commentaries on Old Testament texts. They reflect the mental world of the people in Qumran because they are actualizing interpretations (i.e., they refer to the concrete situation of the community) of such biblical books as Habakkuk, Isaiah, Hosea, Micah, Psalms, and so on. Also included in this group are writings such as the *Rule of the Community* (1QS), *Rule of the Congregation* (1QSa), *Thanksgiving Hymns* (1QH), the *War Scroll* (1QM), and the *Damascus Document*.

This third group, the actual sectarian writings of the community, are the most interesting to scholars. They are important, above all, for answering the question about Qumran's relationship to early Christianity and to Jesus. The reflections in the Dead Sea Scrolls of the life, faith, and organization of the community provide a direct insight into the religious life of the time.

The Qumran community was the core of a separatist Jewish group that was led by priests. In the second half of the 2nd century B.C., it had broken away from the Jerusalem temple cult. Under its leader, the "Teacher of Righteousness," whose antagonist is the so-called Wicked Priest, the group emigrated into the wilderness of Judea near Qumran. There they set up their center. There were subgroups of this sect all over the country. Their members lived apart from the other inhabitants.

All attempts to identify the Teacher of Righteousness and his opponent, the Wicked Priest, with familiar contemporary figures have thus far come to nought. The claim by Baigent and Leigh that the Teacher of Righteousness was the brother of Jesus, James the Just, and that his evil antagonist was the Apostle Paul is simply absurd. Apart from all its other weaknesses, this thesis collapses when faced with the most recently conducted radiocarbon dating, which places the scrolls in the 2nd and 1st centuries B.C.

Some of the Qumran texts that bear witness to lofty poetic power are ascribed to the Teacher of Righteousness. He sees himself, on the one hand, as weak and unworthy, for instance, in one of the songs of praise in the *Thanksgiving Hymns*: "And shaking and trembling seized me / and all my bones cracked, / and my heart melted like wax before fire / and my knees slipped like water descending a slope; for I remembered my faults / and the unfaithfulness of my fathers" (1QH IV:33–34; *TEWFQ*, p. 213). On the other hand, he has the self-consciousness of a religious ruler: "I give Thee thanks, O Adonai, / for Thou hast upheld me by Thy might / and hast poured out Thy holy Spirit within me / . . . and hast established my fabric upon rock. . . . And Thou hast made of me a father to the sons of Grace" (1QH VII:6–9, 20; *TEWFQ*, pp. 222–23).

As two internal Jewish movements, Christianity and Qumran turn out to be quite similar on some points. Both consider themselves the true Israel. Both see themselves as living in the end time, waiting for the imminent end of the world (and both were wrong on that). Both venerate their masters as revealers of divine mysteries. Both are convinced that they were predicted in the Scriptures and consider themselves the fulfillment of these biblical promises.

In both, the cultic meal plays a major role. Josephus writes about the Essenes:

> *They are strenuously employed until the fifth hour [meaning until 11:00 to 12:00 in the morning], when they again assemble in one place and, after girding their loins with linen cloths, bathe their bodies in cold water. After this purification, they assemble in a private apartment which none of the uninitiated is permitted*

to enter; pure now themselves, they repair to the refectory, as to some sacred shrine. When they have taken their seats in silence, the baker serves out the loaves to them in order, and the cook sets before each one plate with a single course. Before meat the priest says a grace, and none may partake until after the prayer. When breakfast is ended, he pronounces a further grace; thus at the beginning and at the close they do homage to God as the bountiful giver of life. Then laying aside their raiment, as holy vestments, they again betake themselves to their labours until the evening. (JW, II, viii, 5; LCL, p. 373)

The cultic element is obvious here: The dining room is a "shrine." The priest plays a crucial role. The heterodox are excluded. Only those who have been purified are allowed to take part in the meal. A special outfit—the white garments mentioned by Josephus shortly before this (II, viii, 3)—are prescribed in lieu of ordinary working clothes. This report by Josephus is confirmed by the Qumran Scriptures (cf. *Rule of the Community* 1QS 6:3–5; *TEWFQ,* p. 85; and the *Rule of the Congregation* 1QSa 2:17–22; *TEWFQ,* pp. 108–9).

The Christian Eucharist, which in many details resembles the Qumran cultic banquet, has been continually stylized to the point that it has completely lost its original character as a real meal. But in the beginning, things were different. Paul criticizes the Christians of Corinth: "Each one goes ahead with his meal, and one is hungry and another is drunk" (1 Cor. 11:21).

For two thousand years Christianity has accustomed its followers to understand the Old Testament as foretelling Jesus and the Christian Church. Now it turns out that Qumran often laid claim to the exact same Old Testament texts as foretelling Qumran and the Teacher of Righteousness.

One such word of promise is the passage in Isa. 61:1–2. In the *Thanksgiving Hymns* (1QH XVIII:14–15; *TEWFQ,* p. 252) the task of the Teacher of Righteousness is described in connection with these verses: "That according to Thy truth [he may be] / the one who announces good tidings [in the ti]me of Thy goodness, [giving them to drink] from the fountain of h[oliness] / [and consoling the co]ntrite of spirit and the afflicted / to (bring them) everlasting joy."

Jesus, too, refers to this prophetic text, in the scene at the Nazareth synagogue (Luke 4:18), where he says, "Today this scripture has been fulfilled in your hearing." As we saw in the last chapter, Jesus drops the phrase from Isa. 61:2b, "and the day of revenge of our God." The text of the *Thanksgiving Hymns* is damaged here. But for Qumran, the day of revenge was crucially important and not a point to be dropped. As we shall see, Qumran's program was as militaristic as Jesus' program was pacifistic. By way of anticipating this, we can note that the *War Scroll* says something about the "poor" that Jesus emphatically did not say about them: "For Thou wilt deliver the [en]emies of all the lands / into the hand of the Poor" (meaning the people of Qumran) "to draw down the reward which is due to the wicked upon [the head] [of] [their] en[emies]" (1QM XI:13–15; *TEWFQ*, p. 186).

But first one more example of common ideas: Both Qumran and the Christians applied to themselves the saying of the prophet Jeremiah (31:31) about the new covenant. In the *Damascus Document* (VI:3–11; *TEWFQ*, p. 131) Qumran calls itself the "community of the new covenant." And the *Rule of the Community* (1QS IV:22; *TEWFQ*, p. 82) declares: "For God has chosen them (the just) for an everlasting Covenant." In the New Testament, the Christian community also sees itself as the new covenant, and so it has Jesus saying at the Last Supper: "This is the blood of the covenant, which is poured out for many for the forgiveness of sins" (Matt. 26:28). Paul, too, speaks of the new covenant: "God has made us competent to be ministers of a new covenant, not in a written code, but in the Spirit" (2 Cor. 3:6). In the Letter to the Hebrews, Christ is described as "the mediator of a new covenant" (9:15).

There are striking similarities even in the details of their teaching: Both Jesus (Mark 10:6; Matt. 19:4) and the Qumran sect point to Gen. 1:27 ("male and female he created them") to stress monogamy and fidelity, not polygamy and divorce, as being originally God's will. Both groups thus opposed the trends toward polygamy and easy divorce in the contemporary male-dominated Jewish world. In the *Damascus Document* (IV:20–V:1; *TEWFQ*, pp. 128–29) it is said of the enemies of Qumran: "[they] have been caught by lust in two things: / by marrying two women during their lifetime, / whereas nature's principle is / *Male and female created He them.* / And those who entered the ark (of Noah), *Two and two they went into the ark.*"

When Jesus—like Qumran—rejects adultery and divorce, his disciples take this as an infringement of their polygamous interests. If you're not allowed to divorce, then it would be better not to marry, because otherwise you lose your sexual freedom and the possibility of getting rid of your wife (Matt. 19:9–10). Jesus answers: "Not all men can receive this saying" (Matt. 19:11). Jesus' wise insight into human shortcomings was not adopted by the Catholic Church. While the other two major Christian Churches, the Protestants and the Eastern Orthodox, permit divorced people to remarry, the Catholic Church singles out remarried divorced persons for special punishment. This despite the fact that Jesus explicitly says about this group, "Not all men can receive this saying."

For two thousand years Catholic theologians have been busy pointing out the unique and unheard of features of the person of Jesus. In the process they infallibly hand out things that either are not true (the virgin birth in the biological sense or miracles as violations of the laws of nature) or that have been done or suffered in exactly the same way by others. To a careful, unbiased observer, this sort of perspective leaves Jesus with not one feature uniquely his own. Nevertheless, Christians should heed what Jesus said even if others have said something similar. What's right isn't made any more right by the fact that no one ever said it before; nor is it made false because someone already said it. The following section will point up the differences between Christians and Qumran. But this is not animated by the sort of theological arrogance that never admits defeat and that has a long tradition of checkmating other religions.

The Qumran community differed from the original Christians, above all, on two points: militarization and hostility to women. To be sure, both those traits made their way into Christianity early on, and in the course of history the Christians have more than caught up on both scores.

Since waging war can't be called an unusual activity for men, the most striking and unusual thing about Qumran is its position on women. The community has often been characterized as an "order of monks," as a "monastery," and scholars have spoken of its obligation to "celibacy" (e.g., in the articles on "Qumran" in both the Catholic *Lexikon für Theologie und Kirche* [1963] and the Protestant standard reference work *Religion in Geschichte und Gegenwart* [1961]). But Shemaryahu Talmon, one of the most eminent contemporary experts on Qumran and professor of Bible at the Hebrew University in Jerusalem, argues on the basis of the most recent research that

> the male members resident in Qumran lived in a sort of pre-Christian, ascetical, monastic community. But they apparently did not bind themselves to lifelong celibacy, and they understood their frugal life not as a principle of faith but as a conditional situation. . . . So we can surmise that a man between twenty or thirty complied with the biblical command to beget offspring and then lived as a celibate in Qumran for ten years. (Address given at the Conference of the Catholic Academy, Munich, 12 January 1992)

Thus far we have heard several voices about the absence of women from the Qumran community. The two Christian voices make Qumran out to be a sort of ancient Vatican. The Jewish scholar Talmon is trying to soften Qumran's antisexuality and to bring it into some sort of harmony with Jewish tradition, which is not—unlike Christian tradition—hostile to sex.

The Old Testament and Judaism had no such hostility. (This is the reason the Christian bachelor theology later did not fail to defame Judaism as "carnal.") The Jewish philosopher of religion Schalom Ben-Chorin even thinks that Jesus, as a rabbi, must have been married. He refers to the saying of Rabbi Eleazar ben Azariah (ca. A.D. 100): "Whoever refuses to marry violates the commandment to increase and multiply, and must be looked upon as a murderer who lowers the number of beings created in the image of God" (*Mutter Mirjam* [1982], p. 92). Rabbi Eliezer (around A.D. 90) had a similar comment: "Whoever does not attend to propagation is like one who sheds blood" (Hermann Strack and Paul Billerbeck, *Kommentar zum Neuen Testament aus Talmud und Midrash*, II, 373).

Given Judaism's negative attitude toward celibacy, the womanless community of Qumran caused a sensation even in antiquity. Philo of Alexandria (d. ca. A.D. 45/50), the most cultivated Jewish contemporary of Jesus, writes in his report about the Essenes that they "forbade marriage and at the same time prescribed a complete continence" (*Quod omnis probus liber sit* 75–91). The famous scientist Pliny the Elder, who died in the eruption of Vesuvius in A.D. 79, writes about the Essenes:

> *They are a people unique of its kind and admirable beyond all others in the whole world, without women and renouncing love entirely, without money, and having for company only the palm trees. Owing to the throng of newcomers, this people is daily reborn in equal number; indeed, those whom, wearied by the fluctuations of fortune, life leads to adopt their customs, stream in in great numbers. Thus, unbelievable though this may seem, for thousands of centuries a people has existed which is eternal yet into which no one is born. (*Natural History, V, xvii, 4; quoted in TEWFQ, p. 37)*

The Jewish historian Josephus writes of them: "The men who practise this way of life number more than four thousand. They neither bring wives into the community nor do they own slaves, since they believe that the latter practice contributes to injustice and that the former opens the way to a source of dissension. Instead they live by themselves" (*JA*, XVIII, i, 5; LCL, p. 19).

Elsewhere Josephus writes of the Essenes:

> *Of Jewish birth, . . . they shun pleasures as a vice and regard temperance and the control of the passions as special virtue. Marriage they disdain, but they adopt other men's children, while yet pliable and docile, and regard them as their kin and mould them in accordance with their own principles. They do not, indeed, on principle condemn wedlock and the propagation of the race, but they wish to protect themselves against women's wantonness, being persuaded that none of the sex keeps her plighted troth to one man. . . . There is yet another order of Essenes, which while*

at one with the rest in its mode of life, customs, and regulations, differs from them in its views on marriage. They think that those who decline to marry cut off the chief function of life, the propagation of the race, and, what is more, that, were all to adopt the same view, the whole race would very quickly die out. They give their wives a three years' probation, and only marry them after they have . . . given proof of fecundity. They have no intercourse with them during pregnancy, thus showing that their motive in marrying is not self-indulgence but the procreation of children. (JW, II, viii, 2-13; LCL, pp. 369-85)

So according to Josephus, there are evidently two kinds of Essenes, married and celibate.

The scrolls found at Qumran also speak of two types of members. The *Damascus Document,* for example (first discovered in the genizah of a synagogue in Old Cairo in 1896; later several manuscripts were also found in Qumran) mentions married people in Qumran. We have already mentioned that in the *Damascus Document,* as later with Jesus, fidelity and monogamy were demanded from men, which was something of a novelty. By contrast, *Rule of the Community* (1QS) presupposes celibacy for the members.

Scholars have tried to right this imbalance by assuming that the male portion of the order lived in the Qumran center, while the married Qumran people lived in individual communities scattered around the country. The Qumran specialist Shemaryahu Talmon, as we have seen, strikes a compromise by arguing that the celibates who lived in the Qumran center were married men who had already fulfilled their duty to procreate.

In any event, these womanless—but perhaps not celibate—believers, these married—or perhaps unmarried—monks in Qumran are a phenomenon that is unusual in Judaism, and the ancient world thought them unusual, too. But the seven graves of the women in the two smaller cemeteries don't fit in with the roughly eleven hundred graves of men in the large cemetery of Qumran. (The four graves of children could belong to other people's children who had been adopted by the womanless sect and had died young.) But those women's graves have been puzzling the scholars since 1947.

Women were excluded from Qumran from the very beginning. But in Christianity, the hostility to women and sexuality did not come in until after Jesus. Jesus was friendly to women, one might almost say the first and last friend women had in the Christian Church. He had "many women" (Luke 8:3) around him, and not just his twelve male disciples, but many female disciples as well. It was these women who financed Jesus' group "out of their means" (Luke 8:3). This suggests that the Jewish women of Jesus' day were more emancipated than Christian women would be for the next two thousand years, or until yesterday, as it were. (On the decline of the importance of women in the Christian Church and on the increasing hostility to sex up until John Paul II, see Uta Ranke-Heinemann, *Eunuchs for the Kingdom of Heaven* [New York: Doubleday, 1990].)

It is not impossible that Qumran influenced the development of misogyny in Christianity, and that Qumran sayings hostile to marriage and family have been put into Jesus' mouth. The following surprising words of Jesus probably originated with the Essenes: "If anyone comes to me and does not hate his own father and mother and wife and children and brothers and sisters, yes, and even his own life, he cannot be my disciple" (Luke 14:26). This might be called the Qumran variation on, or preliminary stage of, Christian celibacy: Marriage for procreation still takes place for the sake of service to humanity. But after that, everyone and everything is abandoned to serve God alone. The service of God and hatred of humans merge into each other. Because they love none of their own kind, the world thinks, such devotees must love God.

In the parallel passage to this saying about hatred, namely, Matt. 10:34–37, hatred of the family is bound up with the sword, just as in Qumran the contempt for women and family grew out of the military situation, which we shall discuss shortly. Jesus is supposed to have said: "Do not think that I have come to bring peace on earth; I have not come to bring peace, but a sword. For I have come to set a man against his father, and a daughter-in-law against her mother-in-law, and a man's foes will be those of his own household. He who loves father or mother more than me is not worthy of me."

This aggressive sectarian mentality, to which many parents and grandparents who have lost a child or grandchild to sects and cults could supply a bitter footnote, seems to have made its way from Qumran into early Christianity. In reality, Jesus rejected such hate-filled sayings from Qumran, as he shows in the Sermon on the Mount: "You have heard that it was said, 'You shall love your neighbor and hate your enemy.' But I say to you, 'Love your enemies and pray for those who persecute you'" (Matt. 5:43–44). Until the discoveries in Qumran, no one could make sense of this line from the Sermon on the Mount. The Old Testament does tell us to love our neighbor (Lev. 19:18), but nowhere are we told to hate our enemies. It remained unclear where this was "said," or where the Jews might have "heard" it. Since the excavations at Qumran, it's clear whom Jesus means: Hatred of the enemy was a basic tenet of the Qumran community.

The *Rule of the Community* says right at the beginning that there the "man of understanding" is bidden to "hate all that He (God) has despised" (1QS I:4; *TEWFQ*, p. 73). Further, all members of the community are obliged to "love all the sons of light, / each according to his lot in the Council of God; / and . . . hate all the sons of darkness, / each according to his fault in the Vengeance of God" (1QS I:9–11; *TEWFQ*, p. 73). And again: "These are the norms of conduct for the man of understanding in these times, concerning what he must love and how he must hate. Everlasting hatred for all men of the pit because of their spirit of hoarding!" (1QS IX: 21–22; *TEWFQ*, p. 96). This theme continues (cf. the *Thanksgiving Hymns* VII:23; *TEWFQ*, p. 224; and the *Damascus Document* II:3; *TEWFQ*, p. 123).

This hatred will break out in the approaching eschatological war. The end of the world, which the Qumran sect expected to come soon, would be preceded by a war of revenge and retribution, the war of the "sons of light" (the Qumran community) against the "sons of darkness." This war is described in detail in the *War Scroll* (1QM). In keeping with the rules of Roman warfare, it will be fought with the use of phalanxes. It will go on for forty years. In the first twenty years, all the foreign nations will be conquered; in the following twenty, all other Jews.

Toward the end of the struggle, which will mark the beginning of new heavenly-earthly life (ideas of this world and the next, of heaven and earth, interfuse and blend, eschatological hopes are painted in the colors of an earthly apocalypse), two messiahs will arise. One will be a high priestly messiah from the house of Aaron, and the other, a royal messiah from the house of David. Both will have their retinue, the high priestly messiah a sacerdotal one, the messianic king a band of military followers. The royal messiah will be the longed-for son of David. He will found the Kingdom of God by intervening in the final battle and victoriously concluding it. He will liberate the Holy Land and establish the dominion of Israel. At the center of this pacified world will be Qumran-Israel. The priestly messiah will forgive sins and open up Paradise (*Damascus Document* VII:20–21; *TEWFQ*, pp. 134–35; *Rule of the Community* 1QS V:20–26; *TEWFQ*, p. 84).

The priestly messiah and the priests will not take part in the final battles, but they will spur on the others through shouts and trumpet blasts: "And they shall not come to the midst of the slaughter lest they be defiled by unclean blood; for they are holy and they shall not profane the oil of their priestly anointing with the blood of a nation of vanity" (*War Scroll* 1QM IX:7–9; *TEWFQ*, p. 183). The freeing of priests from military service while having them serve as chaplains, motivating the troops to battle, is evidently an old tradition.

Both messiah figures bear the title "Son of God," for example, in a messianic fragment from cave 4 (4Q *Florilegium* 10–11; *TEWFQ*, p. 313). The place of dominion of the high priestly messiah is heaven, the royal messiah's is earth. The high priestly messiah takes precedence over the royal messiah. This is especially clear at the messianic banquet. There the priestly messiah has the place of honor. He blesses bread and wine. The next in rank after him is the royal messiah (*Rule of the Congregation* 1QSa II:11–21; *TEWFQ*, p. 108).

This dangerously aggressive eschatological scenario of the Qumran community did not remain a dead letter but became a letter of death. It probably led the Qumran sect to take an active part in the assaults of the Zealots on the Romans and, above all, in the Jewish War (A.D. 66–70), which led to the downfall of Israel in the ancient world.

Tacitus (d. A.D. 120) reports about the beginning of the Romans' siege of Jerusalem in the spring of 70. He tells us that among the Jewish rebels, a utopian vision of world dominion played a crucial role. Admittedly, Tacitus does not mention the Essenes by name, but in his view Christians and Jews were lumped together as potential terrorists, who kept causing the Romans grief. In the case of Christ, it was Pontius Pilate who had to confront them (cf. the chapter on Good Friday). Here Tacitus describes how Emperor Titus attacked Jerusalem. The time is shortly before the storming of the city, which took place in July 70:

> The majority [of the Jews] firmly believed that their ancient priestly writings contained the prophecy that this was the very time when the East should grow strong and that men starting from Judea should possess the world. . . . There were arms for all those who could use them. . . . Men and women showed the same determination; and if they were to be forced to change their home, they feared life more than death. Such was the city and people against which Titus Caesar now proceeded. (Histories V, xiii; LCL, p. 199)

Josephus, the future historian of the Jewish War, was an eyewitness of it. He had at first organized the struggle against the Romans and had been a commandant. When the fortress of Jotapata was conquered by the Romans, he and forty companions saved themselves by taking refuge in a cistern. There Josephus argued that they should surrender to the Romans, whereupon his comrades wanted to kill him as a traitor. Then the decision was reached to commit mass suicide. Josephus delivered a speech to his men on the sinfulness of suicide (briefly mentioned in the chapter on Hell) and proposed a different method: They would draw lots to decide the order in which each one had to kill his comrade, and then be killed in turn by the next man.

"Should one say by fortune or by the providence of God?" (or Josephus's intelligence) that in the end the only two left were Josephus and another man. Since neither of them wanted to kill the other, Josephus convinced his companion to surrender to the Romans. Then Josephus prophesied to the Roman general Vespasian that he and his son

Titus would become emperors (*JW*, III, viii, 7; LCL, p. 687). When Vespasian actually did become emperor—after Nero—in 68, he gave Josephus his freedom and awarded him all sorts of honors. Josephus accompanied Titus to the siege of Jerusalem and tried in vain to convince his countrymen that further resistance was senseless. When he later wrote his history, he condemned the messianic rebellions of the Jews that had led to war and annihilation.

Josephus mentions that a certain "John the Essene" was appointed commandant of "the province of Thamna, with Lydda, Joppa, and Emmaus also under his charge" (*JW*, II, xx, 4; LCL, p. 541). This was "the strategically extraordinarily important triangle . . . that controls communications between Jerusalem and the seacoast" (J. Maier and K. Schubert, *Die Qumran-Essener* [1991], p. 83).

Josephus doesn't tell us whether all the Essenes took part in the rebellion. But his long report on the Essenes indirectly reveals that they were actively involved in the uprisings against the Romans. This is implied by the dramatic and cruel end that they met in the Jewish War:

> *Death, if it come with honor, they consider better than immortality. The war with the Romans tried their souls through and through by every variety of test. Racked and twisted, burnt and broken, and made to pass through every instrument of torture, in order to induce them to blaspheme their lawgiver or eat some forbidden thing, they refused to yield to either demand, nor ever once did they cringe to their persecutors or shed a tear. Smiling in their agonies and mildly deriding their tormentors, they cheerfully resigned their souls, confident that they would receive them back again.* (JW, II, viii, 10; LCL, p. 381)

This account lends support to the idea that Qumran was a center of the anti-Roman resistance and not a pacifist group simply reading their sacred scrolls.

Unlike Qumran, Jesus did not call for a final messianic battle against Rome. And the oldest texts of the New Testament, moreover, the Pauline letters, which were written in the 50s, are highly conformist in politics. They are, in fact, so supportive of the system that critics of the alliance between throne and altar can only shake their heads when they read the famous lines from Romans: "Let every person be subject to the governing authorities. For there is no authority except from God, and those that exist ['the powers that be'] have been instituted by God. So anyone who resists such authority is resisting God's ordinance" (Rom. 13:1f.). The escalation of the uprisings that led to the final struggle in the Jewish War was not the work of Paul or of Jesus. Jesus did not preach the Kingdom of God as the crowning glory of secular Jewish power.

Jesus didn't fit the type of the priestly ascetics of Qumran who contented themselves with "a single course" per meal and about whom Josephus goes on to tell us: "Of Jewish birth, . . . they shun pleasures as a vice and regard temperance and the control of the passions as a special virtue. . . . No clamor or disturbance ever pollutes their dwelling. . . . To persons outside the silence of those within appears like some awful mystery; it is in fact due to their invariable sobriety and to the limitation of their allotted portions of meat and drink to the demands of nature" (*JW,* II, viii, 2–5; LCL, pp. 369–73). Jesus was different from John the Baptist, the son of a priest, who fed on grasshoppers and wild honey. Some critics assume that he was a member of Qumran (*RGG* [1961], V, 751). At any rate, it was said of John that he "came neither eating nor drinking" (Matt. 11:18), whereas Jesus was called "a glutton and a drunkard" (Matt. 11:19; Luke 7:34).

Rudolf Bultmann and many Protestant theologians have challenged the notion that Jesus ever took himself to be the Messiah. Jesus never once confronted the traditional nationalistic idea of the messiah, and he never contrasted to it a corrected, spiritualized concept of the messiah. Texts that say otherwise, or contrary statements from Jesus' own mouth, are, these critics claim, merely legends. And they are right: Only after his death was Jesus made to fit a messianic mold—which completely distorted him and his message.

The Hebrew word *messiah* is an Old Testament term for kings, high priests, and others. It developed into a label for an ideal savior-figure, who would liberate Israel from all foreign domination and make it the ruler of the world. By the beginning of the Christian era, this hope had taken on enormous intensity, and it grew continually until the downfall of the country in A.D. 70. Even then it was not over, as the very last rebellion under Bar Kochba later showed.

The man who recognized Bar Kochba as the Messiah and whom, thanks to his authority, most of the Jews followed, was the most famous of all Jewish scholars, Rabbi Akiba (executed by the Romans in A.D. 135). Akiba was the one who had fixed the canon of the Hebrew Bible—for instance, he had gotten the Song of Solomon accepted into the Bible. The basic reason for Akiba's claim that Bar Kochba was the hoped-for Messiah was the extraordinary strength and dexterity with which Bar Kochba used his knees to fling back the Roman projectiles at the enemy, thereby slaying many of them (Kittel IX, 514).

By contrast, the fact that Bar Kochba was not of the house of David was, in Akiba's eyes, of no consequence (Kittel IX, 514–15). The Messiah's shattering of Israel's enemies in the present is obviously more important than his being linked by the past to the house of David. At all events, Rabbi Akiba announced that he saw in Bar Kochba the fulfillment of the prophecy in Num. 24:17: "A star shall come forth out of Jacob."

If we read the rest of this passage, we realize what the makeup of the Messiah had to be, regardless of whether he was descended only from Jacob (Abraham's grandson and Isaac's son) or from David (who himself descended from Jacob) as well. The text says: "A star shall come forth out of Jacob, and a scepter shall rise out of Israel; it shall crush the forehead of Moab. . . . Edom shall be dispossessed, while Israel does valiantly. By Jacob shall dominion be exercised, and the survivors of cities be destroyed!" (Num. 24:17–19).

Thus, unlike Jesus, Bar Kochba was a messiah in the actual sense, that is, a political and military leader. We are told that his two brothers "never let a Roman pass by without killing him. They said they wanted to take the crown of Hadrian (emperor from A.D. 117 to 138) and put it on the head of Shimon (Bar Kochba)" (Strack and Billerbeck, *Kommentar,* I, 13).

Incidentally, Rabbi Akiba took almost all his disciples (or students, since *mathētēs*—the Greek term for disciple—is the same as *discipulus,* which is Latin for student) with him into death when he summoned them to join the struggle against the Romans on the side of Bar Kochba. Rabbi Akiba, however, failed to convince some people that Bar Kochba was the messiah. His disciple Rabbi Shimon ben Joachai later reported: "Akiba, my teacher, spoke out in public, saying, 'A star has come forth from Jacob.'. . . When my teacher had seen Bar Kochba, he said, 'This is the king, the Messiah.' Rabbi Jochanan ben Tortha replied to him: 'Akiba, grass will grow out of your jawbones (out of your grave), and the son of David (the Messiah) will still not have come'" (Strack and Billerbeck, *Kommentar*, I, 13).

The messianic title, Christ, is applied to Jesus throughout the New Testament, and as early as the Pauline letters it had solidified into a personal name. Modern readers no longer make any distinction between "Jesus" and "Christ." But Jesus was not the messiah, he wasn't the man people had been waiting for. Hence, it is basically quibbling and distorting well-defined Jewish ideas to insist that Jesus was, after all, the messiah. The Jews were looking for a political and military leader; and along came Jesus, who was not the one they were looking for and therefore not the messiah. This naturally didn't prevent the New Testament writers from finding appropriate messianic prophecies (e.g., of the "Suffering Servant" in Isaiah 53 and elsewhere) in the Old Testament and applying them after the fact to the crucified Jesus. Such efforts by New Testament authors and theologians (from then to now) do violence to the text and have no relevance to Jesus.

Consider statements under the heading of "Messiah" such as this one from the Catholic *Lexikon für Theologie und Kirche*: "The manner in which Jesus entered Jerusalem several days before his death can be understood only as a messianic proclamation. He was at once affirming and altering Jewish expectations as he rejected the idea of a warrior messiah." How could Jesus be affirming messianic expectations of a Jewish empire here? Jesus was not the Messiah, and it's a good thing that he wasn't.

Jesus didn't want to be the Christ. Hence Joel Carmichael is partly right (even though he sees Jesus as a political messiah who wanted to set up a "messianic theocracy" and a "national kingdom") when he says: "The famous messianic secret, that is, Jesus' constant warning to his disciples, at least during his mission, to keep silence about his status, can only be understood as an emergency measure to reconcile the attitude of the risen and glorified Jesus with the fact that Jesus never made himself out to be

the Messiah. Nowhere is it reported that he said, 'I am the Messiah'"
(*Leben und Tod des Jesus von Nazareth* [1965], pp. 197–98). The historical
fact is that Jesus never called himself the Messiah, that is, Christ.

Jesus was not the messiah and didn't want to be. At the time, many
Jews, including some of his disciples, would have liked him to be the
Messiah. And this expectation that people had of him must have been the
reason why he was executed. But then the problem arose for Christians that
a crucified messiah is the opposite of a victorious messiah, which is what
the Messiah was supposed to be. They then tried to solve this problem with
their unspeakable theory of substitutionary atonement—in other words,
that God sacrificed his son for us and other such barbaric horrors.

The concept of the Messiah doesn't fit Jesus, and the priestly or military retinue of Qumran's messianic lords is quite different from the people
who followed Jesus. "The blind, cripples, the lame, and the deaf" were not
admitted into the Qumran community. We learn this in fragment 4QDb
of the *Damascus Document* XV:15–17 (*TEWFQ,* p. 161). Handicapped
people would naturally be a hindrance in the approaching final struggle.

The *War Scroll* makes it clear that such people are not suited for the
final struggle: "And all those that strip the dead, and plunder, and purify
the earth and keep watch over the weapons and prepare the provisions,
they shall all be from twenty-five to thirty years old. And no lame man,
nor blind, nor crippled, nor having in his flesh some incurable blemish,
nor smitten with any impurity in his flesh, none of these shall go with
them into battle" (1QM VII:2–5; *TEWFQ,* pp. 180–81).

Jesus, by contrast, did not exclude these military rejects, because he
wasn't summoning people to war or to hatred but to love of one's enemy.
His program was the opposite of Qumran's.

Thanks to the Dead Sea Scrolls, the Essenes are much talked about these
days. But they also made a big stir about two hundred years ago. Back
then, two biographies of Jesus appeared that presented Jesus as a member
of the Essene order. The story was that one of the Essenes, namely, Joseph
of Arimathea, had revived Jesus after the crucifixion, because he had only
appeared to be dead. Three days later he appeared to his disciples. An
Essene in the white garment of his order had approached the women at

the tomb on Easter morning and announced to them the Resurrection of Jesus. The whole story of Jesus is described in the most minute detail.

The two lives of Jesus were written by Protestant theologians, Carl Friedrich Bahrdt (d. 1792) and Karl Heinrich Venturini (d. 1849). Bahrdt's Jesus novel was published in 1782, all three thousand pages of it, Venturini's in 1806, filling a mere twenty-seven hundred. Both books were enormously popular, and to this day, in an unending series of reprints and copies they still influence pious imaginations.

Albert Schweitzer (1875–1965), the musician, medical missionary, and distinguished theologian, discusses both these novels in his *Quest of the Historical Jesus* (1906) in his chapter "The First Fictitious Lives of Jesus." Though they were "imperfectly equipped freelancers," Schweitzer notes, their authors were the first who "endeavored to grasp the inner connection of cause and effect in the events and experiences of Jesus. Since they found no such connexion indicated in the Gospels, they had to supply it for themselves. . . . In a sense, these Lives of Jesus, for all their coloring of fiction, are the first which deserve the name." Schweitzer goes so far as to say, "From the historical point of view these lives are not such contemptible performances as might be supposed. There is much penetrating observation in them. Bahrdt and Venturini are right in feeling that the connexion of events in the life of Jesus has to be discovered; the Gospels give only a series of occurrences, and offer no explanation why they happened as they did" (trans. W. Montgomery [New York: Macmillan, 1948], pp. 38, 47).

But though such novels may give us a sense of Jesus' age and a vivid picture of Jewish customs and folkways, when it comes to the concrete life of Jesus, they are almost pure fantasy. The reason for this is that the Gospels are simply not suitable as the basis of a biography of Jesus. The Gospels deified Jesus. They didn't want to represent Jesus the human being and his real life, but to interpret the figure of Jesus in the light of some guiding theological ideas. Hence, they were indifferent to Jesus' human psychological development, which is indispensable for any real biography. So as far as his concrete life is concerned, Jesus is the great unknown of Christianity. As a person, he is lost or missing in the theological structure that has been built over him. Some of us may regret that.

CHAPTER EIGHTEEN

Redemption
by Execution

WHILE REBUILDING a decrepit church and renovating its cemetery on
his estate at Ferney, Voltaire (d. 1778) wanted to have an enormous
wooden cross, which stood directly in front of the windows of his castle,
set up somewhere else. So he ordered his workmen, "Get that gibbet out
of here! [*Ôtez-moi cette potence!*]" His neighbor, the pastor of Moens, got
wind of the remark and insisted that Voltaire justify his use of the abominable word *gibbet*. Voltaire denied having said it. Six workmen, who witnessed the episode, defended him and assured the clergyman that *gibbet*
was a carpenter's technical term for a T-shaped beam and so could never
have been meant as an insult. But the pastor saw Voltaire's words as an insult to the cross and was not satisfied. The matter came to trial in Dijon,
but Voltaire's friend Tronchin managed to get him off. The punishment
for this sort of blasphemy was to have the culprit's tongue cut out and
hands cut off (see Jean Orieux, *Voltaire*, trans. Barbara Bray and Helen R.
Lane [Garden City, NY: Doubleday, 1979], p. 338).

Voltaire loathed executions. Once, when Madame Suard was visiting
him at Ferney, she came upon an etching that represented the Calas family
saying good-bye before their father, Jean Calas, was broken on the wheel.
"Ah Madame," Voltaire told her, "for eleven years I was preoccupied with
that unfortunate family, and with the Sirvens, and during that time,

Madame, I reproached myself for the least smile that crossed my lips, as though it were a crime" (Orieux, *Voltaire,* p. 449).

Jean Calas (1698–1762), a Huguenot and a rich businessman in Toulouse, had his back, arms, and legs broken and was finally strangled. He was accused of having murdered his son Marc-Antoine (who had hanged himself) to prevent him from converting to Catholicism. In 1765 Voltaire managed to have Calas rehabilitated by the Parliament of Paris, too late for the dead man, but an act of justice for his family. In 1763 Voltaire had written a *Treatise on Tolerance* about the Calas case. Three years later the Church put it on its Index of Forbidden Books.

Sirven, born in 1709, a Huguenot and a land surveyor, was condemned to death by the Parliament of Toulouse but was able to escape. The body of his daughter Elizabeth had been found in a well, and like Calas, Sirven was accused of having murdered her to prevent her from becoming a Catholic. Thanks to Voltaire's efforts, Sirven was rehabilitated in 1771 and thus escaped execution.

In 1766 Voltaire entered the lists for the case of the nineteen-year-old Chevalier Jean-François de La Barre (1747–1766). To his great grief, he failed to prevent La Barre from being condemned to death by the tribunal of Abbeville, and La Barre was tortured and beheaded. At the last moment before the beheading, they dispensed with cutting out his tongue, as stipulated in the sentence. His body was burned and along with it the "Letter on Miracles" and other writings by Voltaire that had been found on his person.

La Barre was accused of not having shown respect to a religious procession and of damaging a crucifix on a bridge. He was convicted of failing to tip his hat to the procession and of singing "indecent" songs. Voltaire couldn't save La Barre, but he did help La Barre's friend and fellow accused, Gaillard d'Étallonde, who had fled. Calas, Sirven, and La Barre are the three most famous cases in a whole series in which Voltaire tried to prevent the execution of people or got them rehabilitated.

The Calas case prompted the Italian jurist Caesare Beccaria (d. 1794) to reject the death penalty altogether. He did this for the first time in a scholarly book, *On Crimes and Punishments,* which appeared in 1764 (Voltaire wrote a commentary on it in 1766) and which the Church put on the Index. The Catholic Church has always stood up for the death penalty. Thus in 1210 Pope Innocent III ordered the Waldensians, who were against the death penalty, to swear the following oath if they wished to return to the Catholic Church: "Concerning the secular authorities, we assert that they can carry out a blood judgment without mortal sin, so long as they proceed to impose the death penalty not out of hatred but out of justice, not rashly but with due reflection." In 1985 Cardinal Joseph Höffner of Cologne wrote in his "Christliche Gesellschaftslehre" (Christian Sociology): "The holiness of the divine order has proved its power even in this age through the death penalty."

The Church is still centuries away from feeling horror at the death penalty. There is reason to fear that someday, when everyone else has bid farewell to the death penalty as an archaic remnant of an exploded barbaric legal system, there will still be Christian theologians demanding state-sponsored bloodshed for the sake of the "holiness of the divine order."

Christianity is a religion that glorifies one concrete execution—the execution of Jesus—because the Church sees in it an act of redemption through blood. Thus for Christians the death penalty is the prerequisite for their redemption. The death penalty has been, as it were, sanctified as the instrument of this redemption. God is the supreme advocate of the death penalty, since he condemned his son to death and willed his crucifixion as the means of redemption. But, of course, the death penalty had to be instituted at some point before Jesus arrived, in time to make the redemptive death of Jesus possible. Thus all the people executed before Jesus are the prerequisite, the precursors, the pioneers of his redemptive death. And all the people executed after Jesus are victims of this idea of redemption through the cross. Because the institution of the death penalty, which was divinely willed with respect to Jesus, cannot be against God's will in the case of other people. From this standpoint all the executed are martyrs of sorts. They died then and die even now for the best of all causes: the redemption of the world.

Whenever it served his purposes, man has always had a liking for death and blood. He has always seen killing as a tool for getting rid of evil, through the death penalty, wars, and the annihilation of wickedness.

Blood has a redemptive function for man. Still, for the Church, blood doesn't just have a "retail" redemptive function; it has a "wholesale" one as well: As Christianity sees it, humanity as a group is redeemed through blood, because God, too, has a liking for blood. It is God's own son who must die, taking the place of and atoning for sinners, so that they may be redeemed from all evil.

A few years ago, Martin Scorsese's film *The Last Temptation of Christ* was showing in movie houses. The film uses grandiose images to tell the story of Jesus of Nazareth, who for our salvation became God's blood offering. Nailed to the cross, he is supposed to die, yet he dreams of being allowed to live. It hadn't been his own will to die, but the will of his divine father. For his part, he had tried in prayer to avert his harsh destiny: "You ask me to let myself be crucified. Is there no other way? You hand me a bitter cup, but I can't, I don't want to drink. Please, let it pass me by, please." But praying did this son no good, nor did mourning, nor a bloody sweat and the long night of his fear. How is a person's despair to reach God's ear when it goes against God's will? And this inexorable will was death.

God insists on the execution of his son. And Christians too insist on it. They will never let Jesus go on living, because without this execution they wouldn't be redeemed—or so they think. Even Jesus realizes this. Scorsese's Jesus says to Judas: "I have no choice. This way I bring God and man together. If I don't die, they'll never find their way to each other." This execution couldn't be stopped, the human sacrifice had to be offered. Anyone who objected to it would no longer deserve to be called a Christian, because being against Jesus' death meant turning against Jesus himself.

According to Christian tradition, even the mother of the victim said yes to his execution. In his second sermon on Mary's annunciation, Photius (d. after 886), the famous patriarch of Constantinople, says: "Mary had at her disposal male virtue and courage. She was not even irritated during the Passion of her son, which she witnessed. She acted differently from the way mothers usually do when they attend the execution of their sons." And Archbishop Antoninus of Florence (d. 1459) argues: "Had no one been prepared to carry out the crucifixion through which the world was redeemed, Mary would have been ready to nail her son to the cross by herself. We may not assume that she was inferior in perfection and obedience to Abraham, who offered his only son as a sacrifice" (*Summa Theologica,* part. IV, tit. XV, c. XII, 1 t. IV col. 1227). Pope Benedict XIV (d. 1758) scolds the painters who depict Mary under the cross as being overwhelmed with pain; likewise, he criticizes preachers who have the same biased view (*Dictionnaire de Théologie Catholique* [1927], IX, 2432). According to Pope (Saint) Pius X, Mary didn't stand "lost in pain at this painful sight, but joyfully" by the cross of her son (encyclical *Ad diem illum,* 1904). John Paul II says that Mary "lovingly consented in a maternal spirit . . . to the sacrifice of the victim that she had borne" (encyclical on Mary, "Redemptoris Mater," 1987).

At long last, the entire contents of Christianity can now be accommodated in a single word. Joachim Cardinal Meisner of Cologne never misses a chance to jolt his flock (who lack Mary's "masculine virtue") with his personal motto: a peculiar German word, *kreuzfidel. Kreuz* means "cross" and the root meaning of *fidel* is "faithful," but since the 18th century, *fidel* has been taken to mean merry or cheerful. So the literal sense of *kreuzfidel* would seem to be merry about the cross. But by a crowning irony, the standard colloquial sense of kreuzfidel is actually something like the English "happy as a lark." Kreuzfidel was the motto of the cardinal Meisner's installation in February 1989. And it was also the motto that he helpfully passed on to Bishop Hubert Luthe of Essen when the latter was installed in the diocese of Essen in February 1992. One wonders that the combination of cross and merry didn't stick in the cardinal's throat. The Essen *Südanzeiger* (21 August 1991) quotes the cardinal of that city—Franz Hengsbach (d. 1991)—as saying he found it right, "that people in the milling excitement of a soccer game make the sign of the cross. This is a genuine joy that can always hold up before God."

These mighty Christian orators, these lions of the pulpit, are forever mouthing the word *cross* with brainless enthusiasm. It leaps to their lips whenever their eloquence threatens to run dry. But, in fact, they duck the issue of the suffering and death facing each and every one of us. These preachers are the reason that Christianity has served to blunt the human sympathies of its followers. Thus, a prayer suggested to Christian married couples says: "The cross, sign of your sacrificial death, adorns our home."

Here is a sample of the address given by Cardinal Meisner at Bishop Luthe's installation: "The installation of a bishop used to be called an 'enthronement.' For the newly appointed bishop back then this was equivalent to 'exalting the cross'"(!) "The pectoral cross is the badge of the bishop's office.... The cross first shows us the horizontal or so-called world-line. It always stands right before our eyes. It runs horizontally both right and left into infinity.... The cross is formed when the vertical line, the God-line, intersects the horizontal line.... We know from experience ... that compared with the conspicuous world-line, the rather hidden God-line is underexposed ... The bishop is placed at the crosspoint. He has to hold it together.... As you do so, dear Bishop Hubert, I and all of us here pray that you will remain happy as a lark—merry about the cross ('kreuzfidel'). Amen."

With all this talk of Jesus' divine father and human mother and all those "cross-merry" cardinals approving human sacrifice, of the cross as a sign of joy and an adornment, it sounds blasphemous to reject the death on the cross and to think of the Son living on. But in *The Last Temptation of Christ*, that is what happens. As Jesus hangs dying, he has a dream: A woman balks his plan and sabotages his redemptive death. She invades the fantasies of the Crucified and has no intention of rubber-stamping Christian execution-theology for the sake of our salvation. First, Jesus' guardian angel appears and assures him that he doesn't have to die. Drawing on the last remnant of his will to live, the poor human Jesus, hanging on the cross, dreams that his Father has allowed him to live. The cinematic angel says: "Your Father is the God of compassion, not of punishment, ... the Lord doesn't want your blood. He said: Let him live his life." Jesus climbs down from the cross, walks down Calvary, and marries Mary Magdalen.

The married Son, however, disturbs the Christian image of God, though the cruel Father doesn't. The Son's love has to manifest itself in a bloody sacrifice, but never in the act of love. And so Christians are comforted by the fact that in Scorsese's film Jesus is punished with the revocation of his messiahship. "I don't have to be sacrificed?" he asks. "No, no," the angel says, "certainly not." Then: "I'm not the messiah?" And the angel: "No, you're not." Thus Jesus has to pay a high price for his father's compassion—namely, no longer being the messiah and certainly not God's Son. Divine sonship and going on with life don't fit together.

Fortunately for the Christians, it's all just a bad dream. Judas has made it clear to him, "Your place is on the cross. God has ordered you there. . . . When death came too close, you broke out into a cold sweat of fear, you ran away. . . . You have turned against God, your Father." The people who have been redeemed by a bloody human sacrifice can breathe easier. But the shock still reverberates. The very idea that this prisoner who was to be executed for the sake of our redemption might be allowed to live on offends the pious feelings of all Christian shouters of "Crucify him!" It's an insult to all those who long to slake their religious blood lust, to those who pray the venerable old hymn to Mary "Stabat mater": "Make me drunk with the cross and blood of your Son [Fac me . . . cruce inebriari et cruore Filii]."

One has to think against the grain of the usual Christian thoughtlessness to recognize that what the angel is saying isn't blasphemy; in fact, it's the real Christian truth that God doesn't want his Son—or anyone else—killed. God, as the angel says, is the God of compassion, who doesn't want any human sacrifice. And Jesus would have had God's justice on his side if he had come down from the cross.

As far as it lies in our power, we should make Jesus climb down from the cross and go on living. In this way we can erase the image of a terrible God that matches the intellectual void of Christian theology. This image of a God who wills the death of his own Son for the sake of a holy cause, and who would if necessary also will the death of other human beings for other holy causes, grows pale and gives way to another image of God: the image of a gentle God, a God of living and not of killing.

God is no hangman. God mourns this death. The dreams of God's compassion are not deviant fantasies. They are the truth, even if in the reality of the world they remain dreams. A "temptation" is what Scorsese (following Kazantzakis) calls this dream of humane existence. But it's no temptation. It's a charge leveled by a victim who has been abandoned by inhuman human beings and an inhuman God.

Humans can be hangmen, so they have made God into one. In an all too easy foregone conclusion, Christians are willing to see Jesus hang on the cross in accord with the will of God. And they haven't the least intention of redeeming him from the cross. It's rare that we see anyone in the Christian world being humane to Jesus. The story is told of Saint Thérèse de Lisieux, the "little Thérèse," that once when she was sick with a high fever, she tried to remove the nails from a crucifix and save Jesus. Another legend tells of a bird, a crossbill, that was present at the crucifixion and, more compassionate than the humans there, tried to pull the nails out of the cross.

The language of the Christians, by contrast, is full of blood. Just as the Spaniards won't give up their bullfights, the Christians can't be persuaded to give up their redemption through blood. They are addicted to blood. On 11 June 1980, Bishop Klaus Hemmerle of Aachen appeared on German television. A journalist asked him what was on his mind every morning upon meeting the first person who crossed his path, to which this otherwise so sensitive and sympathetic man replied: "Upon meeting that first person in the morning, I see the blood of the Redeemer flowing down on him, and I'll know then that we are redeemed. Something like that in any case."

Blood is good. The penitential preacher, castigator of women, and champion of celibacy Saint Peter Damiani (d. 1072) advised his nephew to receive daily communion as a way of maintaining his chastity: "As the enemy of purity, the devil will take flight when he sees your lips stained with the blood of Christ" (*De castitate*).

Saint Catherine of Siena (d. 1380) often had visions of blood when the priest raised the chalice during mass. She would see Christ's blood spilling over the altar. Of all drinks she preferred red vinegar, because it reminded her "of the blissful suffering of Jesus." When the host was broken before her eyes, she saw it turn blood red. Upon taking communion she tasted blood in her mouth and had the sense "of receiving Christ, very small and bloody." For Catherine, the wine in the Eucharist was more important than the bread, because it expressed better the sacrificing of a victim. For this reason she always wanted to drink from the chalice at mass

(André Vauchez, *Les laïcs au moyen-âge* [1987], pp. 262–63). For Catherine of Siena, there was no redemption without blood. She called the pope the "cellarer" of this blood.

In the film *Gandhi* (1982), a Muslim (or Hindu?) says: I know a young girl, a Christian, who drinks blood. The others ask in astonishment: How is that? Answer: The blood of the Lord in the Eucharist. The others: Oh, that. This brief dialogue shows how insane the Christian religion appears to the eyes of unprepared non-Christians. Meanwhile, two thousand years of familiarity with Christians have led people to respond to this cannibalistic Christian drinking of human blood with nothing more than a shrug.

It wasn't always this way. In the first centuries of the Christian era, there were occasional misunderstandings as pagans reproached Christians for eating little children. From the 4th century onward, when Christians were in control, they made this reproach part of the standard repertoire of their pogroms when they persecuted the Jews. The last major trial for ritual murder (accusing a Jew of drinking the blood of Christian children) was held in Kiev in 1913; the accused was one Mendel Beilis. The occasion for the trial was the discovery of the corpse of a thirteen-year-old boy, Andreas Luchtinsky, who had bled to death. (Actually, there were two later trials for ritual murder under the Nazis, in Memel in 1936 and Bamberg in 1937, but these attracted little attention.)

The blood of Jesus is part of customs practiced in pious Christian homes. One German Protestant bedtime prayer for children says: "If I have done some wrong today, / Please, dear God, don't look that way. / For Jesus' blood and your sweet grace, / Will every harm with good replace." Jesus' blood is good for grown-ups, too. Some years ago, newspaper accounts of televangelist Jimmy Swaggart's troubles over a prostitute quoted Swaggart praying to Jesus as follows: "Let your precious blood wash away and purify every stain." But blood doesn't wash stains away; on the contrary, it leaves them behind.

Protestants and Catholics may disagree about many things, but they are bound together in an inexorable blood brotherhood when it comes to the meaning of blood for redemption. They value this execution very highly, and they refuse to do without it. The human race cannot be redeemed without blood. But then what would actually have happened if the Roman Empire under Tiberius had been like the Federal Republic of Germany under Helmut Kohl, or like Italy, England, France, Scandinavia, and so on—countries in which there is no death penalty? Pontius Pilate would not have been able to sentence Jesus to death—and then what? What if Jesus had died of old age or food poisoning? Would the redemption of the human race have come to grief because government had become more humane?

Or would that redemption have only half-succeeded if the Romans had improved their methods of execution by adopting a more technically advanced approach—the guillotine, say, or the electric chair? Christians now pray on the feast of the Exaltation of the Holy Cross (14 September), "O Lord our God, . . . with the unfailing support of the holy Cross uphold us whom thou makest rejoice to do it honor." But would they pray: ". . . with the unfailing support of the holy electric chair uphold us whom thou makest rejoice to do it honor"?

Or if Jesus had died from lethal injection, as is customary in several states in the United States, would we then have redemption by injection? Would that be the golden shot for humankind? Presumably not quite, because no blood would have flowed. We'd be missing half of the Eucharist—the wine, otherwise known as the blood. And at mass, the priests would get to use only half their words for transubstantiation. Incidentally, this shows that our eucharistic feasts stand or fall not only with the death of Jesus, but, above all, with the proper kind of death for Jesus. Practically speaking, then, it was the Romans who redeemed us: Thanks to their bloody, cruel penal justice, the world found salvation.

Rudolf Bultmann has always had a strong influence on Protestant theology, and for some time now on the Catholic variety as well, even though people in general have not followed his radical demythologization of the New Testament. In his book *Jesus* (1926), he wrote:

> *Furthermore Jesus did not speak about his death and resurrection or its meaning for salvation. Of course, the Evangelists have put various sayings about such things into his mouth. But those sayings derive in the first instance from the faith of the community,*

and without exception not from the primitive community but from Hellenistic Christianity. Thus above all the two most important of these sayings, the one about the ransom, and the Eucharistic sayings: "The Son of man also came not to be served but to serve, and to give his life as a ransom for many" (Mark 10:45). "And as they were eating, he took bread, and blessed, and broke it, and gave it to them, and said: 'This is my body.' And he took a cup, and when he had given thanks he gave it to them, and they all drank of it. And he said to them, 'This is my blood of the covenant, which is poured out for many.'" (Mk. 12:22–24).
(p. 196)

This means that Jesus gave neither his flesh to eat nor his blood to drink, in neither the literal nor the figurative sense. Jesus did not sacrifice himself. He did not will his own death, not even out of obedience to the Father. Nor did God want him to die. God neither demanded a sacrifice, nor did the Son carry out any sacrifice. Christians should celebrate the Eucharist as a meal in memory of Jesus. That would make it a real Eucharist (thanksgiving).

The Roman and Hellenistic environment had a crucial influence on the development of the early Christian Eucharist. The religion of Mithra was especially important in this regard. The Christian Messiah increasingly grew into a role that, before him, had been played by Mithra. Mithra, a god of the sky and light, was first worshiped in ancient Persia. Starting in the 1st century B.C., Mithraism began winning numerous followers in the West as well. Many features of Mithra were transferred to Jesus. Mithra was born on 25 December, and so Christians used that date for Christmas. Shepherds were the first ones to adore the newborn king. After he had done good deeds on earth for his followers, he celebrated a last supper with them and went back to heaven. At the end of time, Mithra will return to judge the human race. Mithra became the unconquerable sun (*sol invictus*), a title that was passed on to Jesus. Mithra was the divine protector of the Roman army, until the army, under Constantine, began to fight and win beneath the sign of the cross. And Sunday, which is now the day of the Lord, was and still is the day of the sun god.

The adherents of Mithraism gathered at cultic meals, which so closely resembled the Christian Eucharist that Justin (d. ca. 165), for example, considered them a diabolical imitation: "The Apostles in their memoirs, which are called Gospels, have handed down what Jesus taught them to do; that He took bread and, after giving thanks, said: 'Do this in remembrance of Me; this is my body.' In like manner, he took also the chalice, gave thanks, and said: 'This is my blood'; . . . The evil demons, in imitation of this, ordered the same thing to be performed in the Mythraic mysteries" (1 *Apology* 66). Tertullian (d. after 220) found it diabolical that the followers of Mithra "at the idolatrous goings-on and in so malicious a fashion put into words even the actions by which the sacraments of Christ are performed" (*De praescriptione haereticorum*, XL).

The followers of Mithra were in no way imitating the Christian Eucharist; it was the other way around. Bultmann assumes that the primitive Christian "meals weren't really cultic celebrations, but an expression and bond of fellowship in the sense of Jewish tradition and the historical Jesus himself. They were transformed into sacramental celebrations by Hellenistic Christianity"(*Theologie des Neuen Testament* [1951], p. 149).

As an example of the original Christian Eucharist, which was a "solemn meal quite in the Jewish traditional sense," and in which "any reference to Jesus' death is lacking, and there is no mention of sacramental communion," Bultmann points to the *Didache*. Also known as the *Teaching of the Twelve Apostles*, this work was composed in the first half of the 2nd century. Here we read "concerning the cup": "We give thanks to thee, our Father, for the Holy Vine of David thy child . . . and concerning the broken bread: We give thee thanks, our Father, for the life and knowledge which thou didst make known to us through Jesus thy child" (*Didache*, IX, LLC, *The Apostolic Fathers*, p. 323).

The *Didache* makes no reference to the death of Jesus and has no notion of a divine, sacramental food. Later Christians found that this sort of solemn meal no longer sufficed. The memorial banquet of the community was turned into a priestly ritual of sacrifice.

Eugen Drewermann tells us how this eucharistic sacrificial event, concentrated on Jesus' flesh and blood, appears today from the standpoint of a Catholic priest: "Over twenty years ago when I myself was ordained a priest, I didn't (yet) know how closely the clerics' image of God, if you listen to them long enough, resembles the bloodthirsty-yet-bountiful god of the Aztecs Tonatiuh much more than it does the 'Father' of Jesus Christ" (*Kleriker* [1991], p. 89).

And Hans Küng correctly points out: "Can anyone deny that the very concept of the sacrifice of reconciliation, at least in the popular mind, often gave rise to downright pagan misunderstandings: as if God was so cruel, indeed so sadistic, that his rage could be mollified only through the blood of his own Son?"(*Christ Sein* [1976], pp. 515–16). It should be added, however, that we're not dealing simply with popular notions, but with ideas that are largely to be found among theologians and priests. The question is actually whether this monstrous popular image of God was not passed down from above.

Drewermann points to the consequences that the tale of the death of the Son of God has for children. "He was 'sacrificed,' so that the story of his death must provoke in the soul of every child, first of all, grief, and then repeated guilt-feelings for his or her own 'badness'" (*Kleriker* [1991], p. 395).

Some years ago, a painter named Ernst Seler from Reuting in the Upper Palatinate asked the authorities to remove a crucifix, over two feet long, that hung directly above the blackboard in his daughter Elina's classroom. He wanted to prevent her being harmed by it because, as he said, "The sight of it has a paralyzing effect . . . on the pupils' minds." The Catholic pastor, Josef Denk, was sympathetic, and he replaced the large crucifix above the blackboard with a small one above the door. But in 1988, when Elina entered the third grade, once again she found a large crucifix with Christ's body twisted in pain hanging above the blackboard; and this time, the (lay) teacher refused to take it down. Seler and his wife Renate appealed to the Bavarian State Ministery for Education and Religious Matters, asking whether and why such a large crucifix had to hang directly above the blackboard. The response from Munich, file number III/8–50938, from Assistant Director Kaiser, was as follows: "Displayed in this manner, the cross, as a non-denominational symbol of Christianity [is] especially appropriate for calling to mind the suprapositivistic dimension of the state's educational goals." In addition, "Its universal Christian expressive value contributes to the pupils' character formation" (cf. Rupp Doinet, "Das Kreuz mit dem Kreuz," in *Stern*, n. 11, 3 March 1989).

But Elina wasn't the only one who has suffered from the constant sight of the Crucified hanging above the blackboard for the sake of her "character formation." The sight of the crucifix can disturb adults as well as children. The great painter Nicolas Poussin (1594–1665) was fifty-two years old when, after finishing a painting of the crucifixion, he found he no longer wanted to tackle his next picture, "Jesus carries his cross." As he wrote to a friend: "I don't have enough joy and health anymore to shape such themes. The crucifixion has made me sick. It has become so hard for me. Right now painting Jesus carrying his cross would kill me." From then on, Poussin painted no more crucifixions.

The psychotherapist Tilmann Moser is a man damaged by an "ecclesiogenous" neurosis—that is, a neurosis one catches in church. In his book *Gottesvergiftung* (Poisoned by God) he describes his depressing experiences. As a child he made "terrible sacrifices in cheerfulness and joy" (1976, p. 10). He was constantly depressed by "eternally lurking damnation" (p. 13). "So that I could never believe anyone who said he loved me. I took it to be deception, and didn't let myself be healed by you, but thought contemptuously about anyone's trying to love me" (p. 36).

In Moser's book, the words most frequently met with are *damnation* and *rejection*. The second most common words are *sacrifice, slaughter,* and *cross.* The author's problem is the cruelty of God. "You seem to love the hours before daybreak; that's the time of executions, of self-hatred, and visits from God" (p. 38). His idea of God's cruelty was nourished above all by the biblical story of Abraham, who was ready to sacrifice his beloved only son, Isaac, to God. "As your servants recommended, I have gazed in wonder at your goodness in not letting Abraham slaughter Isaac. It would have been so easy for you to order him; he would have done it *for you*" (p. 20).

The story of the binding of Isaac is in fact a horrible one. It can give a child nightmares and it can leave a theologian, otherwise accustomed to answering all questions, tied up in knots. If Abraham was alive today and had the intention of sacrificing his son, Isaac, on orders from God, and then burning the body, he would be institutionalized. This horror story has nothing to do with Christianity. It must be seen against the background of the corruption of religion against which the story itself is directed, and which we will discuss later on.

Tilmann Moser sees Jesus' death on the cross along the same line of a God addicted to human sacrifice. He is beset by the question of what kind of God would slaughter his own son on the cross, supposedly to redeem the human race in this bloodthirsty fashion. "Perhaps some doubts about his privileged relations with you might yet have crossed good Abraham's mind, if you had first sprinkled him with Isaac's blood. With your own son you were less inhibited and you gave your sadism free range . . . and again I tried, in response to the universal demand, to gaze in wonder at you because you had sacrificed your own son for me, a poor sinner. Naturally that makes quite an impression. . . . None of the preachers ever raised the suspicion that maybe there was something wrong with you and not with us, if out of pure love of humanity you had to have your son slaughtered" (pp. 20–21).

Another case of harm done by the Christian image of God is the Chinese Lin Yu-Tang, the son of a Christian preacher. As he tells in his well-known book *The Importance of Living*, he drew the logical conclusion and in 1958 he abandoned the clerical career for which he was intended and returned to Chinese "paganism." He thought it made no sense that after Adam and Eve had eaten an apple, God became so enraged that he condemned them and all their descendants to suffer; but then when these descendants killed his only son, he was "so overjoyed that he forgave everybody" (cf. Helmut von Glasenapp, *Die fünf Weltreligionen* [1957], II, 463).

Christianity obviously causes misunderstandings when Christians express themselves the way they usually do. Take, for instance, the *Catholic Catechism* issued by the bishops of Germany in 1949. It aimed to be "a book for life . . . a leader and guide for your entire earthly wandering." Then in boldface: "Jesus has earned for us . . . a claim to heaven." Beneath that is the explanation in fine print: "Above all Jesus . . . rendered to his heavenly Father the highest satisfaction through his suffering and death." For some sensitive thinkers there is too much human blood sticking to such entrance tickets to heaven. They turn down their "claim," tendered by the hand of a hangman.

Here is another example from religious instruction (for nine- to ten-year-old pupils) that is the sort capable of making students, once they grow up, flee headlong into paganism. In the textbook *Kommentar und Katechesen zum Glaubensbuch für das 3. und 4. Schuljahr* (1956), from the pen of the Catholic theologian Josef Dreissen:

> The greatness of an offense increases with the person who is offended. Sin is an offense against an infinite divine person. For this reason it cannot be made good by a finite human person. . . . Since God was the offended one, only God could make up for this offense. But because man was the offender, someone from the ranks of human beings had to take the heavy work of reparation on himself. . . . He (the God-man Jesus Christ) is the only one capable of finishing off sin in its uttermost depths and of making not only a sufficient but a superabundant reparation to the father. (P. 348)

Examples of such language could be multiplied ad infinitum.

This barbaric insanity, this calculus of horror about the necessity of Jesus' death on the cross, goes back to the famous Archbishop Anselm of Canterbury (d. 1109). His "doctrine of satisfaction" is no longer very popular with the more insightful theologians, but that's of no use to people (assuming they haven't yet turned pagan) who went to Catholic schools in the mid-1960s—and those who went for ages before then. Reparations to people who have been harmed by religious instruction are still in arrears.

The day in the year, every year, on which Christians transform Christianity into a caricature is Good Friday. In the Prologue to the Gospel according to John, Jesus is called the "Word" who is "with God" (John 1:1). But people didn't listen to this word. They are primarily occupied with elevating their own doings, instead of the divine word, to the status of God's will. So they have understood how to glorify death and to make the best, the very best, of it—the redemption (whatever that is) of humanity. The theology of the cross, not the word of Jesus, became the center of Christianity. The crucifixion became the event that made Jesus interesting. What was done to him, not what he said, is important to Christians. With its theology of human sacrifice, Christianity has replaced the word of Jesus with a hangman's theology. It goes so far as to issue such blasphemous, murderous claims as: God wants to redeem man through Jesus' death on the cross. He wants to save us through the blood of his Son.

It is true, Jesus was killed. But not by his Father, who supposedly sent his only Son to his death and sacrificed him. Neither is God reconciled by this death, nor are we redeemed by it. Jesus was murdered by men. A person who lives in solidarity with all the poor and dependent—in this sense Good Friday means remembering someone who sympathized with everyone—will be seen by many people as siding with the enemy. And so in the world of murderers that we live in, a person like Jesus was placing his life at risk.

Redeemed from what, actually? Redeemed from more murders? That would be something, at any rate. But who is redeemed from murder by murder? And the murdering went further: It was for God, with God, in the name of God. Neither does murder redeem, nor does anyone's suffering, in itself, make other people better. There is no salvation through death.

The false interpretation of Jesus' death began right back in the New Testament, when a false Christian interpretation was substituted for a false Jewish interpretation, when one error was corrected with another. In the Jewish view, a hanged man was cursed by God (cf. Gal. 3:13 and Deut. 21:23.). With the crucifixion of Jesus, the "human notions of messianic splendor were shattered" (Bultmann). The crucifixion of Jesus was a shock for his followers. This appalling event demanded to be integrated into the view that Jesus' followers had of him as the envoy from God. Bultmann assumes that even before Paul, "the primitive Christian community conceived of Jesus' death as an expiatory sacrifice" (*Theologie des Neuen Testament*, p. 47).

Admittedly, this interpretation of Jesus' death makes his personal innocence clear—so he did not die as a criminal for his own sins. But the Christian view that he died for others' sins creates new problems. It is not in fact the case that God's anger fell on Jesus vicariously instead of on us, and that he died vicariously for our sins, as we are always being told. Jesus never died *for* but quite simply *because of* the sins of human beings.

In the effort to give Jesus' death a meaning, one can only produce nonsense. This comes from trying to justify a murder that can't be justified, since no murder can ever be justified. Invoking God and God's will can't straighten out human crimes. Christians shouldn't glorify a gallows. They should sensitize themselves to the terror of the death penalty, of war, of violence, of torture, of military retaliation. Since they can no longer prevent the murder of Christ, they should at least not consent to it after the fact. And, not least of all for the sake of Christ's death, they should not consent to the violent death of any person in the world. So far as they can, they should prevent every such death.

The Christian image of God is at bottom still a pagan image, and a primitive pagan image at that (because only the arrogance of Christians lets them lump all pagan images of God together as primitive). This was made clear by a report in the popular Italian magazine *Oggi* (which supports the pope). In the piece, "John Paul II's Daily Habits," published on 16 May 1990—the occasion of the pontiff's seventieth birthday—we learn that "an old friend of Wojtyla confided to the Spanish journalist Juan Arias, Vatican correspondent for *El País,* that the pope is profoundly convinced that all his success has been paid for by a severe misfortune of someone close to him, perhaps a relative or friend."

To understand the roots of the primitive/pagan image that the pope has of God, as expressed here, we have to descend into the history of human sacrifices and other sacrifices offered to the gods.

God may have made man in his image, but the opposite is also true, that humans have created God in their own image, that is, envious and jealous. Envious, jealous man created envious, jealous gods, who give gifts when they have gotten them, in keeping with the Latin motto *Do ut des* (I give to you so you will give to me).

So one has to give or sacrifice things to the gods, because in sacral language giving is called sacrificing. Moreover, one sacrifices not just this or that, but the dearest thing one has and the thing one most likes to do. The dearest thing one has is one's own children, hence child sacrifice. But sacrificing sons is better than sacrificing daughters, and again, it's better to sacrifice the first son, and best of all the first-born son—the first-born and only son.

The God of the fathers is not the God of the sons. Nor is the God of the Old Testament, if he actually did demand that Abraham sacrifice his son Isaac to him. And most certainly not the God of the New Testament, if there's any truth to the declaration of the German bishops on 17 November 1977: "Abraham, who was prepared to sacrifice his only son Isaac is only a weak preliminary image of the action of our heavenly Father. For the angel from heaven said to Abraham: 'Do not lay your hand on the lad or do anything to him' (Gen. 22:12). But the heavenly Father does not hold back, he sacrifices his only son, his dearest, and thereby himself for us" (declaration on the book *Christ Sein* by Hans Küng).

As the German bishops see it, Abraham is evidently one of those people who may say yes, but in the final analysis don't keep their promise. So the German bishops, when they grumble about Abraham and somehow find him weak, have every reason to be satisfied with God, who at the murder of his son "does not hold back."

The notion that God or the deity demands what people hold dearest was widespread in Palestine and the Mediterranean basin in general. The Greek historian Diodorus Siculus (1st century B.C.) reports that once (in the year 310 B.C.) a great disaster was threatening the city of Carthage. The people ascribed their calamity to the anger of Cronos, to whom they once had sacrificed their best children, but then offered him only bought or weakly children. Thereupon the Carthaginians sacrificed two hundred children from the best families. A child was laid in the arms of a bronze statue of Cronos and would then roll off into a burning oven (*Library* XX, xiv). Philo of Byblos, who wrote a *History of the Phoenicians* around A.D. 100, reports that child sacrifice was customary among the Phoenicians. He tells us that in times of national danger, "The Phoenicians sacrificed their dearest children in a mysterious fashion."

Recently, doubts have been voiced about such reports of child sacrifice among the Phoenicians. Italian archaeologist Sabatino Moscati, the scholar in charge of the great Phoenician exhibit (1988) in the Palazzo Grassi in Venice, stresses that neither in cosmopolitan Carthage nor in the Phoenician city-states were the gods' favors courted by the systematic burning of children. Even the examination of children's corpses in the children's cemeteries (Tophets), which have often been viewed as sites of child sacrifice, showed no sign of violence. Instead the skeletons were of fetuses, stillborn babies, or children dead from sickness who had been interred in the sacred precincts. Moscati thinks the reports of child sacrifice among the Phoenicians are hostile propaganda by Greek and Roman historians, at least as far as any regular sacrifice of children is concerned. This hostility has historical roots: The Phoenician commercial city of Tyre, founded in the 9th century B.C., was leveled by the Romans in 146 B.C., who thus replaced the Phoenicians as the masters of the Mediterranean. In other words, since the Greeks and Romans fought the Phoenicians in Tyre and Carthage, they defamed the Phoenicians by saying that these people sacrificed their children to their gods, which proved that they were subhuman and that the Greco-Roman culture was superior.

The Old Testament also makes frequent mention of child sacrifice, which it criticizes as an abomination. King Mesa of Moab (9th century B.C.), an easterly neighbor of the Israelites, offered up his only son as a burnt offering on the walls of his capital city while it was besieged by the Israelites (2 Kings 3:27). It is reported that Hiel of Bethel (9th century B.C.) "built Jericho; he laid its foundation at the cost of Abiram his firstborn, and set up its gates at the cost of his youngest son Segub" (1 Kings 16:34). It is probable, however, that "the story only means that during the rebuilding and completion of the city of Jericho two sons of Hiel died, which was taken to be the fulfillment of a curse hovering over the site (cf. Josh. 6:26)" (RGG, 4th ed., 3, 868).

The Old Testament finds fault with Ahaz, the king of Judah (8th century B.C.): "He even burned his son as an offering, according to the abominable practices of the nations whom the Lord drove out before the people of Israel" (2 Kings 16:3). The same is told of King Manasseh (7th century B.C.) in 2 Kings 21:6. Such child sacrifices took place primarily in the Valley of Hinnom south of Jerusalem, which is still called the Valley of Fire today, and which gave its name to the New Testament Hell, Gehenna.

But these Old Testament reports are based in large part on vile gossip and hostile propaganda—"according to the abominable practices of the nations whom the Lord drove out before the people of Israel," as the

Bible says apropos of Ahaz. The peoples driven out are the previous inhabitants, the Canaanites. The Israelites thought they were rightly driven out because of such foul crimes as child sacrifice. But the Israelites were not the first ones to come up with the idea of justifying their own wartime behavior by citing horrors on the enemy's side. Nor were they the last. Consider the propaganda lie that the Iraqis ripped 312 babies out of their incubators in Kuwait. With the help of an American advertising agency (Hill & Knowlton) and false witnesses, this lie was used to prime Americans for the beginning of the Gulf War.

But not all the Old Testament reports on child sacrifice are based on hostile propaganda, and not all child sacrifices are rejected as Gentile abominations. It seems there were pious Israelites who thought that God demanded of them the dearest thing they had—their children. One of these people was even praised as a model not only by the Old Testament but by the New Testament. This is Jephtha (12/11th century B.C.) from the Book of Judges. He sacrificed his daughter as a burnt offering in fulfillment of a vow (Judges 11). Jephtha had no sons: "She was his only child; beside her he had neither son nor daughter." So God had to be content with his daughter. The Old Testament author reports this sacrifice without a word of blame; and in the New Testament Jephtha is praised along with Abraham as a hero of faith (Heb. 11:32; 11:17). In general, people sacrifice to God or the gods (or the good cause) their enemies and their enemies' children. Yet the idea that God or the gods demand the dearest thing one has (hence not the corpses of the enemy but of one's own children) is still alive, as in the story of Jephtha.

The sacrifice of one's own daughter is also the subject of *Iphigenia in Aulis*, a drama by Euripides (d. 407 B.C.). The author adopts an old legend: The princess Iphigenia is sacrificed by her father Agamemnon to the goddess Artemis so the goddess will send favorable winds to the Achaean fleet becalmed at Aulis and let it sail on to Troy.

In the 6th century B.C. Polycrates, the tyrant of Samos, sought to escape the envy of the gods by sacrifices. His happy life and his tragic end impressed the Greek world (Herodotus III, 120 ff.): Polycrates was tricked by the Persian satrap Oroetes, who promised him half his kingdom (eight baskets of thinly gilded stones), but had him executed and crucified his corpse.

Schiller's poem "The Ring of Polycrates" describes the phase of his life when he still enjoyed an enviable happiness:

> He stood on his palace's battlements,
> he looked down in satisfaction
> at the Samos he ruled.
> "All this is subject to me,"
> He began saying to Egypt's king,
> "confess that I am fortunate."

But the Egyptian king is mistrustful of fortune:

> "I shudder at the envy of the gods;
> unmixed joy in life
> was never any mortal's fate."

The Egyptian king says that the gods have taken his only son and heir and thus he has "paid for his happiness." He advises Polycrates to sacrifice his dearest treasure to the gods and to throw it into the sea. Polycrates throws his most precious ring into the waves. But the next morning a fisherman presents him with a fish, and in the fish is the ring. At that the king of Egypt takes flight:

> Here turns the guest with horror . . .
> "The gods will your destruction;
> I take flight, so as not to die with you."
> And saying that he quickly sailed away.

Thus, to insure oneself from catastrophes caused by envious-jealous gods, one sacrifices to them what one holds dearest (best of all, children or, as in the case of Polycrates, one's most precious treasure). One can also sacrifice what one most likes to do: everything connected with love and sexuality. Consecrated virginity is supposed to have been introduced in ancient times by the second king of Rome, the wise sacred legislator Numa (d. 672 B.C.). Plutarch (d. ca. A.D. 120) writes: "He [the Pontifex Maximus (greatest priest)] was also guardian of the vestal virgins." The Roman title Pontifex Maximus was later transferred to the pope (the "supreme pontiff"). The vestal virgins, as everyone knows, guarded the sacred fire.

Plutarch continues:

The statutes prescribed by Numa for the vestals were these: that they should take a vow of virginity for thirty years. . . . For this condition he compensated by great privileges and prerogatives; as that they had power to make a will in the lifetime of their father; that they had a free administration of their own affairs without guardian or tutor, which was the privilege of women who were the mothers of three children. [Note: Emperor Augustus (d. A.D. 14) promulgated this "three children law" (jus trium liberorum) to raise the birth rate.] When they go abroad, they have the fasces carried before them [an honor limited to higher level government officials and priests]. And if in their walks they chance to meet a criminal on his way to execution, it saves his life . . . but she that has broken her vow is buried alive near the gate called Collina, where a little mound of earth stands, . . . under it a narrow room is constructed, to which a descent is made by stairs; here they prepare a bed, and light a lamp, and leave a small quantity of victuals, such as bread, water, a pail of milk, and some oil. . . . The culprit herself is put in a litter, which they cover over, and tie her down with cords on it, so that nothing she utters may be heard. Then they take her to the forum; all people silently go out of the way as she passes, and such as follow accompany the bier with solemn and speechless sorrow; and indeed, there is not any spectacle more appalling, nor any day observed by the city with greater appearance of gloom and sadness. When they come to the place of execution, the officers loose the cords, and then the high priest, lifting his hands to heaven, pronounces certain prayers to himself before the act; then he brings out the prisoner, being still covered, and placing her upon the steps that lead down to the cell, turns away his face with the rest of the priests; the stairs are drawn up after she has gone down, and a quantity of earth is heaped up over the entrance to the cell. . . . This is the punishment of those who break the vow of virginity. (Lives, pp. 82-83)

The pagan (that is, universal human) notion of the envy of the gods continues in Christianity. Now as ever, one is supposed to sacrifice, if

possible, the dearest thing one has. As far as sacrificing one's own children
goes, however, an interesting shift takes place: The charge that had generally been leveled at one's enemies is now applied by Christians to God.
Pre-Christian atrocity stories turn into the good news of Christianity:
God sacrifices his first-born, only Son.

Here is how the philosopher Ernst Bloch, quite some time ago, described the insanity of this central Christian tenet:

> But the ultimate source of the doctrine of sacrificial death is not
> only particularly bloody, but also particularly archaic: It derives
> from the most ancient form of sacrifice, the kind so long avoided,
> human sacrifice. . . . Pitiless righteousness now reckoned up the
> debts for which payment was demanded, and the Christ of the
> sacrificial death doctrine paid them with his innocent blood,
> even accumulating through surplus merit a treasury of grace to
> be administered by the Church. (Atheismus im Christentum
> [1969], pp. 221-22)

From the Christian standpoint, the joyous new feature of this
teaching is supposed to be this: God sacrifices his Son not for his own
advantage, but for ours. Thus he is seeking nothing for himself but for
humanity. The most that man ever did for God is what God now does
for man. In Christian terms this is also called grace. In the Old Testament
the story of the binding of Isaac is told to show that God rejects child sacrifice (a ram is sacrificed instead of Isaac). But in the New Testament,
God slaughters his own Son instead of a lamb, and Abraham is seen as
the precursor of such filicide. The progress from Judaism to Christianity
is obvious.

God, "the Destroyer of the first-born," as he is called in the Letter to
the Hebrews (11:28) because he slew the first-born of the Egyptians, now
slays his own first-born. This God with bloody hands has his priests repeat
the bloody sacrifice of atonement "bloodlessly" (Catholics) every day, or
at least he has them recall it every Sunday (Protestants). In any event, the
substitutionary atonement is for all Christians the core of Christianity.

But otherwise it's business as usual. The idea that one should sacrifice to God the dearest thing of all, namely, human life, is as alive among
Christians as it was among pagans. Instead of sacrificing one's first-born

(only God has the competence to carry out such a barbaric act), in Christianity the idea of martyrdom takes over: the sacrifice of one's own life. Christian veneration of the saints begins in the 2nd century at the tombs of the martyrs. Churches are built over their graves. The martyrs, who sacrificed their lives to God, are the first saints. From the 4th century on, when Christianity became the established religion of the state and the persecuted became persecutors, monasticism and virginity became the most important identifying features of the Christian sacrificial mentality.

Of course, bloody martyrdom remains the supreme perfection. Thérèse de Lisieux writes in her autobiography: "And above all I wished to be a martyr! Martyrdom! It was my youthful dream, and in the little Carmelite cell this dream grew in inner strength. I don't long for only one kind of torment. I long for them all. Like you, my divine bridegroom, I would like to be whipped and crucified. . . . Like St. Bartholomew I would like to be flayed, to be plunged into boiling oil with St. John, to be torn by the teeth of wild beasts like St. Ignatius of Antioch, so that I could be found worthy bread for God. With St. Agnes and St. Cecilia I wished to offer my neck to the executioner and with Joan of Arc to whisper the name of Jesus while burning at the stake" (*The Autobiography of St. Thérèse of Lisieux: The Story of a Soul*, trans. John Beevers [New York: Doubleday, 1989], p. 209).

Since martyrdom isn't always a real possibility, consecrated virginity, as a kind of "white martyrdom," has in general become the ideal of people who want to sacrifice themselves completely to God. John Paul II, who according to Juan Arias is convinced "that all his success has been paid for by a severe misfortune of someone close to him," has neither wife nor children, and his parents are dead. So he has no one *that* close to him. For him personally, in accordance with the ancient pagan superstition, the highest price must consist in consecrating his virginity to God. This is explicitly emphasized in the *Oggi* birthday article on the pope: "For the pope the ideal of Christianity is now and always has been chastity." In his Apostolic Letter on "The Dignity of Woman," John Paul II calls virginity the purest essence of Christ's message, as the really new and decisive feature of Christianity (chapter 20).

Normal little Christians are not expected to make the two major sacrifices (martyrdom and virginity), but they can pay God back with smaller sacrifices. Cardinal Hengsbach described such sacrifices at the beginning of Lent, according to a report in the *Westdeutsche Allgemeine Zeitung* (8 March 1984): "Bishop Hengsbach poses the question: 'How we Christians deal with sacrifice.' He emphasizes that in every sacrifice a person bears witness that he or she is subordinate to the creation and the Creator. To be sure, Bishop Hengsbach concedes, this sacrifice must be offered in 'freedom and love,' and not provoked by any sort of constraint such as 'illness, failure, temporary disability or unemployment.'" Here we see the whole mercilessness of a religion to which the genuine sufferings of people are not enough, but which values the causing of additional, artificial pain.

Madonna—the media superstar, not the Virgin—says the following about her Catholic father: "My father made a never-ending impression on me. He had a philosophy, little pearls of wisdom he would drop on us. One of them was, if it feels good, you are doing something wrong. If you are suffering, you are doing something right" (*Time*, 20 May 1991, p. 58).

In the made-for-TV movie *Vom Kloster in die Ehe* (From the Monastery to Marriage) (West German Radio, channel 3, 18 November 1991), a former Carmelite nun tells how she had to whip herself on her bare hips once a week, and every day in Holy Week, for as long as it took to recite a penitential psalm "in memory of the suffering of Jesus." After Holy Week she could no longer sit or lie down. The ex-nun, now married, says: "'In memory of the suffering of Jesus?' I never understood the connection." There is only one connection here: that human cruelty is falsely viewed as God's will. To that extent Christianity is an education in cruelty.

Saint Thérèse de Lisieux, a Carmelite nun herself, writes: "During my postulancy certain external penitential practices that were customary in our convents struck me as very hard. But I never gave in to my aversion. It seemed to me as if I saw the Crucified in the Garden of the Cross looking down at me with a pleading look and *begging* [Thérèse's emphasis] for these sacrifices" (*The Autobiography*, p. 223).

In the TV movie *Leben um zu beten. Marienau, die einzige Kartause in Deutschland* (Living to Pray: Marienau, the only Carthusian Monastery in

Germany) (West German Radio, channel 3, 16 March 1985), a monk says: "Every fourteen days we make a sacrifice of our hair and then sweep the clippings together." Since that time the monastery has moved elsewhere, because of airplane noise. But, as far as "offering things up" is concerned, the roar of jets overhead would have served at least as well as haircuts.

John Paul II has shown to what farfetched extremes the pagan-Catholic sacrifice mentality can go. On 12 November 1988 at the International Congress of Moral Theologians in Rome, he said: "Even for people infected with AIDS or for those who want to use condoms to prevent AIDS," the Church's moral doctrine "allows no exceptions. This sort of rejection of the Church's teaching makes the cross void." Carlo Caffarra, the pope's spokesman for marriage and family issues, added that if an AIDS-infected husband couldn't manage to maintain "total abstinence" for the rest of his life, then it was better to infect his wife than to use a condom, "because the preservation of spiritual goods, such as the sacrament of marriage, is to be preferred to the good of life." That goes without saying, because since time immemorial sacrificing life and sexuality have been proven methods of winning the favor of the gods. Obviously, it's only one step from an absurd theology of the cross to an absurd theology of the condom. The common denominator is inhumanity.

The great Viennese historian Friedrich Heer writes that Goethe and Schiller looked upon Christians as "cruel enemies of life, as venerators of the cross, unhinged by the spasms of penitence, as world-hating killers, as fanatics, as people urgently in need of redemption: in a religion of the human being" (*Europa: Mutter der Revolution* [1964], p. 121).

Yet there have always been theologians who objected to the meaningless offering of sacrifices—for example, the prophets Amos (5:21–25), Hosea (6:6), Isaiah (1:10–17), and Micah (6:6–8), all from the 8th century B.C., along with the prophet Jeremiah from the 7th century B.C. (6:19–20; 7:21–23). Hosea says: "I desire steadfast love and not sacrifice" (6:6). Micah says: " 'Will the Lord be pleased with thousands of rams, with ten thousands of rivers of oil? Shall I give my first-born for my transgression, the fruit of my body for the sin of my soul?' He has showed you, O man, what is good; and what does the Lord require of you but to do justice, and to love kindness, and to walk humbly with your God?" (6:7–8). Yet the ani-

mal sacrifices were destined to go on until A.D. 70, and that was no volun-
tary renunciation, no listening to the prophet's message. It was simply because the Romans had destroyed the Temple.

Even today there are theologians who speak about the cross and sacrifice in a more reflective vein, for instance, Cardinal Joseph Ratzinger,
who was an important theologian before he became a cardinal. He writes
in his book *Einführung in das Christentum* (Introduction to Christianity
[1968]):

> The constitutive principle of sacrifice is not destruction but
> love. . . . How should God find joy in the torment of his creature
> or even of his Son or possibly see in it the currency with which
> reconciliation would have to be bought from him? The Bible and
> right-minded Christian faith are far from having such thoughts.
> It is not pain as such that counts, but the extent of the love. . . . If
> it were otherwise, then the executioner's henchmen at the cross
> would have been the real priests. . . . The fact that the perfectly
> just man, when he appeared, became the crucified one and was
> handed over to death by the law, tells us bluntly what a human
> being is: That's the sort you are, you can't bear the Just One—so
> that the Loving One becomes the fool, the Beaten and Rejected
> One. (Pp. 238ff.)

That's right. We may presume that had he lived at the time, Cardinal
Ratzinger would have revolted against this Crucifixion. But now, after two
thousand years of Christian theology, it's a different story. That same theology has frozen the Crucifixion and petrified it in its dogmatic edifice. It
has built substructures under and superstructures over this death, which it
sees as necessary for everyone and everything. It treats the Crucifixion as a
death without which there is no redemption. Hence, it's no longer so certain now that the cardinal would want to dispense with the Crucifixion.

Indeed, it's not so certain that all Christians aren't in danger of losing their sense of compassion because of the doctrine of the cross, which
they consider the center of Christian teaching. It's not so certain that with
its inhuman theology of the cross, Christianity, instead of making humans
more humane, hasn't just promoted man's inhumanity to man.

Afterword

WHAT'S LEFT? Some people think that once you've set aside all the Christian fairy tales and miracle stories, you've emptied Christianity, leaving nothing behind. But faith composed of, or based on, fairy tales and miracle stories is a sorry, futile faith, a faith that's good for nothing. When the wind of time has swept the fairy tales away, this faith, too, is gone with the wind.

But behind the fleeting, fading belief in fairy tales, something is left that time can't touch: faith in Jesus himself—and this is a more immediate and decisive faith than could ever have existed amid all the miracle stories. It makes no difference in our lives whether Jesus was born of a virgin or changed water into wine, whether he could walk on water or heal the sick. Unless we, too, can be healed by him, that means nothing to us. Likewise, his execution, except that it speaks to our compassion, ultimately means nothing to us either. There were then and there are now too many executed people (each of whom was one too many) who, apart from the fact that they prompt our compassion and stir us to protest against the death penalty, have no meaning for our lives.

The crucial thing for us is Jesus' life. It's his voice that speaks to us and says more to us than any miracles, because it is the voice of God's mercy. We should believe this voice, even more than our own. Jesus says of himself that he is the way and truth and life. This is the way, not to a little life that time sweeps away, but to a true and eternal life that holds good forever.

After this book was first published, I gave a talk at a bookstore in Bielefeld and afterward signed copies. When I had finished, the store owner came up and asked me to sign one more copy, adding that there was something he had to explain. I said that wasn't necessary, I'd sign it in any case. But then he showed me a death notice and said that the parents had really wanted to come that night, but the day before, they had flown to the United States for the burial of their son. I read the obituary: Our only son, . . . Professor . . . There followed the name of a university in America.

I was jolted and wondered how I could say everything in one sentence, how to say something that the Germans call *endgültig*, literally "valid at the end." I thought of the dispute over the resurrection that Jesus had with the Sadducees, who didn't believe in it ("And Sadducees came to him, who say there is no resurrection"), and that Jesus said to them, "As for the dead being raised, have you not read in the book of Moses about the bush, how God said to him, 'I am the God of Abraham, and the God of Isaac, and the God of Jacob?' He is not God of the dead, but of the living; you are quite wrong" (Mark 12:18–27).

So I wrote in the copy, "God is not a God of the dead, but of the living." I don't know whether this line could be a comfort for those parents, but it was and is a comfort for me.

Index